Responsive Teaching for Sustainable Learning

Drawing on Australian and international research, this book presents teaching and support strategies for educators to be responsive to the particular learning needs of each of their students and deliver quality inclusive education in a sustainable way.

Based on the Responsive Teaching Framework, an instructionally-focused approach for teaching that is evidence-based, purposeful, and responsive to students' learning needs, this book assists teachers to build on their current capabilities and strengthen their expertise to ensure that every student in their classrooms can be an effective learner. Part I of the book explains the theoretical and practical basis of Sustainable Learning as a way of thinking about inclusive education through a focus on responsive teaching. Part II unpacks each of the eight steps of the Responsive Teaching Framework. These chapters focus on the reflective questions that guide responsive practice, from whole class and individual student perspectives, outlining practical strategies that can be used, as well as the assessment practices and evidence-gathering needed to support each step of the responsive teaching process. Part III examines the influences that school leaders have on inclusive practice and proposes a Responsive Leadership Framework (RLF). The RLF aligns with the Responsive Teaching Framework to provide a shared language and deepen understanding of *Responsive Teaching for Sustainable Learning*.

Written for practising educators, school leaders, and postgraduate students, *Responsive Teaching for Sustainable Learning* delivers models for inclusive, sustainable teaching practice in an easily accessible format.

Jeanette Berman has been a teacher, school psychologist, and teacher educator in Australia, and teacher of educational psychologists in Aotearoa New Zealand. Since retirement she is Principal Fellow in the Learning Intervention team at The University of Melbourne. Jeanette received an Order of Australia Medal for services to education in 2023.

Lorraine Graham is Professor of Learning Intervention at The University of Melbourne. Her work focuses on the effective teaching of students with learning difficulties, sustainable learning, self-regulation, and teacher professional learning. Lorraine received recognition as a Member of the Order of Australia for her contributions to inclusive learning in 2023.

Anne Bellert is Senior Lecturer in Learning Intervention. She has over a decade of experience in advising school leaders and teachers about the inclusion of students with disabilities in school settings, and a further decade of experience in Initial Teacher Education and postgraduate teaching in inclusive education and leadership.

Lisa McKay-Brown is an Associate Professor in Learning Intervention and has extensive experience as a teacher working in a range of education settings with a particular focus on students with disability. Her research intersects health and education, and focuses on school attendance problems, positive behaviour support, and inclusive education.

Responsive Teaching for Sustainable Learning

A Framework for Inclusive Education

JEANETTE BERMAN,
LORRAINE GRAHAM,
ANNE BELLERT AND
LISA MCKAY-BROWN

LONDON AND NEW YORK

Designed cover image: 'Quito Atrium', Jeanette Berman, 2019.

First published 2024
by Routledge
4 Park Square, Milton Park, Abingdon, Oxon OX14 4RN

and by Routledge
605 Third Avenue, New York, NY 10158

Routledge is an imprint of the Taylor & Francis Group, an informa business

© 2024 Jeanette Berman, Lorraine Graham, Anne Bellert, and Lisa McKay-Brown

The right of Jeanette Berman, Lorraine Graham, Anne Bellert, and Lisa McKay-Brown to be identified as authors of this work has been asserted in accordance with sections 77 and 78 of the Copyright, Designs and Patents Act 1988.

All rights reserved. No part of this book may be reprinted or reproduced or utilised in any form or by any electronic, mechanical, or other means, now known or hereafter invented, including photocopying and recording, or in any information storage or retrieval system, without permission in writing from the publishers.

Trademark notice: Product or corporate names may be trademarks or registered trademarks, and are used only for identification and explanation without intent to infringe.

British Library Cataloguing-in-Publication Data
A catalogue record for this book is available from the British Library

Library of Congress Cataloging-in-Publication Data
Names: Berman, Jeanette, author. | Graham, Lorraine, author. | Bellert, Anne, author. | McKay-Brown, Lisa, author.
Title: Responsive teaching for sustainable learning : a framework for inclusive education / Jeanette Berman, Lorraine Graham, Anne Bellert, and Lisa McKay-Brown.
Description: Abingdon, Oxon ; New York, NY : Routledge, 2024. |
Includes bibliographical references and index. | Identifiers: LCCN 2023010878 (print) | LCCN 2023010879 (ebook) | ISBN 9781032290553 (hardback) |
ISBN 9781032290546 (paperback) | ISBN 9781003299813 (ebook)
Subjects: LCSH: Inclusive education--Australia. | Student-centered learning--Australia. | Reflective learning--Australia.
Classification: LCC LC1203.A8 B47 2024 (print) | LCC LC1203.A8 (ebook) |
DDC 371.9/046099--dc23/eng/20230415
LC record available at https://lccn.loc.gov/2023010878
LC ebook record available at https://lccn.loc.gov/2023010879

ISBN: 978-1-032-29055-3 (hbk)
ISBN: 978-1-032-29054-6 (pbk)
ISBN: 978-1-003-29981-3 (ebk)

DOI: 10.4324/9781003299813

Typeset in Minion
by SPi Technologies India Pvt Ltd (Straive)

Contents

Acknowledgements	x

Part I The foundations of responsive teaching for sustainable learning — 1

1 Sustainable learning — 3
   Teaching that matters is responsive teaching — 4
   Responding to diversity means learning for all — 6
   A capabilities approach for learning that lasts — 7
   Responsive teachers build capabilities — 9
   Summary — 13

2 The responsive teaching framework — 14
   Responsive teaching happens within a complex ecology — 15
   Responsive teachers bring their own influences — 17
   Responsive teachers focus on the class group and on individual learners — 17
   Responsive teachers are reflective and evaluative — 20
   Summary — 21

3 Evidence-based practice — 22
   Research evidence — 23
   Evidence from professional experience — 25
   Evidence from students and their families — 25
   Evidence from within teaching — 26
   WHY do we gather evidence (assess)? — 28
   WHAT do we gather evidence about (assess)? — 30
   HOW do we gather evidence (assess)? — 32

4 Layers of responsive teaching	34
Differentiation	*34*
Universal design for learning	*36*
Changes in intensity of teaching	*38*
Flexible groupings	*40*
Layers of responsive teaching	*41*
Layer 1: Responsive differentiation	*44*
Layers 2 and 3: Small group and individual teaching and learning	*45*
Collaboration for responsive teaching	*46*
Summary of the foundations of responsive teaching for sustainable learning	*47*

Part II Using the responsive teaching framework — 49

5 RTF 1: What frameworks do I need to consider?	51
Introduction	*51*
International conventions and principles	*51*
National legislation	*53*
Education system policies	*55*
Curriculum	*56*
Teacher registration requirements	*57*
Cultural and community contexts	*58*
School culture and organisation	*59*
Learning environments	*62*
6 RTF 2: What do I bring as a teacher?	65
Introduction	*65*
What teaching skills and knowledge do I bring to my teaching?	*65*
What assumptions about learning do I bring to my teaching?	*66*
Using Indigenous and Western theories of learning	*70*
What cultural competence do I bring to my teaching?	*71*
What assumptions about diversity do I bring to my teaching?	*74*
Assumptions about disability	*74*
Assumptions about named disabilities	*76*
Assumptions about giftedness	*78*
Assumptions about behaviour	*80*
Assumptions about learning difficulties	*82*
7 RTF 3: What do my students bring as learners?	85
Introduction	*85*
Assessment of students as learners	*85*
Prior learning and achievement	*87*

Cultural contexts	88
Experiences	90
Interests	91
Educational and developmental casework	92
Gathering information about students as learners	93
Information from school records	94
Information from allied health professionals	94
Information from the family	95
Information from the student	97
What other information is needed?	97
What is the nature of the learning group?	98

8 RTF 4: What do I need to teach now?   103

Introduction	103
Learner readiness, interests, and learning profile	103
Learning profile	105
Ecological map of influences on learners	106
Sustainable learning profile	109
Intended learning outcomes	113
Developmental pathways	114
Learning progressions	115
Theoretical frameworks	116
Defining intended learning outcomes	117

9 RTF 5: How do I teach for all my learners?   124

Teacher-student relationships	124
Teaching approaches	130
Differentiated teaching	131
Culturally responsive teaching	133
Collaborative teaching	133
Explicit teaching	135
Cooperative group teaching	136
Learning opportunities	139
Teaching for all our students	145

10 RTF 6: How do I gather evidence of student learning?   146

Introduction	146
The WHY and WHAT of assessment in RTF 6	146
Criterion and/or norm-referenced assessment	160
The HOW of assessment of learning	161
Assessment-ready and -capable learners	165

Assessment OF learning becomes assessment FOR learning and assessment AS learning   165

11 RTF 7: How do I use feedback to support learning?   168
  Introduction   168
  Quality of feedback   169
  Quantity and timing of feedback   171
  Making sense of feedback within interactions   173
  Self-feedback   175
  Student role in feedback process   176

12 RTF 8: How did my teaching support my students' learning?   178
  Introduction   178
  Outcomes of teaching and learning   178
  Context for teaching and learning   179
  Processes of teaching and learning   180
    Student voice in evaluation   182
    Evaluating teaching approaches   183
    Other teaching approaches   185
    Evaluating layers of responsive teaching   185
  Professional learning for responsive teaching   186

Part III Leadership for responsive teaching and sustainable learning   189

13 Leadership principles   191
  Inclusive and ethical leadership   192
  Leading responsive teaching and sustainable learning   194
  Responsively transformative leadership   196
  Distributed or shared leadership   199
  Sustainable leadership   200

14 The responsive leadership framework   201
  RLF 1. What frameworks need to be considered?   201
  RLF 2. What do I bring as a leader in responsive teaching and sustainable learning?   203
  RLF 3. What is the nature of the educational setting?   205
  RLF 4. What do we prioritise?   206
  RLF 5. How do we lead responsive teaching for sustainable learning?   206
  RLF 6. How will we know what difference we have made?   207

*RLF 7. How have connections and communication
   supported RT4SL?* 207
RLF 8. What worked and what is next? 207
Conclusion 208

References 210
Index 235

Acknowledgements

We wish to acknowledge the lands on which we have learnt and taught, which include Anaiwan, Gubbi Gubbi, Gumbaynggir, and Boon Wurrung country. We recognise that teaching and learning has been carried out for tens of thousands of years on these lands, and we pay our respects to Elders past and present, the original teachers of Australia.

Sustainable Learning was generated within the authors' professional reflection on their teaching over a combined 100 years of practice and research. This third book about *Responsive Teaching for Sustainable Learning* grew out of the collaborative work the authors carried out in Latin America, particularly Ecuador, where we were engaged to provide inclusive education professional learning workshops for hundreds of classroom teachers. We would like to acknowledge:

- all our students from The University of Melbourne, Massey University (Aotearoa New Zealand), Southern Cross University, and the University of New England who have engaged with these ideas and helped us to make them coherent and meaningful
- the teachers in Ecuador who have been involved in the professional development project, *Inclusive Education and Sustainable Learning*, since 2018 and for whom we needed to translate our ideas into practical actions for teachers and leaders.

We also acknowledge Stephanie Chaseling who provided editing and proofreading. In that process she engaged deeply with the ideas and interrogated them from the perspective of a parent with knowledge and experience of special and inclusive education.

You are all in this work. Thank you.

Part I

The foundations of responsive teaching for sustainable learning

Outline of this book

This book is organised in three parts. **Part I: The foundations of responsive teaching for sustainable learning** covers most of the frameworks which underpin *Sustainable Learning*. These are briefly described in the introductory chapter. This part of the book explains the theoretical and practical basis of the Sustainable Learning approach as a way of thinking about inclusive education through a focus on *teaching that matters*, that is, responsive teaching. The approach includes an emphasis on learner capabilities and the consolidation of evidence-based practice through the informed use of assessment information to support teacher responsiveness and reflection.

Part II: Using the responsive teaching framework unpacks each of the eight steps of the *Responsive Teaching Framework* in turn. These chapters focus on the relevant reflective questions that guide responsive practice. These questions are written to encompass both whole class and individual student perspectives and focus on the assessment and evidence-gathering practices needed to support responsive teaching. The final chapter presents an organised compilation of all the reflective questions and frameworks discussed throughout this book. The purpose of this resource is to provide access to the guiding frameworks underpinning Sustainable Learning to those beginning and practising teachers who wish to master the responsive teaching approach.

Part III: Leadership for responsive teaching and sustainable learning is written specifically for school leaders and those who assume leadership roles. Part III makes explicit the links between what responsive teachers 'do' and how leaders can best support their practices, including how to facilitate the kind of professional learning that is essential for sustaining quality teaching and school leadership.

1 Sustainable learning

This book is about the teaching that inclusive classroom teachers do to ensure every student in their classrooms is an effective learner for life. In it, we provide a framework that will assist teachers to strengthen their current capabilities and expertise so that they are increasingly responsive to the learning needs of each of their students. Working within the *Sustainable Learning* model, we explore practical strategies that can be used to ensure responsive teaching. As a first step, it is necessary to establish the foundations of *Responsive Teaching for Sustainable Learning*.

The foundations of this book are in *Sustainable Learning*, a clearly defined approach to inclusive teaching, which was first conceptualised by Graham, Berman, and Bellert (2015) based on their combined teaching and educational casework experience in Australian schools. This conceptualisation of inclusive education aims to support teachers as they provide learning for all students (*learning for all*). Sustainable Learning also aims to facilitate learning that equips young people to flourish in an increasingly complex world with less clear work futures than prior generations have experienced. It does this by teaching capabilities that will continue to be relevant throughout life (*learning that lasts*). Being job-ready is not a matter of acquiring a particular body of skills and knowledge. In contemporary contexts, it means that individuals continue to learn effectively and efficiently throughout their working lives and adapt to new working demands as needed.

The foundations of *Sustainable Learning* are conceptualised as ensuring that:

- teachers understand their essential role in teaching responsively (*teaching that matters*)
- all students can access meaningful learning that supports them to achieve their potential (*learning for all*) and
- the investment in learning required by both teachers and students is utilised purposefully, and learning opportunities are not wasted or depleted (*learning that lasts*) (after Van den Branden, 2012).

When explaining the need for a new vision of education early in the 21st century, Sterling (2001) stressed the need to re-establish relationships between the increasingly discrete aspects of education: ethos; curriculum; pedagogy; management; procurement and resource use; architecture and community

DOI: 10.4324/9781003299813-2

connections. They also need to be linked to the important values of respect, trust, participation, ownership, democracy, openness, and the environment. Conceptualising education in this way and as a proposition related to sustainability is not a new approach.

Van den Branden's (2012) notion of sustainable education, and his analysis of the extent to which education systems fulfil the basic criteria of sustainable development, have influenced the development of our framework for Sustainable Learning. The three fundamental criteria of sustainable development, as identified in the Bruntland report (World Commission on Environment and Development of the United Nations, 1987, as cited in Van den Branden, 2012) are to meet and respond to: the basic needs of every individual and to enable them to reach their potential; current needs without depleting resources that will be required in the future; and threats to the natural systems that support life so individuals and the environment are protected. Van den Branden (2012) proposed that as schools and school systems seek to ensure their effectiveness and sustainability through initiating reforms broadly aimed at improving student achievement and ensuring equity, a "sustainability paradox" (p. 286) emerges. The essence of this paradox is that though schools and educational systems strive to have their students value equality and equity as principles of sustainability, "many education systems themselves fail to live up to (these) basic principles" (p. 292).

Through *Sustainable Learning*, we have taken up the challenge of looking at how to improve equity and student achievement through a focus on learning for all, teaching that matters, and learning that lasts. These three tenets support the growth of learners and their teachers. As a metaphor for sustained and *Sustainable Learning*, the central shapes of Figure 1.1 represent the koru from Aotearoa New Zealand, a representation of fern fronds that if properly nurtured are perpetually unfurling. The elements extending out of the centre of the figure become the basis for the responsive teaching cycle. This graphic representation of *Responsive Teaching for Sustainable Learning* reoccurs throughout this book. The model becomes more complex as the foundations for and the details of the *Responsive Teaching Framework* are explained.

It is important to emphasise that achieving learning for all and learning that lasts depends very much on the powerful and indispensable role of teachers. Teachers frame and filter the curriculum; they design and provide learning opportunities; and they use targeted teaching strategies to facilitate the best possible learning outcomes for their students. This is the teaching that matters, the responsive teaching that relies on expertise and creates the conditions for efficient and effective learning.

Teaching that matters is responsive teaching

The expertise that teachers use in responding to the learning needs of their students is integral to Sustainable Learning. This book discusses what effective and responsive teachers practice every day, that is, how they draw on what they know and can do; who they collaborate with to understand their students as learners; and how they provide authentic classroom learning experiences for all their students.

Sustainable learning 5

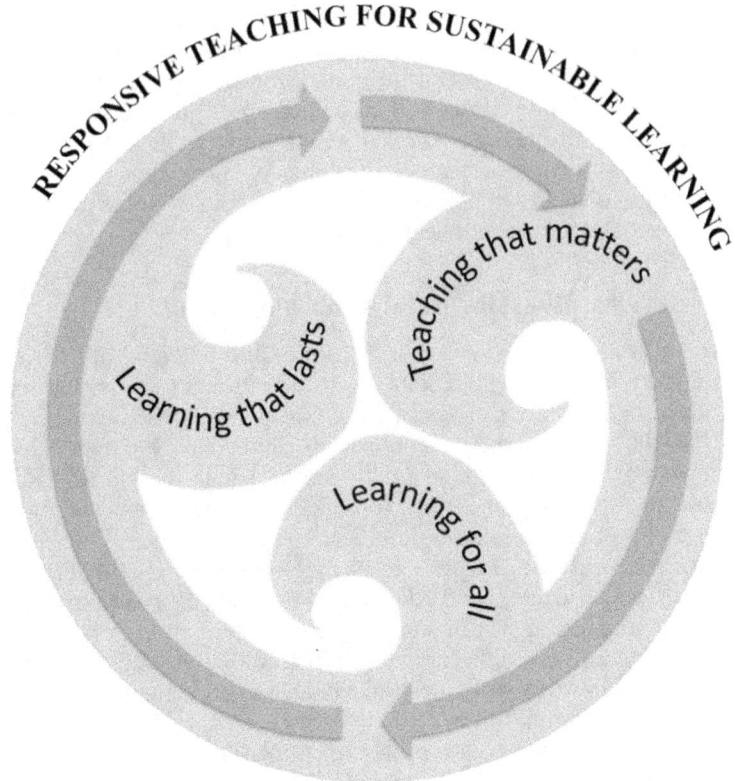

Figure 1.1 Responsive Teaching for Sustainable Learning.
Adapted from Graham, Berman, & Bellert, 2015.

Teaching that matters is responsive to the learning needs of individuals and to groups of students. Within the *Sustainable Learning* model for inclusive education, teaching that matters aims to secure, not only the learning of all students, but also the development of capabilities necessary for lifelong learning. As well, it acknowledges the layers of influence that impact each student and groups of students as they engage with teachers, other learners, and school systems. A useful way to think about this complex situation is as an ecosystem. Learners, teachers, other learners, and learning itself are not discrete entities, but rather function as part of an interactive system or ecology.

As a framework, *Sustainable Learning* supports teachers and schools to respond to diversity; focus on learning, not labels; and develop capability rather than focus on disability. *Sustainable Learning* goes beyond the idea that inclusion is about groups or individuals being educated in the same setting because all learners are considered part of the ecosystem already. Rather than concentrating on groups of students with 'special needs', in *Sustainable Learning* inclusive education is enacted through responsive strategies that support all learners. The focus is on what approaches and strategies individual students, or groups of students need to enable their access, learning, and participation and what curriculum content, skills, and capabilities they need to learn now. In essence, successful inclusive education is reliant on a shared 'learning about learning' process that is recognised as critically important because it directly affects the chances of a more sustainable future for all.

The next two sections establish the basis of *Sustainable Learning* as a response to the diversity of classrooms and the complex and dynamic world where our students continue to learn into adulthood.

Responding to diversity means *learning for all*

Many teachers have an awareness of the power and potential of their work – there are many coffee mugs in staff rooms or satirical t-shirts that teachers wear with pride that have slogans such as: "I'm changing the world one day at a time: I teach". Nelson Mandela famously proclaimed in 1990 that "Education is the most powerful weapon you can use to change the world" (Ratcliffe, 2017), and the inspirational Malala Yousafzai, renowned advocate for education, spoke this powerful, gentle reminder: "Let us remember: One book, one pen, one child, and one teacher can change the world" (UNICEF, Ireland, 2019). As teacher educators and educational researchers, we are convinced of the power that teaching has in shaping people's lives and, more broadly, in shaping society. These beliefs crystallise our thinking around what inclusive education is and how it supports the sustainable development of our world in dynamic and challenging times.

Those of us fortunate enough to live in countries with universal access to education may, at times, be active in expressing our discontent with the current education system or advocating for change and improvement. Whilst these are important views which need to be heard to ensure the most effective educational systems, it is sometimes essential for teachers to remember how fortunate we are to work in such a privileged position – and to consider how ignorance and disadvantage can prevail when access to education is denied or restricted.

What happens in an educational setting has tremendous potential. Students who achieve and progress in learning have increased means to transcend circumstances, to realise their individual potential, to have greater agency and control over the trajectory of their lives, and to influence the future of their families and communities. At its most fundamental, *Sustainable Learning* seeks to maximise the opportunities for education. It is important to emphasise that the opportunity to learn should not be restricted to some students. It is inequitable for teachers to focus only on those who are easy to teach. The work of schools and teachers falls short of its potential unless all students are included, and all students are achieving. The industrial model of education placed all children of a similar age in a grade-based system and assumed they were ready to learn the same content and concepts in the same way (Reigeluth, 2011). The risk inherent in this approach is evident – not only are those who are able to access education forced to think and learn in a similar way, but more importantly, those who are not able to access the learning offered are excluded and vulnerable to failure. Teaching is no longer routine and comfortable. As Tomlinson reflects, "It has never been good practice to teach as though all students in a classroom were essentially alike. As we approach the end of the first quarter of the 21st century, one-size-fits-all teaching seems almost delusional" (2016, p. 38).

The challenge for teachers is to recognise the diversity of their students and to teach in a way that responds to this diversity. The goal is that all students have opportunities to be transformed through education, to reach their potential as learners, and to thrive as members of families, communities, and society. In this vein, *Sustainable Learning* approaches inclusive education from the perspective that diversity 'just is'. This conceptualisation of inclusive education transcends deficit approaches that use categorisation of students. It gets past the tension between broad notions of inclusion that at the same time, focuses on defining categories of students (Armstrong, Armstrong, & Spandagou, 2011). Clearly continuing to categorise students with 'additional' learning needs has the propensity to lead to further exclusion. Furthermore, trying to address student learning needs through approaches that start with whether the student is a member of a particular group are fraught with ethical challenges and lead to exclusion, rather than inclusion. For example, earmarking additional educational resources only for students with a particular disability precludes students who could benefit from accessing these resources but who do not meet the eligibility via the relevant diagnostic label. Similarly, requiring all students from a particular group to attend supplementary programs may waste resources because not all the students may need, or will respond to, the programs on offer. Further, determining students' learning needs based on disability labels and generalisations (for example, that students with autism cannot participate in group work) restricts learning opportunities and further excludes students from learning opportunities. Responsive teachers focus on learning, not on labels.

Inclusion, at its root, implies placing students in settings from which they had previously been excluded. *Sustainable Learning*, however, goes beyond this notion of inclusion; it does not focus on groups or individuals who need to be specifically included, instead, it is recognised from the outset that all students belong in the classroom, the school, and the community. The way forward proposed by *Responsive Teaching for Sustainable Learning* is to recognise the diversity present in any group of learners, to respect and value each student's individuality, and to teach in response to their learning needs.

A capabilities approach for *learning that lasts*

In the context of *Responsive Teaching for Sustainable Learning*, a way to make sense of how to support learners as they move into the post-school world, is to focus on the human processes of learning that are needed while engaging in school and throughout life. A focus on competencies, competences or capabilities is at the core of competence-based approaches (CBA; Anderson-Levitt, Bonnéry, & Fichtner, 2017). Such approaches are increasingly reflected in curriculum development in the past few decades (Nordin & Sundberg, 2020). An instigator of this process has been the focus on competences in vocational education and training in Europe, and the broader notion of 21st century skills

(Halász & Michel, 2011; Hipkins, 2018) which recognises the changing needs of workers. As an example, the Program for International Student Assessment (PISA) which tests the reading, mathematics, and science knowledge of 15-year-old students aims to find out if these young people can "meet the challenges of the future ... can analyse, reason, and communicate their ideas effectively ... [and can] continue to learn throughout life" (OECD, 2000, p. 3).

Contemporary educational systems are increasingly seeking to revise and reform schooling to meet the changing social and economic conditions of the 21st century. Inherent in the shift from an industrial economy to a knowledge economy (OECD, 1996) is an increased focus on managing information, communication, and collaboration. To help the students of today negotiate the challenges of an unknown future, the focus of contemporary schooling is moving away from valuing the transmission of a set body of knowledge, towards enhancing the capabilities of students so they can access, share, and use information in fast-changing contexts.

In school settings, the implementation of flexible pedagogies, for example, co-teaching and personalised learning, and the development of learning environments that are more innovative than traditional 'single cell' classrooms, are key approaches that aim to prepare students for future workforce and societal demands. Generally, effective contemporary educational approaches aim to improve educational outcomes for all students, increase participation in education throughout the lifespan, and build social and emotional connectedness between learners and within their communities.

Articulation of what needs to be learned to engage successfully with the wider world has been important to pedagogical thinking for centuries (Halász & Michel, 2011). A focus on the processes of learning rather than on fixed bodies of skills and knowledge means students can become competent at engaging with, adapting to, and learning about the world – the essence of being sustainable learners.

In terms of frameworks, the European Framework of Key Competences for Lifelong Learning was organised around eight competences and their essential knowledge, skills, and attitudes, which included "critical thinking, creativity, initiative taking, problem solving, risk assessment, decision taking, and managing feelings" (Commission of the European Communities, 2005, p. 12). From the basis of the original European eight competences, other education systems have derived their sets of competences, competencies, or general capabilities as shown in Table 1.1.

Competency-based approaches are now widespread with, for example, the adoption of a Competency Based Curriculum in regional Peru (Ramos Solis, 2020) and the contextualisation of this approach in some African countries (Cheptoo & Ramadas, 2019). Two education systems that have distilled the competencies down to three key skills are British Columbia; Canada (communication, thinking, and personal and social competency; Province of British Columbia, 2022); and Denmark (understanding of citizenship, sustainability, and understanding of own and others' cultures; Mogensen & Schnack, 2010). The very different sets of competencies/competences illustrate how countries and contexts within countries make the focus on human processes their own. In contrast to British Columbia's emphasis on individual

Table 1.1 The European Key Competences and the Australian and New Zealand derivations

European key competences	Australian curriculum general capabilities	New Zealand curriculum key competencies
Communication in the mother tongue	Literacy	Thinking
Communication in a foreign language	Numeracy	Relating to others
Mathematical competence and basic competences in science and technology	Information and communication technology (ICT)	Using language, symbols, and texts
Digital competence	Critical and creative thinking	Managing self
Learning to learn	Personal and social	Participating and contributing
Social and civic competence	Ethical understanding	
Sense of initiative and entrepreneurship	Intercultural understanding	
Cultural awareness and expression		

ACARA, 2010; Commission of the European Communities, 2007; Ministry of Education, Aotearoa New Zealand, 2020.

competencies, exploring the basis of the Danish competencies reveals a foundation in education and action for sustainable development (Mogensen & Schnack, 2010).

Variation across these sets of competences reflect how the activities of individuals within their social and cultural environments are viewed and valued. This is also a key emphasis in *Responsive Teaching for Sustainable Learning*. We are particularly interested in those processes of learning most relevant to our students and how capabilities are enacted within, and influenced by, their environments. Integral to responsive teaching then, is the ATRiUM model of capabilities (Graham, Berman, & Bellert, 2015), which is described in the next section and elaborated on throughout the book.

Responsive teachers build capabilities

The competence-based approach that is a foundation of responsive teaching is represented by the acronym ATRiUM: Active learning (A); Thinking (T); Relating to others (R); Using language, symbol systems, and ICT (iU); and Managing self (M) (Graham, Berman, & Bellert, 2015). ATRiUM (see Figure 1.2) is a strengths-based conceptualisation of the processes that students use when learning and that teachers deliberately build on through teaching. ATRiUM is a reworking of the five New Zealand Key Competencies, with a stronger emphasis given to participation and contribution. These five capabilities encompass what it is we want sustainable learners to develop (Graham, Berman, & Bellert, 2015).

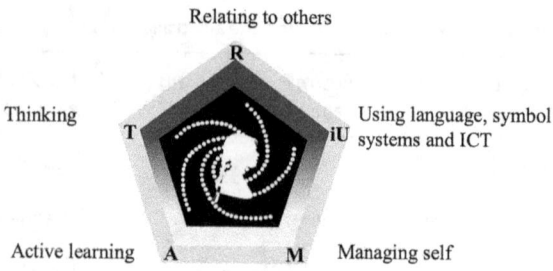

Figure 1.2 ATRiUM capabilities.
Adapted from Berman & Graham, 2018.

This model has been translated into Spanish for use in Latin America and is also used as the organisational cornerstone for student support of a new public secondary college in South Australia (Whyalla Secondary College, 2021).

Active learning

Active learning is represented by the A in ATRiUM. It is an overarching capability that conveys the importance to learning of action and agency and is supported by the remaining capabilities. Vygotskian theory helps make sense of learning as a social, cultural, and individual phenomenon. Learning begins outside learners, in the sociocultural domain. It is a function of what society deems to be important to learn and is framed by the culture within which it is taught. In schools and educational institutions, learning is focused on selected knowledge and skills that have been compiled into the curriculum and are taught through social interactions that rely on the cultural tools of language and other symbol systems. Learning is, therefore, primarily a social activity before internalisation contributes to individual growth and development.

Teachers engineer and manage opportunities for learning, and mediate these activities to optimise learning for their students. Personal learning is more difficult to engineer, as it requires learners to take responsibility. As students become increasingly self-regulated, they become conscious of their own learning abilities and how curious, interested, and engaged they are. They may also note how they become motivated and maintain motivation for learning; how they take risks and use creativity in learning; and how they understand their own growth as learners. Being conscious of these dimensions of being 'active learners' allows students to manage their learning effectively, and to seek support when necessary.

Teaching for active learning and teaching active learners is not easy. It is nothing like traditional teaching that involves a group of students passively sitting and listening, and carrying out individual reading or written work when instructed. Instead, active learning means educational settings will be full of questioning, seeking clarification, searching for information, and challenging of ideas. Contemporary teachers of active learners plan active and generative tasks that require interactions between students, in pairs or small groups, as well as through teacher-managed whole class discussions. Well-designed student-to-student interactions are essential if active learning is to take place.

It is indisputable that the teacher is the more competent other in this kind of classroom and still needs to teach important skills and knowledge explicitly, however, once a culture of expecting interaction between students is established, much learning can happen without the teacher. The curiosity of students, their skills in searching for information, and their motivation can contribute to successful active learning, however, it is the responsiveness of teachers that makes the difference. Students learn more effectively when the teacher designs their activities, equips them with the language and key concepts to use in learning interactions, checks on progress, and contributes to interactions so that learning is supported and extended. *Sustainable Learning* aims for a partnership between teachers and learners that fosters the responsibility of students for their own learning.

Thinking

Thinking is the basic process in academic learning and is the primary tool of student transformation and growth. It is represented by the T in ATRiUM. All learners need to develop and apply their thinking and to learn to be critical thinkers throughout their lives. Traditionally, because of a focus on intelligence, thinking capacity was seen to be biologically determined and limited. We now know that thinking is a capability that can be taught and nurtured. Thinking about everyday matters is seen to be distinct from cognitive processing around intellectual and scientific ideas, but these two layers of thought need to be integrated for individuals to function meaningfully in complex educational settings and the wider world. Teaching needs to link academic thinking with the relevance of knowledge to daily lives.

Using perspectives such as information processing theory, thinking can be broken down into distinct cognitive processes. Such framing can help teachers support their students' learning and identify barriers that exist for some students. Thinking involves sensing, attending, perceiving, comprehending, reasoning, analysing, linking with prior knowledge, memorising, and retrieving, and expressing. All these component skills are in play every time students encounter new ideas or concepts, explore ideas with others, and demonstrate thinking in assessment tasks. Our focus on this capability includes considering all these aspects of cognition.

Relating to others

Interpersonal engagement contributes to active learning within complex social systems of family, community, schools, and classrooms. The relationship between students and teachers is paramount to learning and is the R in ATRiUM. Such relationships rely on social communication and interaction skills, and respond to shared expectations set by teachers and students. In contemporary interactive classrooms where cooperative and collaborative learning activities operate, being active members of the classroom learning community depends on positive teacher-student relationships. Such relationships have a basis of mutual respect, care, and trust that strengthens with increased interaction (Mosley, Broyles, & Kaufman, 2021). The other key relationships in educational settings are those between learners as peers, and these are enhanced by interactive and cooperative learning activities (Johnson & Johnson, 2018). Not only is it good for our students to have strong interpersonal relationships, but it influences these students' social lives as they engage with each other outside educational settings and as they move into their adult worlds.

Using language, other symbol systems and ICT

Language and other symbol systems are essential tools for learning, as are skills for using information communication technology (ICT). This capability is represented by the iU in ATRiUM. Every culture and academic discipline develops elaborate and complex systems of codes for use in social interactions and academic learning. These codes include the language of the educational setting, languages of the community, and specific symbol systems that are embedded in learning areas, such as mathematics, science, and music.

Language is the primary vehicle for teaching and learning. Use of language in learning involves both receptive language, that helps learners access information, and expressive language, which allows their demonstration of thinking and learning. These capabilities are integrally related, as thinking is the internalisation of social language, and uses the concepts and words learners have in their vocabularies. Building vocabulary across all disciplinary areas is a vital step towards strengthening the depth of thinking that is possible for students to achieve. The representation of language through written letters and words requires learners to be able to decode written language (reading) and encode (writing). Much emphasis in early education is on systematically and explicitly teaching these skills so that subsequent learning is supported by this capability.

As innovative technology facilitates communication, language in turn adapts. For example, texting language is an adaptation of written language in response to the use of digital devices and the demands for immediacy of communication. The capacity of learners to adapt to these changes and use different forms of communication is vital, so a significant part of this capability (iU) relates to proficiency in the skills of continual learning, flexibility, and adaptability.

Managing self

The capability of managing self (the M in ATRiUM) is an integral part of active learning, and self-regulation is at its heart. In fact, a general aim of learning is to become a self-managing and self-sustaining lifelong learner. In education settings, teachers provide opportunities for students to explore the skills of self-management and to gradually take over the management of their everyday decision-making as learners. Society expects different degrees of self-management from children and young people of different ages. Strategies for managing self are culturally bound, with certain behaviours accepted in some contexts or settings, but seen as not appropriate in others. The development of self-regulated learning skills that allow individuals to become self-managing active learners has metacognitive, motivational, self-efficacy, and attributional dimensions that can be explicitly taught (Graham & Berman, 2012). These skills are used in managing not only social and emotional reactions to the environment, but also strategies for thinking and learning.

Summary

In conclusion, as teachers respond to diversity of learners and prepare young people to take their places in the world, quality teaching is hugely important. The *Sustainable Learning* approach focuses on supporting teachers and driving inclusive education. In this first chapter, we have articulated the foundations of *Responsive Teaching for Sustainable Learning*, which are *learning for all* (meeting the needs of all students as learners), *teaching that matters* (being responsive teachers), and *learning that lasts* (capabilities for learning and for living). In the next chapter, we carefully consider the dimension of *teaching that matters* through the eight steps of the *Responsive Teaching Framework*.

2 The responsive teaching framework

The process of making sense of what effective teachers do – *teaching that matters* – led to the development of the *Responsive Teaching Framework* (Graham, Berman, & Bellert, 2015). It consists of eight ordered questions that reflect what teachers may ask themselves as they proceed through a teaching-learning cycle and make decisions that guide their teaching. These questions inform both practice and reflection, and together form the organising framework for this book. They are designed to bring focus to the vital parts of inclusive teaching, and to prompt teachers to explicitly consider how to be responsive.

The *Responsive Teaching Framework* (RTF) is set out in Figure 2.1. The three koru (koru are unfurling ferns – a symbol of growth in New Zealand) of *Sustainable Learning* are background to the eight questions of the RTF. The eight

Figure 2.1 Responsive Teaching Framework.

Adapted from Graham, Berman, & Bellert, 2015.

DOI: 10.4324/9781003299813-3

steps of the framework align with key questions that teachers ask themselves as they make decisions about teaching.

These steps fit within three phases. The first is a planning phase, followed by the enactment of teaching phase (teaching and learning, and assessment and feedback); and then by an evaluation and reflection phase which completes the cycle. The RTF cycle may be repeated as many times as necessary based on the evidence generated about what worked and what did not work. Each of the eight questions is introduced briefly in this chapter. A detailed justification and the processes within each step are then provided in the eight chapters, one for each step, of Part II of this book.

Responsive teaching happens within a complex ecology

In the first step of the RTF, we place teaching practice within an ecological context. Teaching and learning occur within a complex system of influences that need to be understood by teachers. Bronfenbrenner (1977) defined systems of influence in an early ecological model that has since been adapted to suit many contexts. For the purposes of *Responsive Teaching for Sustainable Learning*, we combine the key idea of Bronfenbrenner's systems of influence with Zubrick, Williams, and Silburn's (2000) conception of the importance of recognising broad layers of social, structural, economic, political, and cultural impact on education (see Figure 2.2). This model is a visual representation of the important influences that affect teachers and learners.

Figure 2.2 The ecological systems influencing teachers and students as they engage with *Responsive Teaching for Sustainable Learning*.

Adapted from Graham, Berman, & Bellert, 2015.

In nature, ecosystems contribute to the biosphere which in this instance represents the school, families, the local community, society, and at its broadest interpretation, the world. What happens in one small ecosystem, such as an education setting, leads to 'ripple effects' within this biosphere. The learning and teaching that students experience can have important consequences beyond their learning environments.

The quality or 'health' of a learning ecosystem is often determined by the teachers, it is *teaching that matters* and makes the difference. Metaphorically, this ecosystem also requires the effective use of other resources to stimulate student growth and development. Furthermore, these resources need to be used prudently – both 'just in time' responding to what the learners need now and what they need next, and 'just right' in response to the cultural and contextual needs of individuals and the group. Clearly, resources need to be used sustainably, and not depleted so they are available for the future. This metaphor has particular significance for students and their perceptions of themselves as capable learners, and for teachers' responsibility to ensure the active learning of all students in their classrooms.

Another dimension of *Sustainable Learning* consistent with an ecological metaphor is interconnection. Teaching and learning, teachers and learners, and individual students are all interconnected and interdependent in an effective learning environment. *Sustainable Learning*, with its focus on learner capabilities and learning needs, seeks to consistently enable and enhance interconnectivity. For example, as well as students learning from teachers, they also learn from each other and teach each other. Learning itself also connects with the prior knowledge and lived experiences of individual students in different ways. Interconnections and interdependence are essential for sustaining student motivation and engagement with learning.

Essentially these ideas about an ecosystem reflect key underpinnings of the *Sustainable Learning* approach to inclusion. The parallels of this metaphor with an effective schooling system, a supportive classroom, or a lesson that has impact are clear. The essential contribution of teachers is that they have a key role to play in determining the health and sustainability of the learning environment. Under the ecological metaphor of *Sustainable Learning*, every component needs to be in balance for the system to ensure *learning for all, teaching that matters*, and *learning that lasts*.

Another key determinant of a healthy ecosystem is diversity. A healthy and stable ecosystem requires diversity to thrive, and conversely, an ecosystem lacking in diversity is vulnerable. Diversity, not uniformity, is nature's way. This aligns well with the reality of classroom learning, and so teachers should expect, respect, and respond to diversity in *Responsive Teaching*. Consequently, the first reflective question of the RTF focuses on the broad influences on learning and teaching, how teachers understand them, and how they take these factors into account when planning for responsive teaching.

RTF 1. What frameworks do I need to consider?

The frameworks that need to be considered in *Responsive Teaching* include international conventions, legislative frameworks, education system policies and procedures, curricula, teacher registration requirements, cultural and community contexts, school culture and organisation, and learning environments – the contexts within which responsive teaching happens. This list is not fully comprehensive as it varies according to whoever is using the RTF. The purpose of these questions is to prompt teachers to consider external influences that affect their teaching and their students' learning. RTF 1 is examined fully in Part II Chapter 5.

Responsive teachers bring their own influences

Within this complex ecological system, teachers and learners interact and engage. It is certain that each of us, as teachers, bring ourselves into the classroom and into relationship with our students. We influence the effectiveness of our professional practice by who we are and what we represent. We need to be aware of what this means and the responsibility that accompanies our roles. The second reflective question of the *Responsive Teaching Framework*, RTF 2, encourages teachers to be conscious of the influence that their own culture, characteristics, and habits of thought have on their professional practice and how they are seen by their students.

RTF 2. What do I bring as a teacher?

This second reflective question also prompts awareness not only of teaching skills and knowledge, but also teachers' cultural positions and consideration of how these fit with those of their students. It also questions how assumptions about learning, diversity, and education underpin professional decisions about teaching and the nature of students as learners. RTF 2, which sets the basis for being a reflective, conscious, and present teacher, is examined fully in Chapter 6.

Responsive teachers focus on the class group and on individual learners

Traditionally, teachers have focused on a class, have been able to plan with that group in mind, and then adjust for a few students who have a disability or other special needs. That approach to teaching used a hypothetical middle, average, or typical student as the target for planning, with adaptations considered for those who were not able to keep up or who needed extending. By taking this approach to planning, teachers divide their classes into students who fit and those who do not. However, teachers who are highly successful at including students with disabilities tend to see all their students as having individual needs – not just the students who may be diagnosed with a disability (Shaddock et al., 2007). Therefore, responsive teachers need to know their students both as a group, and as individual learners. Inclusive planning which begins with all students in mind should be expected. The third question,

RTF 3, thus sets the expectation that responsive teachers focus on meeting the learning needs of each individual student in their classes.

To guide this responsive teaching focus on individual students as learners, reflective questions have been derived from both the original description of the RTF (Graham, Berman, & Bellert, 2015) and an extension of that conceptualisation to educational casework (Berman & Graham, 2018). These questions support an emphasis on both the group and individual students that is necessary for classroom planning (Figure 2.1).

These questions provide structure for consideration of individual learning needs and can be used whenever teachers focus on the needs of particular students. For example, when asking what the students as a group bring as learners (RTF 3), teachers can also consider the individually focused question: *What does this student bring as a learner?* Similarly for the next five RTF questions, teachers can have a dual focus on the class group and on individual learners. The most important question to ask about any individual student is *How do I teach this student?* (RTF 5). Responsive teachers ask this about every student in their classes, within the context of planning for the group.

The requirement for Australian graduates of teacher education programs to demonstrate their teaching expertise through a Teaching Performance Assessment (TPA) associated with their final practicum (AITSL, 2017a) has emphasised the need for this adaptation of the RTF. For example, the RTF has been used in an Australian University as a scaffold for emerging teachers who are developing their approach to both teaching a class group and teaching each of the students within that group. The individually focused questions are provided for RTF steps 3 through 8. All these questions focus on students as learners. The first of these is about what students bring to their learning (RTF 3).

RTF 3. What do my students bring as learners?

RTF 3 assists teachers' thinking about the class group and individual learners by seeking information about their prior learning and achievements, their cultural contexts, experiences, and interests, and organising that information according to the ATRiUM capabilities. This knowledge of what students bring to their learning is essential to responsive teaching, which at its heart is about meeting the needs of all students in a class. Responsive teaching relies on teacher planning that considers the class and the needs of all members of the class from the outset. RTF 3 is examined more fully in Chapter 7.

Based on understanding the learning needs of each student and knowing what our students bring as learners (RTF 3), the aim of the following reflective question (RTF 4) is to clearly determine students' immediate learning needs and what needs to be taught.

RTF 4. What do I need to teach now?

When engaging with RTF 4, teachers need to think about the sometimes-competing demands of the education system, the community, the learning needs of the group and the needs of individual students. This can be difficult as there are curricular expectations that drive learning opportunities in classrooms, and these do not always match what is needed for a group of individual students. Teaching requires balancing what is to be taught with the needs of the learners. Effective teachers find a way to manage this tension, so they respond to every student's learning needs in the best possible way. Some teachers are strictly bound by the curriculum (for many reasons). For some students this has minimal consequences as they can direct their own learning and get what they need. Other students are less able to do this and rely on their teachers to shape instruction in response to their learning needs. In responsive teaching, we aim to interpret learning needs in relation to both the intended learning set down in the curriculum and the ATRiUM capabilities, and to provide the most appropriate emphasis on what each student needs to engage with and is ready to learn. RTF 4 is examined more fully in Chapter 8.

When it is clear what needs to be taught next in terms of the intended learning outcomes of the curriculum and the ATRiUM capabilities, the logical next question is about how best to teach that content to all students.

RTF 5. How do I teach for all my learners?

RTF 5 of the *Responsive Teaching Framework* is about what teachers provide for students to learn and how they select teaching strategies to support learning opportunities. Responsive teaching starts with acknowledging the diversity of the learners, establishing a growth mindset, and working towards differentiation that will meet the needs of all learners. This approach is based on a Universal Design for Learning foundation (CAST, 2018a) combined with a growth mindset perspective (Dweck, 2006, 2017) which then evolves, as teachers get to know their students as learners, into responsive differentiation. Responsive differentiation depends on a range of strategies within interactive settings that use flexible groupings of students, as well as systematic and explicit teaching of some parts of the curriculum. All this sophisticated teaching happens within carefully organised and managed learning environments, and in collaboration with other teachers, educational caseworkers, and families. RTF 5 is examined in detail in Chapter 9.

Although assessment is carried out throughout this framework, RTF 6 explicitly focuses on what has been learnt and prompts teachers to gather evidence of learning through assessment.

RTF 6. What did my students learn?

In RTF 6, teachers focus on the outcomes of learning and the factors that support or hinder learning. Again, teachers have both a group and individual focus when asking the sets of questions included in Figure 2.1. RTF 6 also brings attention to positive or negative outcomes that may not necessarily have been intended but which need to be considered when planning subsequent learning opportunities. The assessment approaches that allow teachers to gather evidence about what their students have learned are explored in the next chapter of Part I. RTF 6 is examined in detail in Chapter 10.

Responsive teachers are reflective and evaluative

Both RTF 7 and RTF 8 are about reflecting on learning and teaching. RTF 7 uses a retrospective perspective to explore how teacher feedback supported students' learning and what other feedback might be needed. As feedback to learners is one of the most powerful of all teaching strategies, it is the focus of RTF 7.

RTF 7. What feedback supported my students' learning?

Although feedback is provided within responsive teaching as part of teaching interactions, it is valuable to consider its effect and what further feedback may be useful and who it might target. Effective teachers provide feedback and learners respond through deeper or more targeted engagement in learning. Feedback from teachers is ideally provided as part of every interaction. Feedback can also be received from peers, and so an added responsibility for teachers is to establish and nurture supportive feedback interactions between their students. All students also give themselves feedback on their learning and this needs to be considered by teachers. At an organisational level, schools have processes for providing feedback about student learning through reports or parent interviews (also refer to RTF 1). While these reporting processes are included in RTF 7, the main aims of this reflective question are to bring attention to the importance of the feedback that is supplied directly to learners, to acknowledge that it is fundamental to effective teaching, and to prompt teachers to notice what differences it makes to students' learning. RTF 7 is examined in detail in Chapter 11.

To complete the responsive teaching cycle, we use hindsight again to make judgements about the effectiveness of teaching (RTF 8).

RTF 8. How did my teaching support my students' learning?

This final question is necessary because teaching does not always result in learning, and we need to make sure it does. Evaluation in *responsive teaching* depends on teachers gathering evidence of their students' learning (RTF 6), while being conscious of what they bring to their teaching (RTF 2) and what the students bring to their learning (RTF 3). It also prompts teachers to consider their own teaching (RTF 4 to 7) and to use all this information to make well-informed judgments about what has made a difference for their learners. Rather than continuing to do things that may or may not be working, responsive teachers deliberately check what worked so they can make further decisions about what is likely to work again in the future. RTF 8 is examined in detail in Chapter 12.

Summary

To respond to the diversity of learners' needs (*learning for all*), and to teach them so they are prepared for the complex world after school (*learning that lasts*), we have acknowledged the layers of influence on teaching and learning that come from frameworks and systems and from the characteristics of teachers and learners themselves. In this chapter, we have also stressed the need for teachers to focus on their students, both as a group and individually, and emphasised the importance of planning, teaching, assessment, and feedback. Lastly, we have included a reflective and evaluative dimension that supports professionalism in practice. These dimensions underpin the eight reflective questions (RTF 1 to 8) that make up the *Responsive Teaching Framework* (i.e., *teaching that matters*).

Each step of the RTF has been briefly introduced in this section and will be discussed in detail in the eight chapters that comprise Part II of this book. The next chapter in Part I examines how *Responsive Teaching for Sustainable Learning* is not only research-based but also evidence-based, and presents the types of evidence that support inclusive practice.

3 Evidence-based practice

Many professions, like education, have a research-based and evidence-based orientation to practice. In describing the *Responsive Teaching Framework*, we have already emphasised that teaching relies on good assessment information. In this chapter, we explore what evidence is and how it can be accessed, as its use is core to *Responsive Teaching for Sustainable Learning*.

While there are many ways of describing what is meant by research-based and evidence-based practice, in this book research is included as part of a broader conceptualisation of evidence. The term evidence-based practice refers to the practice of drawing from several difference sources of evidence (including scientific research) to inform decision making. Scientific evidence is often the only kind referred to in discussions of evidence-based practice. However, further evidence can be derived from professional insights and from the educational experience of students and their families. Additionally, the very acts of teaching and learning themselves generate important evidence (Berman & Graham, 2018).

To emphasise the need for a range of sources of evidence, we use the metaphor of spotlights which illuminate practice (Figure 3.1). Each of the four

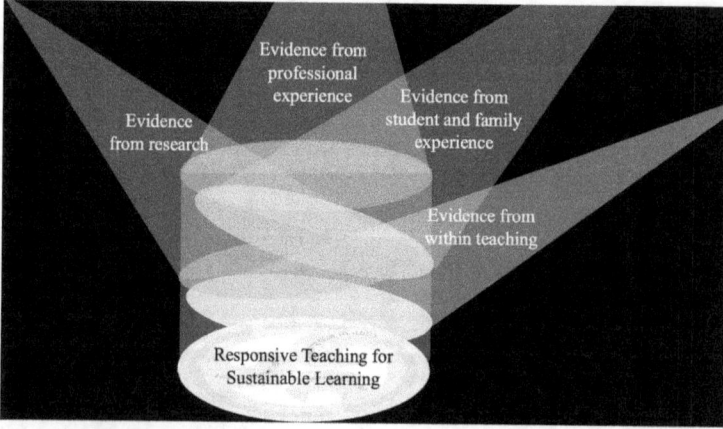

Figure 3.1 Evidence supporting *Responsive Teaching for Sustainable Learning*.
Adapted from Berman & Graham, 2018.

DOI: 10.4324/9781003299813-4

forms of evidence depicted illuminate part of what is needed. Together they provide a strong light that shines on all we do as responsive teachers to enhance our students' learning.

All the sources of evidence shown in Figure 3.1 are valuable and need to be accessed so that teachers can be truly evidence-based and responsive practitioners. In the next sections, we consider all four forms of evidence and what they offer to responsive teaching.

Research evidence

Scientific evidence is generated through research that is published in reputable, peer-reviewed scientific journals. This research-based evidence provides an indication of what factors are likely to be successful in teaching so that practitioners can be informed. Research has been conducted to explore human development and learning and teaching over many decades, and it is possible to find published evidence on every dimension of responsive teaching and sustainable learning. The mass of research in scientific journals has grown over more than 150 years in the context of the West and is a foundational basis of evidence for teaching practice.

Many education systems provide access to research databases for their teachers, with the aim of supporting them to deliver evidence-based practice. However, there is such an enormous body of research that it is impossible to know all of it. It is also sometimes difficult to make decisions about which research is most informative since tension exists between different schools of thought and researchers from diverse methodological backgrounds disagree about the validity of various research approaches. Sometimes research is not as relevant as it could be. For example, a large body of research about dyslexia has been generated using very different definitions of the condition. This has resulted in a lack of coherence across the research base for this condition (Elliott & Grigorenko, 2014). While it is expected that responsive teachers use scientific knowledge, it is important that they are conscious of its possible limitations, as highlighted by Elliott and Grigorenko's work. There can be considerable incongruity within research that necessitates a critical respective, careful reading, and the weighing up of evidence.

For the purposes of *Responsive Teaching for Sustainable Learning*, we organise research evidence about effective teaching and learning according to our ecological map, with a focus on teaching strategies that work to build capabilities in learning within differentiated learning opportunities. Throughout this chapter, we draw on research evidence about teaching practice and student learning, and aim to make sense of the enormous body of evidence that exists. Scientific evidence, along with the professional experience of the authors derived from their combined one hundred years of teaching and research, were drawn on in the conceptualisation of *Sustainable Learning* and in the development of the *Responsive Teaching Framework* (Graham, Berman, & Bellert, 2015). Scientific and professional practice evidence have been used iteratively in all subsequent writing and teaching about *Responsive Teaching for Sustainable Learning*, as will be evident in this chapter.

It is easy to be overwhelmed by the range of evidence for teaching strategies and influencers who advocate for approaches and strategies. Teachers can access individual research studies regarding effective teaching and then assess and make judgement about how relevant the evidence is for their teaching situation. This process is extremely time-consuming and not always feasible. To make research more accessible for teachers, several researchers and organisations have constructed reviews, meta-analyses, and database portals that curate research evidence.

For example, the Australian Institute for Teaching and School Leadership has provided summaries of research evidence relevant to different domains with links to advice from Australian state education systems and international research portals (AITSL, 2021). The US Department of Education set up their What Works Clearinghouse in 2002. It offers practice guides for teachers based on available research (US Department of Education, 2022). More recently, a not-for-profit organisation, the Education Endowment Foundation in the UK, supported by the UK Department for Education with a partner organisation in Australia, have developed portals of international research evidence specifically for teachers (Education Endowment Fund, 2022; Social Ventures Australia, 2022). These portals present the predicted impact of teaching strategies, evaluations of the quality of the research, and implementation costs. Other work in this field of translation of evidence includes Hattie's *Visible Learning* (2009, 2017, 2018), and Mitchell's *What Works in Inclusive Education* (2014, 2016, 2018; Mitchell & Sutherland, 2020).

The original conceptualisation of responsive teaching (Graham, Berman, & Bellert, 2015) organised the strategies or factors influencing learning according to ecological layers: family and community; learning environment; learning opportunities; and teaching strategies. This ecological perspective has been reflected in the work of John Hattie and colleagues in a volume of research summaries from around the world which focus on aspects of teaching, and influences on teaching and learning arranged as follows: student, home, school, classroom, teacher, curriculum, teaching strategies followed by chapters on understanding student achievement, and international perspectives on student achievement (Hattie & Anderman, 2013). These layers of influence have been used more recently in Hattie's online database which contains references for meta-analyses. These data sources have been organised according to whether they are related to the student; teacher; student learning strategies; teaching strategies; classroom; school; curricula; home; technology; and schoolwide and out-of-school strategies (Corwin Visible Learning Plus, 2023). Information is also included indicating whether there is confidence in the approach and potential for considerable acceleration, acceleration, positive impact, small positive impact, or negative impact on student achievement.

Another source of translated research about effective teaching within an ecological model is Mitchell's (2018) compilation of effective strategies specifically for inclusive education. His advocacy for research-based and inclusive practice is based on making available reputable evidence across layers of influence from teachers to systems, so that policy makers, educational leaders, and teachers can make sense of and use research evidence. This approach is helpful for distilling factors that support effective teaching and learning, and those pertinent to leadership (see Part III).

Evidence from professional experience

The second source of evidence that responsive teachers draw from is their own professional experiences. Teachers are lifelong learners who continue to grow throughout their careers. As they gain experience in applying their knowledge about learning and teaching in different situations, teachers become more and more knowledgeable. Working with students and their families and professional colleagues over the years constitutes a considerable body of evidence upon which to base decision-making.

On the other hand, there are challenges related to an over-reliance on professional experience. These include the need to make sure successes and failures of professional practice are evaluated carefully and professionally to inform future decisions. Evidence from professional practice needs to be used deliberately, consciously, and reflectively to continually improve practice. In the experience of the authors, it is not unusual for teachers to argue that a particular strategy or intervention was not effective because, "I tried it". However, when further discussion occurs, it is clear that the strategy was not implemented as intended and could not be evaluated with confidence.

The valid use of professional experience depends on the professionalism of teachers and their awareness of any biases that may influence their conclusions about practice. Reflective teachers are honest about the complexity of teaching and learning situations and draw from their professional experiences in reliable and meaningful ways. The approach we take in this book is to value professional experience and to support teachers to build their reflective and critical capabilities so that they can make informed judgements that support their teaching and their students' learning.

Evidence from students and their families

The third source of evidence about teaching and learning comes from the experiences of students and their families. It includes their encounters with educational settings, previous teachers, and school contexts. For families of students with disabilities, there is likely to be a long history of engagement with intervention professionals, often from birth or early childhood. Their many years of experience constitute valuable information which can be considered when making teaching and intervention-related decisions. Responsive teachers need to access this kind of evidence so that decisions can be made in light of what has previously worked to support particular learners, what has not been successful, and under what conditions approaches have been successful. The RTF is a framework that cues the gathering of information about the student in preparation for planning for teaching, accessing evidence of what has worked (or not), and what might work in the future.

Sometimes teachers may say they do not want to read previous teachers' comments, or be told what works or does not work from student or parent perspectives. They may say, "I want to make up my own mind about these students and what is best for them". This approach means teachers avoid taking on others' biases, but it might also mean that they dismiss useful evidence about what has been successful. Relationships with students are core to everything teachers do as responsive teachers, so considerable amounts of valid evidence can be obtained by including the voices of our students as much as possible (Berman & MacArthur, 2018). Furthermore, partnerships with parents are vital, and responsive teachers establish and nurture these partnerships so that teaching decisions are informed and justified.

Evidence from within teaching

The fourth type of evidence integral to responsive teaching is generated within teaching and intervention. Assessment is central to all teaching. It results in evidence of what students bring with them to their learning (RTF 3); what they need to learn now (RTF 4); how best to teach (RTF 5); what students have learnt (RTF 6); and how teaching has successfully supported their learning (RTF 8). Much of the evidence gathered is not only for teachers' use but is also the basis of feedback to students (RTF 7), reporting to families, and a source of substantiation for the impact teachers have as agents of change.

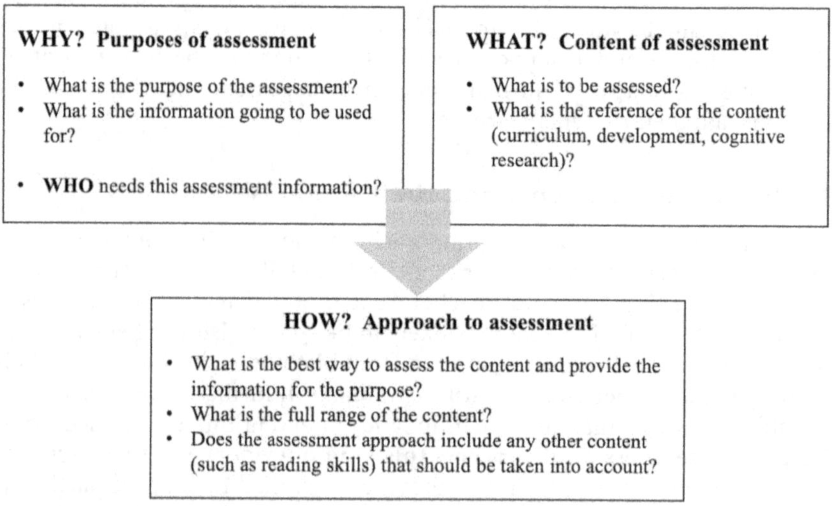

WHY? Purposes of assessment

- What is the purpose of the assessment?
- What is the information going to be used for?
- WHO needs this assessment information?

WHAT? Content of assessment

- What is to be assessed?
- What is the reference for the content (curriculum, development, cognitive research)?

⬇

HOW? Approach to assessment

- What is the best way to assess the content and provide the information for the purpose?
- What is the full range of the content?
- Does the assessment approach include any other content (such as reading skills) that should be taken into account?

Figure 3.2 Assessment decision-making.
Berman, 2001.

In the context of responsive teaching, assessment is the process of gathering evidence, it is relevant to every step of the RTF, most particularly as articulated in the paragraph above, to RTF 3 through to RTF 8. In Table 3.1 details are not included about assessment for RTF 1 and RTF 2, but there are still relevant teacher-focused reflective processes for gathering information that informs these steps (see Chapters 5 and 6). The nature of evidence gathered for the other six steps of the RTF is outlined in Table 3.1.

Table 3.1 Assessment as evidence gathering in the *Responsive Teaching Framework*

	Step of the RTF	Evidence to be gathered in assessment
3	RTF 3. What do my students bring as learners?	Assessment to gather information about cultural contexts, needs, interests, experiences, capabilities, prior learning, and achievements that the students bring to their learning; the nature of the learning group they create; what the students' families bring to each student's learning and the learning group.
4	RTF 4. What do I need to teach now?	Assessment specifically related to defining intended learning outcomes and ATRiUM capabilities.
5	RTF 5. How do I teach for all my learners?	Assessment embedded in learning activities to monitor learning in reference to intended learning outcomes, unintended learning outcomes, and factors that support and hinder learning including ATRiUM capabilities.
6	RTF 6. What did my students learn?	Assessment of how each learner and the learning group responded to instruction in relation to the intended learning outcomes, unintended learning outcomes, and factors that support and hinder learning.
7	RTF 7. What feedback supports my students' learning?	Assessment information is provided as feedback to students to support their learning.
8	RTF 8. How did my teaching support my students' learning?	Assessment information is used to evaluate the effect of teaching on the group and individual learning. Assessment to point to what students are ready to learn next and what the teacher needs for professional development.

Adapted from Graham, Berman, & Bellert, 2015 and Berman & Graham, 2018.

Gathering evidence through assessment is a vital component of responsive teaching and is not just what teachers do at the end of a unit of work to check what students have learnt (RTF 6), although that form of assessment is a significant part of the process. Guided by the decision-making model for assessment used in *Responsive Teaching for Sustainable Learning*, appropriate assessments are used to gather information needed after considering WHY (the purpose), WHAT (the content), and subsequently HOW (the procedures) assessment will be carried out. The arrow in Figure 3.2 is positioned as a reminder that decisions about HOW to assess should be based on previous decisions about the WHY (and WHO) and the WHAT.

Each of these aspects of assessment will now be considered in the order that they would ideally be implemented in practice. Determining WHY an assessment is to be administered and WHO needs the assessment information addresses the context for deciding WHAT needs to be assessed, and then HOW to do it. In practice this is not always what happens. Assessment is sometimes determined by the tools available or the routine practices of educational settings. However, it is always preferable to consider the WHY of assessment first.

WHY do we gather evidence (assess)?

A framework that is used widely in education systems to help teachers clarify their purposes for assessment is described by the phrases *Assessment OF Learning*, *Assessment FOR Learning*, and *Assessment AS Learning*. If we use these three purposes as a starting point, we can link them to another common conceptualisation that characterises assessment as either summative or formative. To assist with this alignment, we have defined each of these terms in Table 3.2.

The primary purpose of assessment is to inform practice and instructional decision making. This means Assessment FOR Learning is the fundamental purpose of assessment for responsive teachers. The goals are to be well informed and make good decisions about what to teach and how to teach it; to acknowledge student growth and learning; and to evaluate and reflect on teaching decisions; and make changes as needed. As shown in Table 3.2,

Table 3.2 Purposes of assessment

Assessment OF learning	Teachers use evidence of student learning to make judgements about student achievement against goals and standards, curriculum competences, or developmental progressions.	is summative
Assessment FOR learning	Teachers use inferences from evidence about student learning to inform their teaching.	is formative
Assessment AS learning	Students reflect on and monitor their progress to inform their future learning goals; or when the assessment task is also a learning task.	is both summative and formative

Adapted from Berman & Graham, 2018.

assessment OF, FOR, and AS learning can be determined to be summative and/or formative. Summative assessment is assessment that is looking back in time and gathering evidence of what has been learned. In contrast, formative assessment is about looking forward and using assessment information to help make decisions about future teaching and learning. Furthermore, there are two other purposes of assessment that are pertinent to responsive teaching: selection and diagnosis. Any use of assessment for placing students in programs is selective and draws on both summative and formative information. Assessment is also used to evaluate the success of teaching and intervention, and relies on both summative and formative assessment as evidence for this purpose. In addition, often diagnostic assessment is discussed either explicitly or implicitly after a referral for assessment has been obtained.

The diagnosis of any developmental or other disability is related to criteria that are set for specialist education or health services or programs. Conversations about such assessments are really about selection but are often referred to as being diagnostic. It is important to think about why the exploration of a diagnosis might be appropriate, and that it can be for selection purposes. In medicine, it is often just enough to focus on diagnosis since that provides direction for treatment. The recent move to individualised medicine (Cortese, 2007) echoes the constant need in education for more individualisation in relation to diagnostic assessment. Even if assessment results in a diagnostic label, there will be variations in how conditions present themselves. Each learner will experience and engage with their learning differently, and although a diagnostic label may point to possible ways to teach students according to common characteristics, this will be insufficient for teachers who are responsive to individual learning needs. In *Responsive Teaching for Sustainable Learning*, we interpret labels in terms of the ATRiUM capabilities when we define learning needs (see Chapter 7).

Consideration of WHY we are assessing also focuses on who is going to use the assessment information. Assessment is wasted unless it is acted on, and within responsive teaching that action is all about enhancing learning through teaching. Responsive teachers use assessment information to inform their teaching, to draw conclusions about student learning, to evaluate their teaching, and to plan for subsequent instruction. The other people who are interested in assessment information, and who will act on it, include students and their families, and those who work in educational settings and systems, and other professionals (Table 3.3). It is helpful to be clear about what actions accompany each purpose of assessment and who is involved in initiating those actions.

Being explicit about the purpose (WHY) of any assessment is important and needs to include consideration of what the information is going to be used for and who is going to use it (WHO). These assessment purposes are not mutually exclusive, but instead blend to support responsive teaching. Once it is clear WHY the assessment is to be carried out and WHO is going to use the evidence generated, it is appropriate to consider the content of that assessment, the WHAT.

Table 3.3 Actions that are supported by assessment for different purposes

WHY?	& WHO?
Summative	Teachers and learners, families, educational settings and system, and other professionals make determinations of achievement and progress.
Formative	Teachers and learners, families, and schools make decisions about learning opportunities and teaching strategies, and about their management of influences on achievement and progress.
Selective	Schools, education systems, and families make decisions about access to support services and management of influences on achievement and progress. Other professionals use assessment information to determine eligibility for diagnosis and intervention (health and allied health).
Evaluative	Teachers and learners, schools, education systems, and families make determinations of effectiveness of teaching, and impact of influences on achievement and progress. Other professionals use assessment information to determine effectiveness of intervention (health and allied health).

WHAT do we gather evidence about (assess)?

The second dimension of assessment decision-making is the content of assessment (WHAT is to be assessed; see Figure 3.2). The type of evidence needed for specific purposes and actions will depend on WHY the assessment is being carried out, and WHO is going to act on it. A summary of the WHY and WHAT of assessment is provided in Table 3.4.

There will be different references for the WHAT of assessment for each purpose, and even within each purpose. For example, summative assessment is about the curriculum, and can refer to the knowledge and skills from a learning area, or

Table 3.4 The WHY (& WHO) and WHAT of assessment

WHY?	WHAT? *(Content of assessment; type of evidence needed)*
Summative	Evidence of student learning in reference to intended learning outcomes and ATRiUM capabilities.
Formative	Evidence of student learning (as above), of effective and ineffective teaching strategies and learning opportunities, and of influences on learning.
Selective	Evidence of student learning (as above) and development, of effective and ineffective teaching strategies and learning opportunities, of influences on learning – drawn together in reference to set criteria for eligibility including for diagnosis of condition or disability (diagnostic).
Evaluative	Evidence of student learning (as above), of teaching strategies and learning opportunities, of influences on learning and teaching, and of teacher knowledge and expertise.

a curriculum-defined competence. Alternatively, it can reference learning progressions. This is the focus of RTF 6 in the *Responsive Teaching Framework*.

When evidence is needed by an educational system, it may be merely encapsulated into a grade (e.g., A, B, C, D, or E). These grades are codes within the system and allow collation of levels of achievement across educational settings or systems, which can inform selective and evaluative decision making. In contrast, when this type of evidence is needed by an educational caseworker, it needs to be much more specific. For example, evidence about emerging literacy can include demonstration of phonological awareness and manipulation skills; phonics skills; developing vocabulary (oral and written); comprehension strategies, writing and spelling. Each of these components of literacy can be further broken down into subskills that can be assessed, and which provide important information for professionals who will be supporting learners. Because all assessment is linked to a particular time, caseworkers also need access to results of a series of assessments, so the pattern and pace of students' learning can be determined.

Formative decision-making based on evidence requires analysis of information about student learning and information about what may have influenced student learning. To be responsive, teachers need to make determinations about what worked and what did not, so they can provide effective learning opportunities for each of their students. The evidence needed by responsive teachers is further detailed in Part II when each RTF step is considered in more depth.

Evidence needed to support assessment for selection purposes includes all of that previously outlined, as well as any other information required to address eligibility criteria for diagnostic labels or access to specialist educational provisions. Some of these circumstances use assessment information generated through usual school assessment, while others require additional specialist assessment as part of the process of selection. For example, referral for an investigation of mood disorder means that students are involved in the assessment of their behaviour within clinical settings, in combination with reports from their educational and home settings. The types of information required will not be the typical focus of teachers, but they will be involved through reporting on the educational life of these students. Psychological professionals then interpret the information gathered against norms, to determine whether students have the intensity and pervasiveness of indicators to substantiate a diagnosis at this time.

The evaluative purpose of assessment requires the analysis of all information about students' learning and about teaching, so that reflective practitioners can make determinations of how educationally effective they have been (RTF 8). This process also includes reference to frameworks for teacher knowledge and expertise (see Chapter 12).

Although different evidence is needed for the four purposes of assessment, as a foundation they all require valid evidence of student learning. Compiling evidence of student learning over time allows students and their teachers to see progress and achievement, to notice what they have learnt recently, and what they are working towards learning. Decisions about how best to teach (i.e., formative), about selection of students for more intensive teaching or other supports (i.e., selective), and about strengthening teaching expertise (i.e., evaluative) are all informed by evidence, not only about student learning, but about the context for learning, including the teaching that has been provided. Next, we consider HOW assessment information is collected to fulfill these purposes.

HOW do we gather evidence (assess)?

Gathering evidence to support responsive teaching happens in many ways and is informed by the purposes (WHY & WHO) and content (WHAT) of the assessment. With this in mind, it is useful to consider the range of assessment strategies that teachers can use to gather evidence about student learning.

Traditionally, assessment in education has used formal tests or examinations at the end of a period of learning (a term, semester, or year). Written language and other symbol systems are the vehicle for the questions and for the student responses, which can be of varying lengths from short answer to extended writing and essays. Conventional tests use a range of question types (multiple choice questions, true-false questions, short answer questions, matching questions, cloze questions). They can ask direct or indirect questions of students; present students with stimulus materials to respond to, or provide tasks or problems to be solved.

In less formal assessment students can be asked to demonstrate their knowledge and skills by using oral or written language, graphic representations, video recordings, and creative works. They can also demonstrate learning when asked to teach others or carry out problem solving or creative activities collaboratively. Assessment activities can be contrived, naturalistic, static (i.e., with no input from teachers) or dynamic (i.e., with embedded teaching).

All these possibilities provide opportunities for students to demonstrate what they have learned, and each of these contexts presents challenges for teachers who need to interpret the demonstrated learning and judge the evidence. Responsive teachers can navigate the complexities of student learning and make sure that no students are disadvantaged by inappropriate assessment that does not allow them to demonstrate their learning. And yet, educational settings place some students in this situation every year – because they are not able to demonstrate what they have learnt in formal examinations. This can happen because of misplaced notions of equality and fairness, which are often used to justify formal, individual, written examinations. The practice of giving all students the same conditions is not responsive and can be unfair. Instead, equity is the foundation of assessment decision-making in responsive teaching. A range of opportunities are offered for students to demonstrate their success, and for educators to understand what supported their students' successful demonstration of learning.

In an educational system that uses external examinations and performance assessments, it is imperative that teachers, as far as possible, remove barriers to students' demonstration of learning. If, for example, students' literacy development does not allow them to show what they know, then assessment requiring that capability is not an appropriate choice. Instead, an oral interview, a conference, instance of applied problem solving, a creative activity, or a portfolio, project, or exhibition may be more successful at demonstrating evidence of learning.

Within the context of state-wide assessment of students with learning difficulties, or disabilities, or illness or accident, this issue has been addressed by special consideration procedures. These procedures are an additional layer of assessment for selective purposes that are necessary when students have shown that they will be disadvantaged without access to alternatives which provide the opportunity for them to show what they know and can do. This system has been shown to be more accessible for students from wealthy schools (Baker & Gladstone, 2021) than others and, therefore, may not reduce inequity but exacerbate it.

Just as responsive teachers need to consider their teaching and whether it has led to their students' learning, links also need to be made between assessment activities and the learning that is demonstrated in educational settings. Teachers can provide a range of assessment opportunities and record the learning demonstrated by their students under those particular conditions. The evidence, then, is not just what has been learned, but also under what conditions learning was demonstrated.

The WHY (& WHO), WHAT, and HOW of assessment-led decision-making is revisited in Part II where we explore what evidence is needed within each step of the *Responsive Teaching Framework*.

4 Layers of responsive teaching

Responsive Teaching for Sustainable Learning is about teachers' routine use of a variety of strategies to respond to their students' range of learning needs. It is enacted through flexible and dynamic approaches to the organisation, delivery, and intensity of teaching. *Responsive Teaching for Sustainable Learning* is also about being jointly responsible for all the students in the educational setting. In the past, teaching was focused on 'the class', and any 'special' learning needs were seen to be the responsibility of others, including specialist teachers, allied health professionals, families, and communities. This is no longer the case. All teachers are responsible for providing individual learners with differentiation of instruction, that is, with the intensive and targeted teaching appropriate to their needs. The model of *Layers of Responsive Teaching* supports teachers in thinking about how to respond to the needs of all their students. In this chapter, we explain the derivation of this model for differentiation, its key principles, and the way this works in practice. This information is elaborated on in Chapter 9.

Differentiation

Responsive teachers focus on the class group and on individual students, getting to know them as learners, and designing learning opportunities and teaching strategies that respond to individual learning needs. This approach to teaching has led to the development of the field of differentiated instruction, which has become established practice over the past two decades. It is a genuine response to the diversity of students that can be simply defined as "teaching things differently according to observed differences in learners" (Westwood 2001, p. 5). It is also a process of instructional planning and implementation which seeks to provide all students with authentic access to the curriculum. While some teachers have always included different points of entry and options for learning content in their instruction, differentiation became more established as a pedagogical concept in the late 20th century. It emerged largely in response to the recognition that a 'one size fits all' approach to teaching and learning perpetuated a lack of engagement and educational disadvantage for some students (Tomlinson, 2011, p. 13). An increase in accountability for teachers and school systems and the necessity to show learning progress for all students has added further impetus. Furthermore, differentiation entails taking student differences into account in a way that focuses on enhanced engagement and participation, and uses this information to shape the way the curriculum and learning activities are presented.

In the context of responsive teaching, differentiation is an essential approach that aims to ensure all students are engaged in learning and can demonstrate achievement. In Australia differentiated practices are specified in teacher registration as part of the first standard, that teachers 'know their students and how they learn' (AITSL, 2011, Standard 1). This fundamental focus aligns with RTF 3, which emphasises teachers' need to know what students bring to their learning, so they can decide what needs to be taught next (RTF 4) and how best to do that (RTF 5). Tomlinson, a key thinker in this domain, defined what we know about students in terms of their readiness for a particular domain of learning, their interest in that learning, and their learner profile (Tomlinson et al., 2003).

Before we look at how responsive differentiation works in practice (Chapter 5), it is valuable to look at what differentiation is *not*. An interesting approach to the definition of differentiated instruction is the identification of prevalent misconceptions including: the perception that it is merely a set of strategies; that it is only pertinent for struggling or advanced learners; that it is about different goals for different learners; and that it is the provision of individualised instruction (Dack, 2019). These four ideas are seen to be barriers to the effective use of differentiated instruction since they take the teacher back to the notion of teaching to the middle of a class, with extensions for faster or slower learners, or the use of additional or different activities for those students who experience difficulties or need acceleration.

Differentiation has a premise that learning goals are not changed; the principle is that teachers do not 'dumb down' the intended learning outcomes. Many people have stories about how students were supposedly included within a differentiated lesson by being given a colouring-in page that had a picture of whatever the content of the lesson was about. This is not what is meant by differentiation, and it is not teaching, unless an aspect of colouring-in was the intended learning outcome. Instead, it keeps a student who is not ready for the intended conceptual learning busy. Such a situation reminds us that we need to be very clear about what we want our students to learn from our teaching, and to think carefully about whether a range of learning outcomes is appropriate. There will be times when these need to be different across the class because that is what students need at the time. These intended learning outcomes need to be explicitly linked to individual learning plans, and not delivered by accident or as part of classroom management. It is always important that intended learning outcomes are focused and explicit and able to be extended as students are ready for the next level of depth in any learning.

This conception of differentiation can be further extended by considering the factors included in the *Differentiated Instruction Questionnaire* (DIQ; Coubergs et al., 2017). Three factors (use of flexible grouping, teachers' information gathering, and assessment and feedback practices) are about practice (see Chapter 5). The remaining two factors (growth mindset and ethical compass) are about teacher thinking.

Teachers need to have a mindset that anticipates and encourages student growth and learning, that is, a growth mindset (Dweck, 2006, 2017). They not only need a belief that all students can learn, which is fundamental to inclusive education, but also high expectations and a sense of responsibility for the learning of all students. The items in the DIQ focus on the teacher belief that intellectual capabilities are not fixed but can be developed through classroom experiences by means of teaching that promotes motivation for learning and creates success (Gheyssens et al., 2017).

The questions in the DIQ about growth mindset focus on perceptions about the influence of teaching on intellectual capabilities (Coubergs et al., 2017) since growth mindsets related to students who bring intellectual disabilities and/or giftedness into their classrooms are particularly challenging for teachers to hold. Teachers need to constantly question their expectations of students and assumptions about student potential and how these are affected by factors of diversity, disability, learning difficulties, and culture (Chapter 6).

At times teachers face ethical dilemmas, for example, when differences are evident between curriculum or system demands and what some students need to learn (Brighton et al., 2015). Tensions around whether teachers follow the system or respond to what they see as student needs were highlighted in the DIQ (Coubergs et al., 2017). Within this context, responsive teaching includes advocacy for students as learners and their right to an education that meets their needs.

Universal design for learning

A way to establish differentiation as central to teaching and not an add-on is by using *Universal Design for Learning* (UDL) as the foundation for planning and lesson design. Universal design is a concept that was developed by Ron Mace and colleagues at North Carolina State University in 1988 (Dalton, 2020). As both an architect and a person with a disability, Mace's work focused on designing environments that were accessible for all people. Article 2 of the Convention on the Rights of Persons with Disabilities (UN, 2006) defines universal design as "the design of products, environments, programmes and services to be usable by all people, to the greatest extent possible, without the need for adaptation or specialized design" (para 5). Elements of universal design can be seen in today's built environment with features such as automatic doors, building ramps, touch taps, and reception areas with desks of different heights. A key feature of universal design is that the environment is considered in the planning stages so that retrofitting need not occur.

In the 1990s, researchers at the Centre for Applied Special Technology (CAST) in the United States found that while universal design reduced physical barriers, students with diverse needs faced other barriers to learning within traditional education models (Dalton, 2020). This led researchers to explore how universal design principles could be applied to educational environments to support the inclusion of all learners. Their findings suggested that curricula were often designed for homogeneity of students and that designing learning experiences based on typical students meant that there were inherent barriers inadvertently built into learning experiences (Meyer, Rose, & Gordon, 2014). This led to an extension of universal design to Universal Design for Learning. Educators working within a UDL framework understand that curriculum design and delivery needs to be considered at the planning stage before educators reach the classroom. Meo (2008) encapsulates this idea in the following quote:

> *by addressing the diversity of learners at the point of curriculum development rather than as an afterthought or retrofit, UDL helps educators to develop curricula that truly leaves no child behind while maintaining high expectations for all students, including those with disabilities.*
>
> (p. 22)

Before we explore the principles and guidelines for teachers, it is important to be clear about what UDL is *not*. UDL is not about providing specialised adjustments or accommodations for a select group of learners (Waldron, 2016). It is not about lowering academic expectations and simplifying the curriculum; high expectations and challenges that engage learners are still required. UDL is not a 'magic bullet' or 'fix' for all students and it will not solve all curricular or pedagogical problems (para. 4). Finally, UDL is not based on a prescriptive formula. Educators still need to use their professional discretion and make their own decisions about how they use UDL in the classrooms. There is no checklist that will ensure teachers create perfect UDL-based lessons or classrooms.

UDL is a planning framework that focuses on making the curriculum accessible for all learners by examining at the outset the barriers that might occur in the delivery of teaching and learning activities. As noted previously, this avoids retrofitting or changing instruction at the point of delivery (Chita-Tegmark et al., 2011) which can impact teachers' confidence in delivering teaching and learning activities to diverse learners. While UDL was originally developed for learners with disability, a recent meta-analysis suggests it is effective for all learners and useful across all school settings (Capp, 2017).

Table 4.1 below highlights some of the key differences between traditional instruction and UDL. UDL aims to accommodate all learners through flexible

Table 4.1 Traditional and UDL instruction compared

Traditional instruction	Universal design for learning instruction
• Teachers typically deliver content one way	• Teachers deliver content in multiple ways
• Students are passive learners who acquire information through memorising, practising, and taking tests	• Students are active learners who engage and analyse the content to gain understanding by themselves and collaboratively
• The learning environment encourages students to sit quietly and work on identical tasks	• The learning environment encourages students to explore content based on personal interests, preferences, or abilities
• Students' skills and knowledge of content are assessed using one method	• Students are allowed to demonstrate their skills and knowledge of content using one of several methods

Adapted from Council for Exceptional Children, 2005.

instructional practice and assessment. It includes being adaptable when delivering content, drawing on student strengths and interests, encouraging active learning, and ensuring that assessments are varied and target the skills and knowledge taught.

UDL draws on research from the field of neuroscience where there is an understanding that the brain is seen as "a complex web of integrated and overlapping networks" with learning being the "changes in the connection within and between these networks" (Meyer, et al., 2014, p. 30). Neuroscientific research can help educators understand more about the variability of learners with an understanding that each learner is unique and that it is important to recognise the complexity of unique differences.

Further, UDL harnesses this understanding and refers to the affective, recognition, and strategic networks of the brain. The *affective networks* enable the learner to evaluate patterns and assign them emotional significance as well as to engage with tasks and learning (Hall, Meyer, & Rose, 2012). The *recognition networks* sense and assign meaning to patterns to identify and understand information, ideas, and concepts (p. 3). The *strategic networks* are related to executive function. They produce and manage mental and motor patterns and are also linked to actions. All three of these UDL networks need to be engaged for high-quality learning (Meyer, Rose, & Gordon, 2014).

Changes in intensity of teaching

Responsive teachers need to think about how to provide multiple ways to access curriculum, to engage with it, and to demonstrate learning. A central aspect of differentiation is variation to the intensity of teaching. Teachers make deliberate changes in the intensity of their teaching in response to assessment information about student learning. For the purposes of responsive teaching, intensity of instruction is considered in a range of ways (Table 4.2).

There are times when more-of-the-same learning activities, some practice, or a repetition of learning opportunities is needed for learners to progress. This may be appropriate for students who are responding to teaching less quickly than might be anticipated, or when students understand part of what is being taught but not all of it. All of us know that we engage in learning differently if we are familiar with the content and activities, and therefore repetition can be among the most effective and easily provided ways of enhancing learning, especially when fluency is the aim.

Another key component of intensity of teaching is the degree of explicitness required in both content and feedback. Some learners will recognise connections within content, while others will need to be provided with each part of the learning and then scaffolded to put their understandings together as a whole. Explicit, systematic teaching is central to effective teaching (Hattie, 2018) and is vital for many students, for example, those who would not develop literacy skills without it (Hempenstall, 2020). Explicit teaching depends on having structured lessons with clear goals. It includes planning for multiple exposures and practice opportunities, such as worked examples, and supports learning through expert questioning and task-related feedback. These are all components of expert lesson planning and core competencies for responsive teachers.

Table 4.2 Changes in intensity in responsive teaching

Intensity as …	Appropriate when …
Repeated learning experiences	• a skill is not yet consistently demonstrated, and more opportunities to consolidate learning are needed • a skill is established, and it is useful for that skill to become more automatic or fluent • domain-specific concepts or vocabulary need to become established and remembered • a student has an intellectual disability, specific cognitive difficulty, or other condition that means more practice is needed for the skill or understanding to be established
Increasingly explicit content, monitoring, and feedback	• the delayed responsiveness to teaching may be because of misconceptions, partial learning, or skills that are developing
Smaller learning group	• a teacher needs to focus closely on students as learners; the smaller the group the more intense the focus, and the more direct the teaching and assessment
More frequent opportunities and varied length of activities	• more frequent opportunities are needed; shorter intense periods of teaching are accessed more easily than longer sessions; or longer periods of instruction allow for depth of learning
Increasing challenge	• a student needs to develop more depth of learning or extension of skills, or requires opportunities to apply knowledge or skills
Access to specialist expertise	• it is determined that specialist assessment of learning needs, and/or access to specialist intervention is needed; a student becomes the focus of educational casework

Adapted from Berman & Graham, 2018.

It is also important to recognise when the explicit teaching of some content is not applicable, and to not subject students to lessons they do not need. This is avoided thorough monitoring assessments that help teachers know how students' learning is progressing. Monitoring progress and assessing what is already known is particularly important for gifted students, and even more so for gifted students who experience learning difficulties. These twice exceptional students need learning opportunities that match their complex needs. For example, some students may not have acquired what are considered the basic skills of a topic but despite that, are developing complex understandings. It is unethical for these students to be restricted to establishing basic skills when they are actually ready for higher-order problem solving, albeit with basic skill support.

Small group teaching is a practical way to increase the intensity of teaching. This flexible arrangement allows teachers to target students who need explicit teaching and provide more opportunities for practice, or alternately, a different concentration of time on aspects of learning. The smallest group, and therefore the most intense, is when one teacher works with one student. This can be appropriate at times and may be the most effective way for teachers to provide what is needed. One-on-one interactions mean identified teaching needs can be acted upon immediately. As this is logistically difficult, though, a compromise is to flexibly organise and reorganise students into learning groups. If students become accustomed to being grouped differently for various activities, this can become a routine and effective way to adjust instruction.

Responsive teachers need to be able to mix and match intensive learning opportunities to students' learning needs – extension and enrichment should not be for selected students only. All students need to experience the possibilities of learning alongside other students who are thinking deeply or are expert in particular skills. Students need to be able to build their own knowledge and skills.

The final point in Table 4.2 refers to the need for specialist involvement in responsive teaching. This is the process of educational casework that complements responsive teaching. The specialist may be another teacher, an allied health professional, or a specialist assessment professional. Teachers work with other professionals to better understand their students as learners and to collaboratively provide the appropriate intensity of teaching and intervention. For those who are particularly interested in this topic, in-depth exploration of the educational casework process is offered in Berman and Graham's (2018) book on *Learning Intervention*.

Flexible groupings

As outlined in the previous section, flexible groupings of students allow students to engage in collaborative learning with other students, while teachers target small groups and individuals to provide more intensive and explicit teaching. The flexible use of groupings is essential for responsive teaching as it establishes the expectation that teachers will deliberately and strategically engage with the whole class group, small groups, or individual students at times.

When combined with the explicit teaching of learning behaviours, routines underpin the success of flexible groupings in differentiated classrooms (Bellert & Graham, 2017). As Richmond (2007) emphasises, the teaching role needs to be less about managing and more about teaching. Within a well-organised classroom, it is possible to create rich opportunities for dialogue between students. This is a key teaching strategy that has been shown to be effective through the "joint construction of knowledge, understanding, and learning" and instrumental for both academic and social growth and development (Gillies, 2019, p.200). A recent review of research literature focused on collaborative learning groups and classroom dialogue (Gillies, 2020) concluded that teachers need to set expectations and processes for:

- positive interdependence
- individual accountability
- active listening, mutual acknowledgement, non-judgemental statement of ideas
- constructive critique of ideas, sharing of resources and taking turns

- promoting interaction
- group processes

By setting up opportunities for students to engage in academic dialogue, teachers nurture the development of the ATRiUM capabilities. The interactive setting of small groups allows students to develop their capabilities for relating to others (R) in the context of learning, thereby using their capabilities in language and other symbol systems (iU) to engage in dialogue and deep thinking (T). The capabilities used in managing the self (M), both in these interactions and in learning, are further developed, while the opportunities for engaging in active learning (A) are enhanced by collaborative small group learning. The nature of learning in this context is truly sustainable, with learning capabilities instigated and nurtured by collaborative groupings in classrooms.

Additionally, dialogue in classrooms can be thought of as academic talk (Gillies, 2019) and the more expertly a teacher can generate classroom talk, the more effective students' learning will be. From these interactions students grow intellectually as they internalise the ideas discussed (Vygotsky, 1978). This approach takes the best of traditional teaching (i.e., talking, interaction and questioning) and increases its sophistication, so that all dialogue in classrooms is deliberately designed to support learning.

We can consider the use of flexible groupings and what is to happen within those groupings through looking more closely at the interactions between teacher and students (Alexander, 2018; Berman & Graham, 2018). Teachers have always used groupings in their classrooms. The default group is the whole class, with a focus on teachers who provide much of the talk supplemented by direct student contributions. To complement whole class teaching, teachers can place students into groups and set up opportunities for student dialogue. They can also engage in more intense teacher-student interactions.

Therefore, classroom dialogue, within flexible groupings, plays a major part in responsively differentiated classrooms. Such learning environments are organised using the principles of UDL to ensure all students can optimise learning. In response to assessment information, teachers fluidly arrange groupings which provide opportunities for learning, for practice of developing skills, and for explicit teaching and feedback. Responsive teachers also alter the intensity of their teaching according to student needs by varying the length of activities, increasing challenge, and providing access to specialist expertise. Changing intensity of teaching in response to evidence of student learning is integral to the *Layers of Responsive Teaching* model explained next.

Layers of responsive teaching

The idea of layers of teaching has come from the development of the *Response to Intervention* (RtI) model (e.g., Preston, Wood, & Stecker, 2016). RtI has three tiers (Figure 4.1). The principal level (Tier 1) is universal instruction. When quality universal instruction is provided through research-based differentiation, most students will learn effectively. However, it is accepted that up to 20% of students may require teaching that is more intensive (i.e., through Tier 2 or

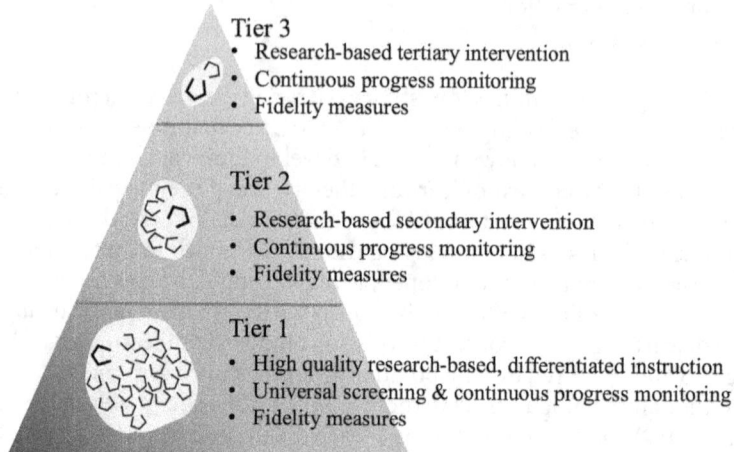

Figure 4.1 Response to Intervention (RtI), a tiered model.
Adapted from Berman & Graham, 2018, p.43, with text from Bradley, Danielson, & Doolittle, 2005.

Tier 3 intervention). When a student is not responsive to classroom instruction, a secondary intervention is implemented, which is more intense or targeted. Progress is monitored as this happens, and if learning progress is not as anticipated, even though appropriate instruction has been delivered, then a third tier of intervention is provided. At Tier 3, learning is monitored, other professionals like educational psychologists or speech pathologists are involved, and the implementation of the intervention is checked to make sure it is being provided with fidelity.

RtI was first articulated within the context of rethinking the process of assessment for the diagnosis of learning disabilities (LD) in the United States. It began with two premises: that appropriate education should not wait for a diagnosis of LD; and that assessment for the purposes of diagnosis can use evidence that is generated within intervention. As such, RtI has become more than an alternative for determining LD. Integral to this model is the idea of responsiveness to teaching and intervention. By including the context of learning and assessment, RtI acknowledges the relationship between teaching and learning, and the importance of the responsiveness of both teachers and learners.

At the same time as the processes for diagnosis of LD were being questioned, there was a move towards using evidence-based effective classroom teaching, universal screening, and curriculum-based assessments to track the progress of all students (Heller, Holtzman, & Messick, 1982). In this way, the possibility that student difficulties are the result of inadequate opportunity to learn is eliminated. Strengthening classroom teaching is done by using scientific evidence about what works and embedding assessment, both as a way of screening to identify difficulties and as systematic measures that monitor learning.

The RtI model is still evolving. It has been subsumed in a growing number of instances by *Multi-Tiered Systems of Support* (MTSS), which extends the

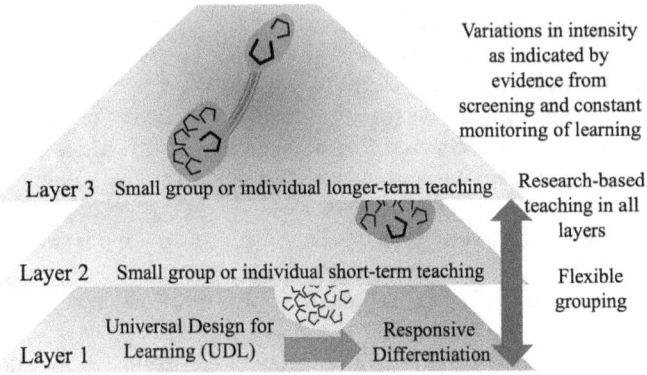

Figure 4.2 Layers of responsive teaching.
Adapted from Berman & Graham, 2018.

focus of RtI from academic learning to also include behaviour, and social and emotional learning (Sailor, Skrtic, Cohn, & Olmstead, 2021). RtI, with efficacious teaching, rigorous assessment, and changes in the intensity of teaching as needed, is one of the highest-ranked teaching strategies that makes a difference to student achievement (Hattie, 2018). *Responsive Teaching for Sustainable Learning* accepts the principles of RtI and MTSS articulated above and adds the notion of overlay (Figure 4.2) so that short-term and longer-term intensive teaching is complementary to evidence-based classroom teaching and not seen as an alternative. This results in a model of *Layers of Responsive Teaching* (Berman & Graham, 2018).

This model depicts increased intensity of teaching as overlapping. It shows how access to increased intensity of teaching, in small groups or individually, is based on evidence of what is working and what is not. Flexible grouping and processes of problem solving are included, as they are in more recent models of RtI (Berkeley, Scanlon, Bailey, Sutton, & Sacco, 2020). We also recognize that many students, not just 20%, may need access to increased intensity of teaching at times because of acute adverse circumstances. Responsive teaching could apply to one teacher and a group of students, but it also extends into other learning opportunities, both within and outside, the educational setting. The principles underpinning the *Layers of Responsive Teaching Model* are:

- Appropriate education should not wait for a diagnosis or specialist assessment; teachers should not wait for students to experience significant lack of success, but as far as possible, prevent failure through early intervention
- Tiered or layered teaching or intervention can be provided as soon as it is needed
- Teachers need to embed assessment and act on that assessment information, so they make the best decisions about what to do next for all their students

44 The foundations of responsive teaching for sustainable learning

- All learners may need increased intensity of teaching or different learning opportunities at times; teachers can provide layers of responsive teaching as needed in fluid, dynamic and responsive ways
- Evidence-based, intensive teaching can be provided as needed with appropriate transitions between different learning opportunities
- Collaborative teaching and shared responsibility for student learning is fundamental
- Assessment for the purposes of diagnosis uses the evidence (i.e., student responsiveness to the intervention) that is generated within the layers of responsive teaching as an important source of information

Layers of Responsive Teaching is how teachers can think about and organise variably intensive learning opportunities for all students. In the next sections of this chapter, each of the three layers of the model will be considered in more depth.

Layer 1: Responsive differentiation

In Layer 1, teachers enact the *Responsive Teaching Framework*, starting with considering the context in which they are to teach (RTF 1) and what is expected of them. They also ask themselves about their own teaching skills and knowledge, cultural positions, and assumptions that influence teaching (RTF 2). These two steps set them up to understand the influences on their teaching and what they bring as teachers to their classes. The focus is then on students as learners. This means that teachers set out to understand what their students bring to their learning (RTF 3) and what they need to learn now (RTF 4). This is when some ethical tensions may arise, and teachers need to justify their planning decisions.

In terms of how best to teach their students (RTF 5), responsive teachers start with *Universal Design for Learning* and move towards responsive differentiation as they gather more information about their students as learners through screening tasks and curriculum-based assessment. In Layer 1, flexible groupings are used to respond effectively to changes in the learning needs of students. The use of small group or individual teaching increases the intensity of the teaching for students as needed and can be provided for as long as it is working, as depicted in Figure 4.3. All other aspects of differentiated

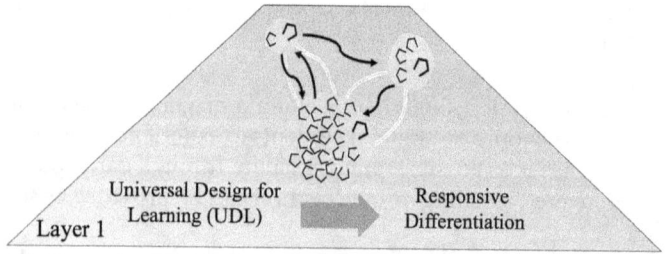

Figure 4.3 Layer 1 Responsive, differentiated classroom teaching.
Adapted from Berman & Graham, 2018.

instruction, including changes in intensity of learning activities and flexible grouping, are used by classroom teachers as they provide responsive differentiation.

The finer details of teacher practice are examined in Chapter 5, where the research-base is more thoroughly considered. For example, effective teaching strategies that have been identified in large scale research (Hattie, 2018) are explored in the context of responsive differentiation. Those strategies that can be adjusted in intensity to meet learner needs and which can be used within a collaborative environment (Meyer, Rose, & Gordon, 2014) and those that support explicit teaching are included. Responsive differentiation combines the provision of research-based teaching strategies and learning opportunities with constant monitoring of learning (assessment), so that the best possible opportunities for student learning are provided.

Layers 2 and 3: Small group and individual teaching and learning

Responsive differentiation can be extended beyond the classroom to include other instances of small group and/or individual teaching or intervention. In smaller groups, teachers focus more closely on individual students, and teaching and assessment interactions are more direct. Increased immediacy also accompanies giving feedback to students and the selection of specific teaching strategies in response to evidence of student learning.

Layer 2 is about short-term, more intensive teaching or intervention which is an appropriate response to the learning needs of many students. For example, Layer 2 intervention may be appropriate when students have been absent or have experienced an adverse event that has interfered with their learning. Layer 2 may also be useful when students have difficulty with part of their learning and need more practice or scaffolded explanation for a short while. Many school-based interventions fit this layer, including intensive literacy or numeracy programs. Education systems and other organisations also provide these kinds of short-term interventions through specialist reading classes in districts, or camps focused on particular domains of the curriculum. There are also short-term therapeutic interventions within Layer 2, such as individual speech therapy for articulation, small group social skills development provided by specialist teachers, or grief and loss support with school psychologists. In addition, responsive teachers can also support their students in less formal ways, including spending a session or two consolidating knowledge. Students can also take part in small-group study sessions in preparation for an examination or project. Families may also organise short-term group or individual tuition or intervention at times, for various purposes, including preparations for entry examinations.

In RtI models, the distinction between Tiers 2 and 3 is usually about whether the students need instruction in small groups or individual intervention. In *Layers of Responsive Teaching* the size of a group is not pre-determined, and instead, we make a distinction based on length of time allocated to the intervention. Layer 3 is about longer-term, higher-intensity teaching or intervention. The longer-term intervention groups or individual interventions are most common for students who have been identified with a disability or chronic condition, and whose development and learning requires consistent support. Such interventions often include the involvement of educational psychologists and other allied health colleagues. They can also be organised by families who want to ensure their child has support for all their learning, as they are seen to be at risk of learning difficulties. Layer 3 learning opportunities may include individual tuition or therapeutic intervention that is provided by out-of-school agencies, private allied health, or education professionals.

Instruction and intervention at Layers 1, 2 and 3 are not mutually exclusive or separate. They should complement each other and all inform quality classroom teaching. According to this model, all instruction and intervention should be research-based and carefully monitored so that evidence of student learning is generated. Decisions about which layers are most appropriate at any time are based on evidence of what is working and not working in response to student learning needs and whether resources are available in particular education settings. It is important to remember that all learners may need increased intensity of teaching, or different learning opportunities, at times. Ideally, the aim of responsive teaching is to provide layers of learning opportunities, as needed, in a fluid and dynamic way.

Ideally, teachers will collaborate with students, families, and other teachers, and with other professionals and organisations to provide these layers of teaching or intervention. This optimises the coherence of learning experiences that students can access and, therefore, their learning. It also means that a larger body of evidence of learning from multiple perspectives can be brought together to inform future teaching.

Collaboration for responsive teaching

It is evident that the successful implementation of the *Layers of Responsive Teaching* model depends on collaboration and an ethos of shared responsibility for all student learning. Given the sophisticated level of responsiveness expected of contemporary teachers, and the necessity to focus on both the group of students and individual learners, classroom teachers cannot easily accomplish their work alone; they need to work with teacher colleagues, specialist teachers, and other allied professionals, both within the school and in the wider community. In this way teachers access different knowledge, experience, and expertise that complements their own. By learning from others and offering their own knowledge contributions, teachers extend and strengthen their professional experience. Collaboration with allied health professionals, for example, provides a more individual-focused perspective that contributes to a deeper understanding of students and helps to ensure that small group and individual interventions are targeted and effective.

Education systems have many ways of organising the involvement of specialist teachers and other professionals and of shaping their roles and responsibilities. Schools often organise their staffing so that some teachers are responsible for classes, while others are responsible for the caseload support of individual students. In this way, schools use their resources to cover the dual focus of work with groups and individuals. Responsive teachers work with specialist teachers and other professionals, both within and outside schools. For example, a teacher can refer a student to a school psychologist for specialist assessment of learning and developmental needs, or to a speech and language pathologist to provide access to small group or individual interventions that build on teaching in the classroom.

The process of collaboration between teachers and other professionals who focus on individual students is integral to educational casework. Nothing a caseworker does is effective unless there is a flow of information and, ideally, a partnership with students' teachers and families. When this does happen the "collaboration between the class teacher and the caseworker will support well-founded decisions about the classroom learning opportunities and teaching strategies. Such casework will also support consideration of the possibilities of small group or individual short term or longer-term intervention for any particular student" (Berman & Graham, 2018, p. 46).

According to Hattie (2018) collective teacher efficacy is the highest-ranking aspect of teacher influence on student achievement. This ranking is derived from three meta-analyses that include 85 studies (Corwin Visible Learning Plus, 2021) which indicate that collaboration builds teacher knowledge and can result in a powerful sense of efficacy that flows into a positive effect on student learning. This will also be the case when collaborators are not necessarily teachers but professionals who bring their expertise to educational decision-making. Sometimes partners are within the same educational settings; at other times they are in different systems like Health Departments or in private practice. These partnerships should be fostered so that teaching is most effective for students who are the focus of educational casework, usually those with disabilities or learning difficulties.

Summary of the foundations of responsive teaching for sustainable learning

Part I of *Responsive Teaching for Sustainable Learning* has presented the conceptualisation of inclusive education as *Sustainable Learning* (Chapter 1). We defined *teaching that matters* using the *Responsive Teaching Framework*, which consists of eight reflective questions that support instructional decision making. As responding to the diversity of learners is central, *learning for all* is the aspirational goal of working towards universal and inclusive education. Responsive teaching uses a capabilities approach which values students as they build *learning that lasts* in order to engage actively in our complex and changing world. The ecological nature of education recognises the influences from wider society, in combination with community, family and educational systems. All these factors are important to acknowledge as teachers partner with students to enact responsive teaching that results in *Sustainable Learning*. The main actions of teaching are captured in the *Responsive Teaching Framework* (Chapter 2) which is elaborated on in Part II of this volume.

To inform decision making in the *Responsive Teaching Framework*, teachers rely on evidence that comes from scientific research, from within their own professional expertise, from the experiences of students and families, and from within their teaching (Chapter 3). In addition, the WHY, WHAT and

HOW of assessment supports processes for gathering evidence within practice, so that teachers know what their students have learnt, can make determinations of their own effectiveness, and engage in the next phase of planning for teaching.

Responsive teachers focus on groups of students, as is conventional, and also on individual learners. In responding to the diversity of students, responsive teachers plan for changes in the targets for, and intensity of, teaching to meet the differing needs of their students. *Responsive Teaching for Sustainable Learning* relies on a model of *Layers of Responsive Teaching* (Chapter 4) which is derived from tiered models of intervention. Within these layers of responsiveness, teachers work collaboratively to enhance teaching and learning for all. Not only do they partner with students and their families, but they also work with other teachers and professionals, and draw on available systems of support both within and outside their educational settings to strengthen the influence of their teaching.

Responsive differentiation, as the foundational approach to teaching, extends into increasingly targeted and intensive teaching, which is delivered, as needed, within class activities and in collaboration with specialist teachers, or other intervention professionals. The caveat placed on this approach to responsive differentiation is that it needs to be manageable; this means that teachers do not teach differently for each student. Teachers do, however, use ways of thinking, and frameworks and structures to help them provide different learning opportunities and effective teaching strategies for their students.

In conclusion, Part I of *Responsive Teaching for Sustainable Learning* secures the foundation for our evidence-informed, layered, and responsive framework designed to assist teachers in making instructional decisions. This framework guides teachers to respond to the learning needs of all their students. Each of the eight steps of the *Responsive Teaching Framework* are examined in detail in Part II.

Part II
Using the responsive teaching framework

In Part II of *Responsive Teaching for Sustainable Learning*, we elaborate on what it means to be responsive teachers who facilitate sustainable learning for all their students. There are eight chapters, with each chapter describing one of the eight steps of the *Responsive Teaching Framework*.

These chapters aim to empower teachers to build their knowledge and implement the RTF as part of their teaching. Part II also includes activities that guide reflective practice and allow readers to explore and personalise aspects of each step.

5 RTF 1: What frameworks do I need to consider?

RTF 1. What frameworks do I need to consider?

What international conventions, legislative frameworks, education system policies and procedures, curriculum, teacher registration requirements, cultural and community contexts, school culture and organisation, and learning environments do I teach within?

Introduction

The first step of the *Responsive Teaching Framework* (RTF 1) focuses on the context within which teachers teach. In this step the organising question is: What frameworks do I need to consider? Frameworks provide structure for actions and are fundamental to the way we learn. We learn by linking new understandings to established schema; judging information in relation to mental structures already in place and making decisions based on understandings; and by expanding or changing frameworks depending on knowledge and experience. The reflective question for this step reminds teachers of the frameworks within which their work is situated. What international conventions, national legislative frameworks, curriculum requirements, culture and community contexts, education system policies and procedures, school contexts, teacher registration requirements, and physical environments do I need to consider? These broad frameworks shape what teachers teach and how they teach it.

International conventions and principles

Since the Second World War the number of influential human rights frameworks has increased markedly. These rights-based frameworks have moved the debate towards embedding inclusive education into state systems. A commitment to universal education has been the foundation of the increased focus on education for students with disabilities. This goal is clearly stated in the United Nations Convention on the Rights of the Child (UN, 1989). In tandem with this development of an international commitment to universal education is an increasing focus on the rights of people with disabilities. The Universal

DOI: 10.4324/9781003299813-7

Declaration of Human Rights in 1948 and then a world conference on education for all in 1990 concluded that global education initiatives should aim to develop the capabilities, knowledge, values, and attitudes necessary so that everyone is able "to live and work in dignity, to participate fully in development, to improve the quality of lives, to make informed decisions, and to continue learning" (Inter-Agency Commission, 1990, p. 32).

A subsequent world conference on access and quality in special needs education resulted in the Salamanca Statement and Framework for Action on Special Needs Education (UNESCO & Ministry of Education and Science, Spain, 1994) which has become the bedrock statement on inclusive education. The Salamanca Statement called on international and national organisations to commit to education for all, and within that, inclusive education by "enrolling all children in regular schools, unless there are compelling reasons for doing otherwise" (p. ix). The Salamanca Statement continues to influence education around the world, with wide acceptance that inclusion is justified educationally, socially, and economically (Ainscow, Slee, & Best, 2019). The United Nations Convention on the Rights of Persons with Disabilities (UNCRPD; UN, 2006) has continued this international emphasis on inclusive education.

Activity

International conventions influence responsive teaching. Explore whether your country is a signatory to, and has ratified, the UN international conventions on the rights of children and people with disabilities. Consider what this means for the education system within which you work. A list of signatories is available on the United Nations Treaty Collection page (UN, 2022).

More recently the United Nations' Millennium Development Goals (MDGs; UN, 2015) drove international efforts to reduce poverty at the turn of the 21st century. Subsequently, the Sustainable Development Goals (SDGs; UN, 2016) have provided important international direction. One of the outcomes of the MDGs, which aimed to achieve universal primary education, has been a near halving of the number of out-of-school children of primary school age worldwide "to an estimated 57 million in 2015, down from 100 million in 2000" (UN, 2015, p. 4). The figures here are significant as there are still in excess of 50 million children of primary age not accessing schools globally. The goal to achieve universal primary education is integral to all other goals, which depend on education becoming increasingly universal and inclusive. For example, eradicating poverty and hunger, empowering women, developing global partnerships for development, and ensuring environmental sustainability, all depend on educated people. Sustainable Development Goal #4 aims to ensure "inclusive and equitable quality education and promote lifelong learning opportunities for all" (UN, 2016). Again, this educational goal is fundamental to the achievement of the SDGs which are focused on improving our human and environmental conditions.

As well as global goals that provide frameworks for national responses to education, there are more specific international frameworks that influence teaching. An example is the publication of the Organisation for Economic

Co-operation and Development's principles of learning, that aim to change the understanding of learning and the roles and agency of teachers and learners (Dumont, Istance, & Benevides, 2010). The seven principles proposed are concerned with: learners being at the centre; the social nature of learning; that emotions are integral to learning; recognising individual differences; stretching all students; assessment for learning; and building connections between areas of knowledge and their context of the wider world. Building on these principles the OECD has continued its exploration of what teaching should and could be and landed on a dynamic systems model that aligns with *Sustainable Learning*. The seven principles of learning have thereby evolved and are now the principles of Innovative Learning Environments (ILEs; OECD, 2017). These principles align with *Responsive Teaching for Sustainable Learning*.

The profound change in how learning environments are defined in these OECD documents is a refocusing on relationships that are acknowledged as the centre of teaching and learning. This points to a time when teaching and learning will be carried out in a much less institutionalised and regimental way. For example, although many educational settings already provide distance education and online learning, this way of teaching became necessary for all institutions because of the Covid-19 pandemic which began in 2020. The inequities regarding technological resources were highlighted, as was the significant role of parents in their children's education.

This major disruption prompted schools, education systems, and families to rethink how teaching and learning might work best for young people and dismissed some of the institutional imperatives that many students find difficult to manage. It is clear that some students learn better when not having to attend formal classrooms and conform to organisational rules. From the responsive teaching perspective, the use of flexibility in attendance and grouping could be extended further into the everyday organisation of teaching and learning. Therefore, from international considerations about education, we move to the documents that guide teaching and learning within nations.

National legislation

Each country has their own legislative frameworks that support education. Education in Australia is provided by the states and territories in response to a national requirement that school education must be available and accessible to all, as is articulated in international conventions (Commonwealth of Australia, 2022a). State and territory legislation then sets out how this will happen, for example the Australian Capital Territory has the Education Act 2004 (ACT Government, 2022). A range of other laws contribute to how education is set up and administered. At the national level there are four anti-discrimination acts that are pertinent to education and focus on age, race, sex, and disability (Commonwealth of Australia, 2022b). As an example, the key Australian legislation concerned with disability is the *Disability Discrimination Act* (1992). This legislation clearly defines what is lawful in relation to the actions of educational authorities and educational providers. The salient unlawful actions include: refusing or failing to accept a person's application for admission as a student; setting terms or conditions regarding the admission of the person as a student;

denying students access or limiting their access to any benefit provided by the educational authority; expelling the student; subjecting the student to any other detriment; developing or accrediting curricula or training courses having content that will either exclude the person from participation or subject the person to any other detriment (Disability Discrimination Act, 1992, s22).

There are also practical frameworks that help education settings enact their legal responsibilities with regards to students with disability. In Australia, the *Disability Standards for Education (2005) plus further Guidance Notes* (DSE) have been developed (Australian Government, 2005). The DSE (2005) documents the rights of students with disabilities and the responsibilities of educational authorities. It also describes the measures required to provide evidence of compliance in each of the key areas. These are enrolment and admission; participation; curriculum development, delivery, and accreditation; and harassment and victimisation. It is important for teachers to understand that students with disabilities have the right to access education "on the same basis", that is, with the same opportunities and choices as other students, and that "reasonable adjustments" must be made for them to access educational opportunities. While "reasonable adjustments" are defined in the legislation, descriptions of what adjustments look like are specified at three distinct levels (supplementary, substantial, and extensive) as part of the Nationally Consistent Collection of Data (NCCD). These are:

- Support provided within Quality Differentiated Teaching Practice
- Students receive minor adjustments reasonably expected as part of quality teaching/school practice
- Supplementary adjustments happen at specific times, and involve modified or tailored programs and instructions, with accessible materials
- Substantial adjustments involve frequent teacher-directed individual instruction with adapted materials and instructions
- Extensive adjustments are personalised at all times and may involve assistive technology (Commonwealth of Australia, 2022c).

In addition, the states, and territories of Australia each have further legislation concerned with disability that affects educational practice. For example, in NSW education is provided for under the legislative framework of the Education Act, 1990 (NSW Government, 2020) and the more recent Disability Inclusion Act, 2014 (NSW Government, 2022). The latter expects education systems and local governments to clearly articulate their plans for disability inclusion and to comply with reporting requirements.

It is clear that these legislative and regulatory guidelines influence how systems and schools manage issues around disability. Their influence also flows through to teachers by setting imperatives about collecting data, reporting on student learning, and providing language around teaching and inclusion. For example, the structure of adjustments within the NCCD (Commonwealth of Australia, 2022c) is reflected in how teachers talk about provisions for students with disability and has been matched to the three tiers of Response to Intervention (RtI) by some practitioners. Within the inclusive classroom (Tier 1), quality differentiated teaching is the basis for minor and supplementary adjustments, whereby substantial adjustments are Tier 2, and extensive adjustments are related to Tier 3.

Activity

Find out which legislation in your country is relevant to your teaching. Which laws are pertinent to inclusive education in your context?

Education system policies

While all education in Australia operates under national and state or territory legislation, the states and territories have also developed educational policies that reflect regional differences. Independent education providers also operate within each state and territory which results in a complex system of policies in the education sector.

Education system policies encompass everything from attendance, behavioural expectations and discipline, to teacher practice and inclusion. An example of inclusive education policy is Queensland's Inclusive Education Policy (Queensland Government Department of Education, 2021) that defines inclusive education to mean "that students can access and fully participate in learning, alongside their similar-aged peers, supported by reasonable adjustments and teaching strategies tailored to meet their individual needs" (p. 1). This policy lists the legislation and regulations under which it has been developed. These reference anti-discrimination law, human rights laws, and Disability Standards for Education (Australian Government, 2005).

In response to disability anti-discrimination law, the NSW Department of Education, the largest education system in Australia, has developed a Disability Inclusion Action Plan 2016–2020 (NSW Government, 2016), specifically related to inclusive education. Its goals include (4.4 to 4.7):

- Improved teacher knowledge and skills in recognising and responding to the learning and support needs of students whose learning is impacted by disability and making adjustments
- Improved processes for accessing additional specialist support for students with disability
- Increased number of students who have evidence based personalised learning and support provisions
- Increased number of children with disability in quality preschool programs (these children will primarily be in the year before school or disadvantaged three-year-old children).

Most schools also develop their own policies, some of which are distinctive while others reflect wider policy. Policy framing of issues influences how teachers, students, families, and communities use them to share understandings and justify local decisions. Sometimes schools write policies for their students using accessible language. For example, Katherine High School in remote Australia provides policies written in accessible language on their web page

(Katherine High School, 2018) to foster shared understanding between student, families, and the school.

Teachers need to know what policies apply in their educational settings and what they mean for their practice. As a reflective practitioner, it is important to consider the way policies and their implementation can affect how students and families think about schooling and their relationships with teachers and schools. Many staff meetings and professional learning sessions ensure teachers are familiar with the current policies that affect their work.

Activity

Find out which policies in your education system guide your teaching. Which policies are pertinent to inclusive education? Review policies in your educational setting to see how they reflect the broader systemic policies and relevant legislation. Take time to explore policies from other settings to see what is similar and what is distinctive about your context.

Curriculum

Curriculum in Australia is national, but then again it isn't! While there is a national Australian Curriculum, the states and territories have developed their own versions with varying degrees of alignment. In addition, independent education systems and schools all have curricula that reflect their philosophical approaches, albeit within the frameworks provided by the accreditation bodies that oversee them.

Curriculum is variably prescriptive. In some systems, it includes not only the content to be taught, but also the ways that the content is to be taught, and the standardised assessments that are to be administered across the system. Each of these dimensions of curriculum are frameworks within which teachers apply their expertise. Such situations provide varying amounts of discretion for teachers, with some teachers 'trained' in particular teaching strategies, and others able to use their professional expertise to choose teaching strategies flexibly. The latter context is an assumption underpinning the *Responsive Teaching Framework* – that teachers can make decisions based on how they see their students' learning needs and how they draw on their expertise to meet those needs.

The structure of the Australian Curriculum includes not only learning areas but also General Capabilities (ACARA, 2022a) that are a useful reference for a capabilities approach to teaching, such as *Sustainable Learning*. As already explored, this trend towards competencies/competences/capabilities is worldwide. It allows teachers of students with disabilities to share meaning around what needs to be taught now and what capabilities will be needed in life after school.

In inclusive education, the curriculum is often a source of negotiation with respect to student learning needs. In such cases, it is important for teachers and families to decide which parts of the curriculum are essential for students and which parts are not as important at this time. In some systems, this can involve selecting learning outcomes from earlier stages of the curriculum or from a separate curriculum which is designed for students with disabilities. The NSW version of the Australian curriculum includes a Life Skills strand (NESA, 2021a), designed for students with disabilities for whom barriers to accessing curriculum are not able to be reduced through adjustment.

Teachers need to know the curriculum and how it is to be implemented in practice. Knowing the portion of the curriculum that is pertinent to the age of students and the learning area being taught is important. It is also important to know how parts of the curriculum fit within the whole. In the Australian context, this means knowing about the learning areas, the general capabilities, and the recently included learning progressions (ACARA, 2020a).

Activity

Take time to explore the sections of your curriculum that focus on the diversity of students. Consider how these sections are framed. Are they about adjustments? Are they about inclusion through planning? Are there references to the tenets of *Sustainable Learning* (i.e., learning for all, teaching that matters, learning that lasts)? How do the curricular guidelines and expectations around teaching and learning align with the *Responsive Teaching Framework*?

Teacher registration requirements

Systems of teacher registration also influence teachers' work. In many education systems there are sets of standards against which teachers need to report so they can become registered. How the standards are worded and what they emphasise, influences how teachers reflect on their own teaching, what they emphasise in their work, and what they want to build in terms of their own professional capabilities.

In Australia, the Australian Institute of Teaching and School Leadership (AITSL) Standards are comprehensive. This framework defines what it is to be a good teacher in the national context. Teacher candidates in Australia must demonstrate their emerging teaching expertise through a Teaching Performance Assessment, which is a final assessment task for all graduating teachers. This task is linked to the developmental progressions for practising teachers that guide registration and continuing professional learning from graduate teacher, to proficient, to highly accomplished, and then to lead and mentoring roles. As frameworks, the Australian Teaching Standards aligns with *Responsive Teaching for Sustainable Learning* because they share the underpinning principles of inclusion and equity and the starting points of knowing the students and how they learn, as well the need for supportive and safe environments within which to plan for and implement effective teaching and learning (AITSL, 2011).

All teachers are responsible to registration bodies for their professional accreditation. In doing so, they connect to processes for establishing and continually developing their competence. This process is important for guiding teachers' professional learning and career progression.

Activity

As you plan your professional learning, refer to the AITSL registration standards, or other standard of relevance to you. Consider how the requirements match those set out for *Responsive Teaching for Sustainable Learning*. How are these frameworks compatible? What questions arise for you? How will you resolve these?

Cultural and community contexts

The cultural contexts in which teaching and learning occur have a profound impact on outcomes. Cultural mismatches can be the basis of ineffectual teaching and may lead to the management of students rather than focusing on their learning (Richmond, 2002, 2007).

In many settings, particularly where settlement has been a significant part of the history, there will be a cultural mainstream that is colonial. Such framing of schools and classrooms creates a mismatch for many learners. This cultural mismatch, based in an oppressive past when Indigenous peoples were limited in their access to education and their own cultural teachings were actively blocked by authorities, continues to hinder the engagement and learning of a sizeable proportion of the school population. Acknowledging the impact of colonisation, which has been reality for generations, is imperative for teachers. An understanding of what it means to be culturally representative of the colonising group whenever teaching children from the colonised group is fundamental to being able to bridge the cultural gap that is inherent in many teaching-learning relationships.

There is also considerable evidence that cultural difference has been interpreted by education systems as deficits, and in some cases disabilities. For example, cultural difference has been built into many of the standardised tests that determine level of disability, such as language and intelligence tests, as well as into definitions of giftedness. In these circumstances, children who belong to cultures different from the one considered when developing the tests are disadvantaged. They are assessed outside their cultural context and then, by definition, deemed to be lacking.

The development of cultural competence by teachers is a strong focus for many education systems and national contexts. This is important for minimising negative impact on students, particularly those who are part of voluntary and involuntary minorities. Aotearoa New Zealand is explicit in relation to this dimension of professional expertise and provides frameworks for teachers to use to assist their development of cultural competence (Teaching Council of Aotearoa New Zealand, 2022).

What does cultural competence look like? A search of research literature and educational writing using the term 'responsive teaching' will lead to many articles and books that focus on *culturally responsive teaching*. Bishop and Berryman's (2006) definition of culturally responsive teaching highlights the need for culture to 'count'; for learning to be interactive and dialogic; for teaching-learning relationships to involve shared power and strong connections; and for expectations to be high. For further discussion of frameworks for teachers to use in the development of cultural competence see Chapter 6, where 'what teachers bring to their teaching' (RTF 2) is explored.

Activity

Do your own search for cultural competence frameworks and consider how these fit your context. If the ones you find are not a match, see if you can develop guidelines for you and your colleagues based on the information you have found.

School culture and organisation

Even if the frameworks within which schools operate in systems are the same, there is always a distinctive flavour to any school. Each school is a unique organisation of people in a particular place with a particular school culture. Getting a sense of how schools are organised and how students are grouped helps to form a picture of who is important and how all students are valued. Schools group students together for organisational purposes and in doing so reveal their positions towards marginalised students. Sometimes schools with segregated classes or units see the existence of these specialist teaching contexts as recognition of their strength in catering for diversity. However, this organisation can also suggest that these students are not considered part of the school.

School culture has been defined and explored in terms of its relationship with student learning. A study in the United States recently demonstrated that the key factors of school culture relative to student learning are a sense of importance around academic achievement; student support; trust and respect; optimism; and a professional learning community consisting of "shared responsibility, reflective dialogue, derivatised practice, and organizational learning" (Lee & Louis, 2019, p. 91). School culture is complex and influences both teachers and students in overt and covert ways. Erickson (2004) noted that cultures can be "shaped by the learning and teaching that happen during the practical conduct of daily life within all educational settings we encounter as learning environments throughout the human life span" (p. 32). Further to this, Erickson acknowledges that cultures are constantly changing as we absorb new cultural ideas and discard old cultural ways. Finally, he also accepts that everybody is cultural and that everybody is multicultural – that is, that every human group possesses both culture and cultural diversity (Erickson, 2004).

When considering the question "What do I bring as a teacher?" understanding how school cultures are maintained and reproduced and how they influence teachers and students is important. Schools are part of broader societies that have been shaped by their historical, economic, political, and social contexts (Breunig, 2005) which, in turn, impact the delivery of teaching and learning. As Hanley (2006) concludes, "Education is a cultural project" (p. 52) and schooling cannot be separated from culture.

Education plays a vital part in the transmission and transformation of culture, and while schools try to convey through the curriculum the cultural knowledge of most worth, this enterprise can be seen as a search for control, comfort and meaning by the dominant culture (Hanley, 2006). As a result, the cultural inequalities found in the wider society may be replicated within schools (Chen, 2005). This can create tensions when attempting to create inclusive school communities, as societal messages around disability, socioeconomic status, ethnicity, and gender may not align with the developing school culture. It is useful to realise that the culture that a school transmits to its staff and students can be part of, or separate to, the wider community. Specifically, social relations impact school culture and its associated practices, ideologies, and values. As Owens (2004) asserts, the culture of a school develops over time and is shaped by values and beliefs; traditions and rituals; history; stories and myths; heroes; and behaviour norms.

To understand school culture more deeply, it is worth exploring the work of Schein (1992, 1997, 2004) who developed a widely accepted understanding of organisational culture. Schein (2004) asserts that culture can be analysed at various levels, with each level suggesting the degree to which each part of the culture is visible to observers. This is an important way of thinking for teachers to encounter, otherwise they may not be aware how the visible and invisible levels of culture impact their day-to-day work with students. These levels are artefacts, espoused beliefs, and values and underlying or basic assumptions (Schein, 2004). In this instance, artefacts include the visible parts of a culture including the school's physical presence, language, technology, artistic output, clothing, myths and stories, rituals, ceremonies and published information about values, and organisational products such as charters, improvement plans, and ways of working (Schein, 2004). Espoused beliefs and values include the strategies, goals, and philosophies that are developed over time by the members of the organisation (Schein, 2004). These beliefs are usually begun by organisational leaders based on what they think will and will not work to solve problems and manage various situations. These espoused beliefs are adopted by group members and become part of the way the organisation 'thinks'. Underlying assumptions are "unconscious, taken-for-granted beliefs, perceptions, thoughts and feelings" (Schein, 2004, p. 26). There is often minor variation in how assumptions are interpreted, as consensus comes from the repeated success of implementing the beliefs and values demonstrated within the culture (Schein, 2004). Schein believes that until the underlying or basic assumptions of an organisation are understood, then the other levels of culture cannot be adequately deciphered.

Schools are organisations, and as such, display each of the three levels of culture. Brady (2005) notes that in schools, artefacts can include documents that form a school's operational routine such as their timetables, codes of conduct, and other policies that describe how a school works on a day-to-day basis. Espoused values and beliefs are the ways that the artefacts are enacted. While a policy or procedure may stipulate the way something is done, the reality can be different (Brady, 2005), and the values and beliefs of the school are only really learned by students and staff through participating in the culture. Basic assumptions in schools develop out of the preconceived ideas of group members about how schools should operate (Brady, 2005). When developing inclusive schools, it is this level of culture that presents the most challenge. Basic assumptions help to form the 'hidden curriculum' experienced by staff and students which can restrict the outlook of students and the inclusivity of the setting (Apple, 2004).

As noted, school cultures are created through the intertwining of artefacts and creations, values, and basic assumptions (Evans, 1996; Schein, 1992, 1997, 2004; Sims & Sims, 2004). Artefacts and creations are how school operations are made routine; values are those principles that guide a school's daily behaviour; and basic assumptions are institutional practices and values that are so ingrained in the group's collective consciousness that behaviour based on any other premise is unimaginable (Schein, 1997). Each of these three levels will reflect the dominant groups within the school system, as the values and privileges of the dominant culture are reproduced (Chen, 2005). As noted by Sustainable Development Goal 4, all students have the right to learn in an inclusive environment. However, if there are underlying beliefs about certain groups in society and their ability to engage in the learning, a school may become a place of exclusion for these students. Teachers need to understand how culture shapes their engagement with all learners.

At the artefacts and creations level, schools reproduce the dominant messages about what constitutes good educational practice. Artefacts and creations can be found in the general operational routine of a school in procedures such as codes of conduct and timetabling of classes, as well as in classroom organisation, school management and curriculum. Government imperatives will also be found in policy documentation, for example, student engagement policies that outline school responses to inclusion initiatives. These artefacts and creations are used to transmit the permitted cultural knowledge of a school.

The values level is more complex. Values can be defined as "the principles and fundamental convictions which act as general guides to behaviour, the standards by which particular actions are judged as good or desirable" (Halstead & Taylor, 2000, p. 169). When discussing schools, Evans (1996) suggested that values are used to guide work and collegial behaviour, however, school values are often mapped to those of a specific, usually dominant group (Apple, 2004) and not necessarily common to all. Values about inclusion can be developed through the enactment and re-enactment of policy directives. Values can also be held by teachers based on their own individual experiences and beliefs about the diverse learners they teach. For example, a teacher might hold values and beliefs that students with disability will get a better education if they are taught in segregated settings. Teachers may feel that they will not be able to provide effective teaching and learning opportunities for these students, and this may create tensions for them working in an inclusive setting.

Basic assumptions can be positioned as the deepest level of culture and defined as "underlying shared convictions that guide behaviour and shape the way group members perceive, think and feel" (Evans, 1996, p. 43). Basic assumptions are invisible, and it has been suggested that they can only be understood by participating in the life of the school (Evans, 1996). This level is most challenging when attempting to understand assumptions held about inclusive education within school cultures and by individual teachers. Basic assumptions, that part of culture where the dominant groups hold the most power, are the hardest to change. It is at this level of culture where diverse groups become silenced and marginalised in education and where barriers to including all learners impede progress.

Studying culture and understanding what assumptions teachers may bring to their work is a complicated undertaking and is discussed further in RTF 2 (Chapter 7). It can be a challenging experience to honestly consider how one's own cultural experiences affect work with a diversity of students. Teachers need to consider how they incorporate artefacts and creations, what values they hold about diverse learning communities, and how basic assumptions support or hinder their work with all students.

Activity

School culture is another way of thinking about what it is that makes schools safe learning places that support sustainable learners. There are many aspects of school context that affect how responsive teachers function; however, the following dimensions are a starting point for teachers to be aware of and reflect on.

- Write down your understandings about the artefacts and creations, values, and basic assumptions relevant to inclusive education in your school setting.
- Repeat this by identifying the levels of culture related to inclusive education that you recognise in your setting.
- Do the understandings that emerge from your reflections and the analysis of your setting align? If not, what can you do as a teacher to address these differences?

Learning environments

To complete this discussion of the frameworks that influence our work as teachers, we want to draw the various influences discussed in this chapter together under the term 'learning environment'. Learning environments have been defined by the Organisation for Economic Co-operation and Development (OECD) over the past decade to mean more than buildings, rooms, furniture, and playgrounds. Under the umbrella of innovation in education, Innovative Learning Environments (ILEs) have been conceptualised as organic wholes that encompass the experience of organised learning for given groups of learners around a single 'pedagogical core' of learners, educators, content, and resources. ILEs are larger than classes or programs; they include the activity and outcomes of learning rather than simply the location where learning takes place; and refer to the importance of leadership in making design decisions about how to optimise learning (OECD, 2017, p. 16).

This definition of ILEs allows the acknowledgment of the interactions and dynamic nature of what it is that we do when we responsively teach and what our students do when they actively learn. This definition and the body of work that has been generated affirm the ecological and multidimensional model that is *Responsive Teaching for Sustainable Learning*. As we have explored many of the dimensions of learning environments in the previous sections, we will conclude this chapter by focusing on the physical environment within which the teaching and learning interactions are instigated and nurtured.

The places, spaces, and buildings where teachers engage in teaching and learning, and their arrangement of spaces are the focus of considerable investment. Traditionally, learning and teaching has been carried out within community spaces. Since the establishment of school buildings, there has been a focus on multiple classrooms, one for each grouping of students and their teacher. These separate spaces were organised for passive learning, with individual desks facing the front so students would pay attention to a teacher who provided information using 'chalk and talk' and directed responses from the students. Fixed furniture arrangements are not aligned with the pedagogy of contemporary education, although there are still times when expository teaching is appropriate.

Responsive teachers need to be able to rearrange the furniture to accommodate separate groups and activities that require flexible learning spaces. It is interesting to note that although flexible learning spaces have been provided in new schools, at times these have been "retrofitted by the schoolteachers themselves to recreate classrooms" (Newton & Fisher, 2009, p. 134). Apart from practical issues like acoustics, this situation reveals a mismatch between teaching approaches and the physical environment. Resolution will only come about when architects and teachers work together to design spaces for teaching and learning (Newton & Fisher, 2009). In fact, a recent collaboration shows how this can be achieved.

In South Australia, the establishment of Whyalla Secondary College has required three schools to combine to create a brand-new learning environment. As part of the architectural brief, teachers, parents, and students were asked "what they wanted to do, hear, say, think and feel". This resulted in the design of seven spaces for different teaching and learning activities, which have become the touchstones of the College's design (Whyalla Secondary School, 2019, p. 5). These are:

- Quiet Spaces, where students undertake solo activity without distraction or breaking of their sense of 'flow'
- Group Spaces, where natural affiliations come together collaboratively
- Publishing Spaces, where we put our ideas up for anyone to see
- Performing Spaces, where we adopt roles that are not our usual ones, or where we prototype ideas before committing to them
- Participation Spaces, such as markets, events, and meetings, where those who are not part of the same 'group' might come together
- Data Spaces, which include technology such as sensors and displays that record data to help us learn to better use data. For example, environmental data might nudge our choices in energy use; other data can help us work out whether students are engaged or not
- Watching Spaces, where most people view and listen, rather than participate (p. 8).

This collaboration between those who were to use and create the school community and the building designers has resulted in clear understandings of "how students might learn in different ways, [and] … provoke[d] questions about the way teachers teach" (Whyalla Secondary College, 2019, p. 9). Many teachers have little control over the architecture or the materials within which they work. As any teacher who has worked in more than one school can testify, though, the place and the spaces affect teaching, and how groups of students work together. Of course, not every educational setting has the privilege of being able to design spaces from the ground up, but it is possible to think about how to mix and match spaces and use the ideas that accompany Innovative Learning Environments creatively.

Activity

Consider the actions you engage in when teaching. Think about what you do and what you want your students to do as they learn. Design ideal spaces that would match your teaching and your students' learning. You can also ask your students to respond to this challenge. They can design their own learning spaces and explain how they would be used.

- What would these spaces look like, feel like, sound like?
- How would you resource them? What do you need?
- How would you navigate in them? How would you move in and between these spaces to interact with your students and offer layers of responsive teaching?

In summary, this chapter has responded to the first of the *Responsive Teaching Framework* questions: *RTF 1. What frameworks do I need to consider?* The chapter is not exhaustive as the number of frameworks to select from is extensive. However, those that have been included will prompt teachers to consider other frameworks that are important to their work and their contexts. In this chapter, we have noted the influence of international conventions and principles guiding education, national laws and frameworks, policy and curriculum produced by education systems, teacher registration requirements, cultural and community contexts, and learning environments.

6 RTF 2: What do I bring as a teacher?

RTF 2. What do I bring as a teacher?

What teaching skills and knowledge, cultural competence, and assumptions about learning, disabilities, giftedness, behaviour, and learning difficulties do I bring to my teaching?

Introduction

The second step of the *Responsive Teaching Framework* (RTF 2) is about the influence, both implicit and explicit, of teachers. Not only do teachers bring their professional expertise, their knowledge, and skills, which are recognised by tertiary qualifications and teacher registration, but also the entirety of themselves as cultural, physical, cognitive, interpersonal, and intrapersonal beings who engage in social interactions and relate to others. This chapter responds to RTF 2 which asks: What do I bring as a teacher? It focuses not only on teachers' professional skills and knowledge but also on assumptions about learning and diversity, and their cultural competence.

What teaching skills and knowledge do I bring to my teaching?

The professional core of what individuals bring to their roles as teachers is embodied in their teaching skills and knowledge, that is, their expertise. It is important for teachers to take stock of what it is that they bring in terms of skills and knowledge, to know what they do well, and to be conscious of what they need to develop to further strengthen their teaching expertise. While teachers have already spent up to four years in initial teacher education, there is then an expectation of continued professional learning, through practice and postgraduate study. As teachers, we recognise that we never get to a point where we know it all and can do it all; teachers are life-long learners. Responsive teachers need to be learners. This part of being a professional is acknowledged and supported by teacher registration and associated professional development requirements and processes. Teacher registration frameworks are the current means of defining the expected skills and knowledge required in teaching. The Australian Standards for Teachers (AITSL, 2011) cover three

DOI: 10.4324/9781003299813-8

domains of teaching, (professional knowledge, professional practice, and professional engagement) which are explicitly defined in the following seven standards.

- Know students and how they learn
- Know the content and how to teach it
- Plan for and implement effective teaching and learning
- Create and maintain supportive and safe learning environments
- Assess, provide feedback, and report on student learning
- Engage in professional learning
- Engage professionally with colleagues, parents/carers, and the community.

Responsive Teaching for Sustainable Learning is aligned with what teachers are expected to be able to know and do in Australia, and supports the professional reflection they are expected to engage in. Whatever the framework for judging professional expertise that is relevant, however, responsive teachers must be sustainable learners who reflect on the continued development of their skills and knowledge. As the *Responsive Teaching Framework* provides a sound structure for reflecting on all aspects of teaching practice, it has been used to scaffold the final mandatory teacher-education assessment for final year initial teacher education students from several teacher education institution in Australia.

What assumptions about learning do I bring to my teaching?

All teaching skills and knowledge are underpinned by what teachers know and what they assume about the process of learning. This aligns with the first Australian standard focused on knowing how students learn. Assumptions about learning and the theoretical perspectives on which teachers rely, influence how they teach and what they look for in student learning. What teachers know, or think they know, about learning is significant and affects every decision in relation to learning and teaching. In this context, assumptions are the rationales teachers use to make sense of learning; they help to explain the effects of teaching and why learning does not always lead to the intended outcomes.

Activity

Before continuing, take time to explain your understanding of how students learn by completing this sentence: *Learning is...* Then compare your statement with the theoretical positions summarised in Table 6.1.

Indigenous ways of seeing are complex and the oldest theories in existence. More recently, Western educational psychology has examined small areas of human functioning and generated enormous bodies of peer-reviewed scientific evidence about learning. Over time, the field of psychology has gradually acknowledged the complexity of learning, and learning theory has, therefore, become increasingly ecological, strengths-based, inclusive, collaborative,

Table 6.1 Theories of learning and how learning is explained

Learning theories	Learning is …
Indigenous theories	… cultural belonging and growth
Behaviourist theories of learning	… change in behaviour
Social learning theories	… changes in behaviour and thinking through social engagement or observation
Cognitive and neurological theories	… changes in thinking and in neurological pathways
Information processing theories	… changes of thinking through processing information
Ecological theories	… response to environment
Sociocultural theories	… the use of cultural tools (language) for social interaction and changes in thinking
Dynamic systems theories; transformative theories	… transformation of multiple systems of human functioning

Berman & Graham, 2018.

ethical, and sustainable. It is still appropriate for science to examine, with intensity, small components of learning, but in the practice of teaching, it is necessary to make inferences about what happens in the human learning as a whole experience.

There are consequences that follow teachers' reliance on theories. For example, if teachers rely on behaviourist theories of learning they may accept changes of behaviour as evidence of learning, without acknowledging the limits of this theoretical position. A learning theory that does not refer to thinking has major limitations and operates under the assumption that a change in behaviour means there have been changes in other aspects of student functioning (i.e., their thinking and emotions) which are not observable. This raises a major issue for teachers – that changes in thinking are not visible or easily measured. Behaviours, actions, or explanations (written or verbal) are often used as evidence upon which inferences about thinking are made, therefore, teaching requires expertise in accessing and interpreting evidence of learning.

Each aspect of the learning processes can also be interpreted according to learning theories and result in implications for teaching and learning. The analysis of how growth and fixed mindsets, and aspects of ATRiUM capabilities are framed within different learning theories (Campbell, Craig, & Collier-Reed, 2019) in Table 6.2 illustrates how powerful underlying explanations can be. Every aspect of learning (and teaching) can be interpreted from different theoretical perspectives which provide a range of problem-solving solutions. For example, persistence and effort, which contribute to active learning (A) and managing self (M), are understood differently from the viewpoint of behaviourist and sociocultural learning theories, and in reference to growth mindsets or fixed mindsets (Campbell, Craig, & Collier-Reed, 2019).

These excerpts from a larger study, which also examined challenges, praise, the success of others, and learning goals (Campbell, Craig, & Collier-Reed, 2019),

Table 6.2 Effort and persistence interpreted according to sociocultural and behaviourist learning theories

	Sociocultural theory	Behaviourist theory
Persistence	A persistent student continues to learn through internalising individual meaning from interactions with more competent others.	Persistence means responding to feedback (in the form of positive or negative reinforcement or punishment) by adjusting behaviour and practising in response to feedback.
How can persistence after setbacks be encouraged? (supporting a growth mindset)	Offer scaffolded activities that are not too far beyond a learner's current state of knowledge and provide opportunities to recover from failure. Give partial credit for failed attempts that follow problem solving steps.	Feedback on poor achievement should emphasise that improvement is possible, suggest alternative strategies, and allow repeated attempts.
How can giving up easily be (unintentionally) encouraged? (suggesting a fixed mindset)	Repeated attempts at assessments too far beyond a student's current ability may bring further setbacks and confirm beliefs that 'I don't have what it takes'.	Feedback such as public displays of ranking or low scores may encourage giving up, especially if the feedback creates shame and there are no opportunities to improve.
Effort	Effort involves working through scaffolded problems to develop meaning; questioning rather than accepting results; exploring alternative approaches to the same problems.	Effort involves observing and modelling the behaviour of an expert (a teacher or tutor) and using feedback to practice and develop mastery.
How can students be encouraged to put effort into their work? (growth mindset)	Use checkboxes/rubrics listing sub-steps of expert behaviour and indicating which steps are optional as expertise improves. Ask learners to rate how much effort they put into a task. Include extension options on assignments.	Encourage and reward repeated attempts at a task when feedback has been used to make changes. Show graphs of time on task without feedback compared to improvement from students who use feedback to improve. Provide differentiated activities to keep all students in a class engaged.
How can students be (unintentionally) discouraged from putting effort into their work? (fixed mindset)	Distant deadlines without interim deadlines may encourage work avoidance. Using only a single type of assessment that favours some learners (e.g., timed tests) can reinforce a fixed mindset.	Comparisons with peers who appear to achieve with little effort may make students feel discouraged. The reuse of test questions which have model answers may reward low effort rote learning.

Adapted from Campbell, Craig, & Collier-Reed, 2019.

illustrates the power of teachers' differing theoretical explanations in supporting or hindering their students' learning.

Activity

The Deans for Impact group have developed key questions to assist reflection on how teachers understand their students' learning from a cognitive perspective. These questions can be used to check assumptions irrespective of how learning is understood and explained. Take time to consider what you think about these aspects of learning, and the implications that your answers have for your teaching.

- How do students understand new ideas?
- How do students learn and retain new information?
- How do students solve problems?
- How does learning transfer to new situations in or outside of the classroom?
- What motivates students to learn? (Deans for Impact, 2015)

A further question of interest focuses on common misconceptions about how students think and learn. An OECD project into brain science at the turn of the century identified a set of myths (neuromyths) that influence education (OECD, 2002). For example, a devolution of autonomy in the NSW public school system led to some schools spending professional learning funds on programs that were not evidence based. The two prevalent neuromyths were that teachers' attention to learning styles would improve student achievement and that activities could target left-brained or right-brained learning. A small study conducted in NSW showed that 65% to 91% of the learning support and special education teachers surveyed accepted these two misconceptions (Bellert & Graham, 2013) although they are not based on evidence (OECD, 2002; Dekker et al., 2012) and do not make a difference to academic outcomes (Willingham et al., 2015). This example illustrates the susceptibility of teachers to ideas anchored in neuroscience which can spread quickly and are difficult to challenge (Grospietsch & Lins, 2021). There is no doubt that as innovation continues, theories of learning informed by educational neuroscience will become more useful to educators.

The most recent Western theories of learning (Table 6.1) are holistic and acknowledge the interplay of multiple systems of human functioning. For example, dynamic systems theory grew out of physiology (Thelen & Smith, 1998) and its application to aspects of cognitive, linguistic, and behavioural learning continues to be explored (Perone & Simmering, 2017). This theory recognises learning as transformations not only in behaviour and thinking, but also in physical, social, and emotional development. The focus on transformation is also part of transformative learning theory, which grew out of adult learning contexts (Mezirow, 1985). Adults (and therefore teachers) have developed a coherent frame of reference or set of coherent "associations, concepts, values, feelings, conditioned responses" which "selectively shape and delimit expectations, perceptions, cognition, and feelings" (Mezirow, 1991, p. 5). Transformative learning theories provide a way to explain the influence of teacher assumptions on practice and justify the critical questioning of assumptions that is part of *Responsive Teaching for Sustainable Learning*.

Each of the theoretical perspectives listed in Table 6.1 is complex and involves much more depth than we have scope to cover. Exploring how teachers describe learning is an entry point to this enormous field of theory and research.

Using Indigenous and Western theories of learning

Indigenous learning theories have been in existence for many more years than Western theories. These ways of seeing are complex and deep, and define learning as related to cultural belonging and growth. Indigenous learning theories focus on the essential connections of people with place, with the past, and with meaning and responsibilities, rather than trying to establish absolute truths about discrete aspects of human functioning (like behaviour). Indigenous models of human functioning have become more visible through their applications in mental health. For example, a model called The Dance of Life (Milroy, 2006) guides professionals to take the following into account that: physical development and health is about connection to country; psychological development and wellbeing is about meaning, identity and shared learning; social development is about early autonomy, collective responsibility, and two-way sharing; spiritual development and presence is about experiences, belonging and wisdom; and cultural development and learning is about language, cultural lore and law, and cultural identity (Milroy, 2006). This same interconnectedness is evident in Māori models of wellbeing such as Te Whare Tapa Wha (Durie, 1998) and Te Wheke (Pere, 1997), which stress the need for individuals to build all capabilities to support their development and learning.

Apart from these holistic models of human functioning and wellbeing, there are some key concepts from Indigenous cultures that are helpful for understanding learning and teaching, and have been incorporated into education systems. For example, ako and tuakana teina are two concepts from Māori mātauranga (knowledge) which are central to education in Aotearoa New Zealand. The NZ Ministry of Education recognises that "Ako is a dynamic form of learning where the educator and the student learn from each other in an interactive way. Ako is grounded in the principle of reciprocity and recognises that the student and whānau cannot be separated" (Ministry of Education, 2013, p. 3). Similarly, tuakana teina refers to a dynamic reciprocal teaching and learning relationship. Both concepts align with sociocultural theories of learning and illustrate how education has much to gain from the diversity of worldviews that explain what teachers and their students do.

Processes for drawing from both Western and Indigenous theory have been developing around the world. Geographic metaphors have been used in Aotearoa New Zealand and Australia to describe the blending of Western theories with Indigenous ways of seeing. These two metaphors refer to the blending of waters and are distinctive to their contexts. He Awa Whiria references the braided rivers of Te Waipounamu (the South Island of Aotearoa New Zealand). The braiding represents the integration of Pākehā (European) bodies of knowledge and Māori knowledge (Fergusson et al., 2011; Macfarlane &

MacFarlane, 2019). This process results in 'culturally reasoned' meanings and a distinctive evidence base for professional practice (MacFarlane, Blampied, & MacFarlane, 2011). Northern Australian Aboriginal meaning-making has drawn on a similar metaphor involving the mixing of waters in a lagoon (Ganma process; Marika, 2000; Thraves et al., 2021). In this metaphor from the Yolngu people, the salt water of the sea represents Western knowledge while the fresh water is Indigenous.

Another example of this same process from Canada refers to weaving Indigenous and Western knowledges together and to "two-eyed seeing" (Bartlett, Marshall, & Marshall, 2012). These examples of combined ways of seeing, or theories, are situated in the context of European colonisation, where Western knowledge has been the primary (or mainstream) knowledge of countries for centuries, and Indigenous knowledge has only recently begun to regain its value. Ancient ways of seeing are increasingly being recognised and drawn on in contemporary psychology and education (Commonwealth of Australia, 2018; University of Melbourne, 2022).

Responsive teachers need to be conscious of their assumptions about learning, and the theories, or ways of seeing, that they rely on. It is important for teachers to note that the more recent Western theories of learning and Indigenous ways of seeing learning and development all emphasise integrated and holistic phenomenon. Indigenous ways of seeing are insightful and allow responsive teachers to draw from perspectives that include a diversity of explanations about what it is to be human and to be learners and teachers. The integration of Indigenous knowledges into curriculum and educational research moves us towards a richer, more authentic world view.

Activity

What theories do you rely on? What do your perspectives mean for your teaching and assessment, and for how you provide feedback about learning to your students?

Use the descriptions in Table 6.2 to articulate your theoretical position. What are the implications for your practice? Think about whether you draw on any Indigenous theories, or if some of your perspectives align with Indigenous theories, and how you might combine multiple perspectives. What does this look like for you as a responsive teacher?

What cultural competence do I bring to my teaching?

Teachers are complex, cultural beings who bring much more than their professional knowledge and skills to their practice. Cultures, personalities, and fallibilities are all intrinsic and influential in the daily lives of teachers. We accept that what teachers bring to their teaching has profound effects on their engagement and relationships with students. Cultural contexts and competence are fundamental to how teachers are seen by students and families and how families connect with schools. Therefore, teachers need to be conscious of how their culture is perceived by students and how this influences teacher-student and teacher-family relationships.

Teachers need to make classrooms and schools culturally safe. Success in achieving this depends on teacher cultural competence and awareness. In the Australian context, cultural competence involves building opportunities for visible and valued cultural identity for Aboriginal students. This is a responsibility of all teachers (AITSL, 2022). In bicultural contexts, developing cultural competence is essential for all teachers. Bevan-Brown's (2003) model of cultural competence in Aotearoa New Zealand education provides the basis for assisting teachers to reflect on what they bring culturally to their teaching, and to build on that by:

- Increasing understanding of your own culture and the influence it has on you and your teaching
- Understanding how Pākehā culture influences New Zealand education
- Learning about the cultural background of the learners, how this influences them, and how to use that knowledge to make learning relevant, meaningful, affirming, and effective.

Aotearoa New Zealand is an increasingly multicultural country, as is Australia, which provides another complex situation within which teachers need to consider and develop cultural competence. However, there are models of multiculturalism within which to make more sense of what it means to be culturally competent. These include Erdem's (2020) Multicultural Competence scale which can be used to focus teachers on issues of awareness, skills, and knowledge.

Awareness:

- My cultural belonging can make me distant from students in diverse cultures and I can behave [with bias] towards students of other cultures
- I can understand the diverse characteristics of students
- I am aware of and can critically examine my prejudices towards diverse cultures and can notice if I discriminate against students.

Skills

- I can arrange the educational environment for students from diverse cultures
- I can prepare exam questions, adapt teaching materials, handle course subjects for students from diverse cultures
- I can build activities to reduce students' prejudices towards cultural differences.

Knowledge

- I care about student' beliefs, values, and traditions
- I treat student differences sensitively

- I find it necessary to have knowledge about the communication styles of students from different cultures (Erdem, 2020).

A third approach to building cultural competence is to broaden this concept to intercultural competence. In the context of Peru, the Ministry of Education (Ministerio de Educación, 2013) has defined the characteristics of interculturally competent teachers which include qualifications and professional education and written and spoken communication skills in both the native language of their students and in Spanish. The aspects of intercultural competence in Peruvian schools (Ministerio de Educación, 2013, p. 42) can be framed as reflective questions:

- Do you have a solid and harmonious cultural and linguistic identity that allows you to be a cultural mediator?
- Do you have knowledge and appreciation of the native culture of your students and of your own culture?
- Do you value and respect the children in your care with all their physical, social, cultural, linguistic, and gender characteristics?
- Do you speak and write in the first language of your students and in Spanish, and continue to develop communicative skills in these two languages?
- Do you encourage the participation of the parents and the community in the pedagogical and institutional management of the school?

The notion of being a 'cultural mediator' in these questions places responsibility on teachers to be able to engage with all students and to interact with them as a diverse group. The intercultural competency approach aims to build shared understandings and encourage mutual valuing amongst the students and their community in the educational setting. In the Peruvian context, bilingualism is expected of teachers, which is not the case in many other contexts. As in this example, teachers need to be sustainable learners so they can be responsive to their students. Responsive teaching also brings with it a responsibility to build the cultural competence of students, through attention to their ATRiUM capabilities and access to knowledge from diverse cultures integrated into learning opportunities.

Activity

From the cultural competence frameworks anchored in bicultural, multicultural, and intercultural contexts, it is possible to develop a set of explicit reflective questions for responsive teachers to adapt to their own situations. Choose from the questions below or adapt them to develop a list of prompts that will support professional reflection on your own cultural competence.

- What is my understanding of my own culture and the influence it has on my practice as a teacher? How do my students see my cultural identity? How can I find out?
- What is my understanding and appreciation of the culture(s) of my students? Do I know where they are coming from? How do I value the culture

of my students? Am I aware of any unconscious bias I may have? How can I check for this? How do I continue to learn about the cultures of my students and my colleagues?
- Do I have a strong and harmonious identity that allows me to be a cultural mediator? How do I enable expression of culture (e.g., products, practice, and interactions) in the classroom? How do I notice and address cultural biases and prejudices?
- How do I teach to develop and enhance the cultural competence of my students?

What assumptions about diversity do I bring to my teaching?

Assumptions about diversity crucially affect how teachers assess and instruct their students. These assumptions are interwoven with assumptions about learning and culture (explored in the previous sections of this chapter) and also affected by previous and current experiences with disability. Responsive teachers need to explore their assumptions about disabilities, giftedness, behaviour, and learning difficulties. It is important to acknowledge that underlying assumptions affect all teaching decisions and interactions and, if unexamined, can disadvantage some students.

Assumptions about disability

In the context of *learning for all*, assumptions about diversity are fundamental to how teachers respond to individual students as learners. It is important that teachers are aware of their default thinking about *disability* as a construct, and its consequences. Assumptions can colour decision-making about teaching students with a disability – those learners who most need effective and responsive teachers.

Many teachers do not have deep knowledge about disability studies or the theorising that is basic to disability research and advocacy. Instead, they have varying levels of understanding based on their personal and professional experiences and informed by study and professional learning. Some teachers will have considerable experience of disability, either their own or that of family members, and this will influence how they respond to, and advocate for, students with disabilities.

In general, teachers need to ask themselves how they see disability and consider in what ways their attitudes and beliefs impact on relationships with students with a disability and how they will approach teaching these students. Assumptions about disability that need to be considered are a focus in the field of disability studies, which grew out of activist movements and focuses on the critical analysis of assumptions about disability (Dirth & Branscombe, 2018). Models of disability that have been theorised in disability studies are provided in Table 6.4 as a reference for reflection. The summary of models in Table 6.3 is superficial; it is not possible to convey the complexities of models with such brevity. However, responsive teachers can use these models as starting points, and further research them as part of their examination of their own perspectives on and assumptions about disability.

Table 6.3 Assumptions within models of disability

Model	Definition of disability	Assumptions
Moral and/or Religious	Curse; punishment for sins or immoral actions; a challenge of faith; opportunity for character development; sacred infringement or divine affliction	There can be judgement and shame associated with disability for individuals and families; Compassion, kindness and protection should be provided for less fortunate people; value and dignity of people
Charity/Tragedy	Victims of impairment or circumstance	The suffering deserves pity and charity for helplessness and dependence
Medical	Disease or impairment, physical or mental limitations, abnormality	Can be diagnosed; treatment, cure, and care are needed; professionals are experts and can access resources
Social	Situation with physical and social disadvantages; environmental, attitudinal, and institutional barriers	There is need for reduction of barriers in the environment
Human rights	Reduced human rights because of disease or impairment, physical or mental limitations, abnormality, and situation with physical and social disadvantages	There is an emphasis on human dignity and rights to independence and autonomy
Identity (affirmation)	A social and political experience; a minority identity	Self-identification with minority group forms the basis of group advocacy
Cultural	Depends on different notions of disability and non-disability in specific cultures; some cultural definitions will be influenced by religion	Negotiated meaning is needed
Economic	Disability is a challenge to productivity	There needs to be a cost-benefit analysis to inform any decision about people with disabilities
Educational/Resources	Special education needs (SEN); additional needs; disabilities, difficulties, and disadvantages	There should be equity of resourcing based on needs

Derived from Bevan-Brown, 2015; Hickey, 2015; Nikora et al., 2004; OECD, 2008; Retief & Letšosa, 2018.

These models can be simultaneously active in educational communities and contribute to mismatches between the views of teachers, students, and families. The most common models of disability in education are the medical, social, and human rights models. Education has rejected the purely medical model, while the social model of disability has been used in inclusive education textbooks for many years. By making a distinction between an impairment and disability, the social model focuses on reducing the barriers within an educational setting. Inclusive education has adopted this approach. The social justice or human rights model of disability (Degener, 2017) is also integral to inclusive education. It is supported by the *International Convention on the Rights of Persons with Disability* (UN, 2006), national anti-discrimination legislation, and regulations such as the Australian *Disability Standards for Education* (Australian Government, 2005), education system policies, and practices for inclusive education that have been developed to ensure the human rights of students with disabilities (see Chapter 5).

The economic or actuarial model (Retief & Letšosa, 2018; Smart, 2004) is used by systems to develop policies for the allocation of resources. Education systems struggle with the costs of education, and casework in schools focuses considerable time and personnel on assessment and subsequent committee time to determine students' eligibility for resources. Economic models also include a framing of people with disabilities as customers who take responsibility for the management of financial resources and supports (Nikora et al., 2004). Empowerment through choice and control of supports by individuals with disability is the approach taken in the Australian National Disability Insurance Scheme (NDIA, 2021), a particularly complex process when the customers are adults with intellectual disabilities or young children (Brien, 2018; Brien, Page, & Berman, 2017; Lloyd et al., 2021). In line with this empowerment in relation to resources, people with disabilities are increasingly seen to hold valid knowledge about disability and are identified as "insiders and experts" (Dirth & Branscombe, 2018, p. 1302).

The alignment of the Māori concept of *whānau hauā* with the identity model of disability and a focus on the extended family (Hickey, 2015) is an example of a specific cultural model that recognises the sociocultural complexity that exists around experiences of disability (Waldschmidt, 2017). The social identity approach to disability acknowledges the social and cultural complexity of disability, and the place of students themselves as experts on their learning and development. The broader focus on a student as a whole person, and a member of a family group (Hernández, Gutmann Kahn, & Cannon, 2018; Hickey & Wilson, 2017) aligns with *Responsive Teaching for Sustainable Learning*. This approach reflects the need to consider social and human rights, identity, and cultural models to begin to understand disability.

Activity

Carry out an online web-browser search using the keywords 'assumptions about disability' and select one or more links to explore. See what you can find about societal assumptions about disability and test your own identified assumptions against what you find. Could your assumptions contribute to you limiting your expectations or the provision of opportunities for students with disabilities? How can you make sure this does not happen?

Assumptions about named disabilities

Assumptions about specific identified disabilities can also be interrogated as they also affect how teachers interact and engage with individual students and their families. It is common for a disability label to be provided to teachers before any other information is shared. In this situation, a teacher reacts based on what they already know about that diagnostic label, which may not be relevant for the student. Therefore, it is appropriate for responsive teachers to ask what assumptions are related to labels.

Specific disability labels come from the medical/psychological sciences and from within education systems. As we have already stressed, it is not useful to know about all these labels, but instead to be able to find out what they mean in the context of the school and classroom experiences of a particular student.

Activity

Read through the terms in Table 6.4 and see if you have any emotional response to any of them. Next, explore why this might be the case for you. Alternatively, you can select a diagnostic label from the table of terms, interrogate what it means to you, and then research the label to test your assumptions. The labels that students bring with them are derived from medical science, from psychological science, and from social and cultural descriptions (Graham, Berman, & Bellert, 2015). The ones we are interested in in this context of responsive teaching are those used in medical, allied health, and education system contexts (Berman & Graham, 2018).

Some labels are common currency in education, and teachers may describe their classes using ages and labels, for example, "I have a year seven class which has three students with ASD, one with ADHD, one with epilepsy and two with anxiety". This creates a picture of a class of typical or 'normal' 12–13-year-olds

Table 6.4 Selected specific disability terms from medical and psychological science and those used within education systems

Medical science	Psychological science	Education systems
• Spina bifida • Cerebral palsy • Trisome 21 • Cystic fibrosis • Multiple sclerosis • Acquired brain injury • Asthma • Sensory impairment • Quadriplegia • Chronic illness • Fragile X • Angelman Syndrome • Cri du Chat Syndrome	• Specific learning disorders • ADHD • Autism Spectrum Disorder • Obsessive compulsive disorder • Oppositional defiant disorder • Conduct disorder • Borderline personality disorder • Mood disorders • Intellectual disability	• Intellectual disability • Physical disability • Multiple disability • Vision impairment or blindness • Deaf or hearing impairment • Autism/Pervasive developmental disorder • Severe behaviour disorder • Severe language disorder • Social emotional disorder • Highly able

Adapted from Graham, Berman, & Bellert, 2015; Berman & Graham, 2018.

and seven with special or additional needs. The implication from this kind of description is that the teacher will need to spend more time and effort teaching those seven students. There are so many assumptions in this scenario that need to be questioned. Using this information meaningfully depends on teacher knowledge and understanding of each of the diagnostic labels, and, importantly what each label means for the individual students. Because teachers are so busy it is easy to rely on assumptions related to diagnoses and yet, that can be misleading and detrimental to the process of understanding each student as a unique learner.

An early study into the mainstreaming of students with severe levels of disability showed that teachers transformed as they got to know the students more fully and recognised that "their initial expectations regarding the student with disabilities were based on unsubstantiated assumptions" and that they had to "reflect and reconsider previously assumed positions" and instead were "beginning to view the child as a person rather than as a disability" (Giangreco et al., 1993, p. 367).

What is known about developmental conditions changes as new research and framing of issues affects both what we know and how we see disability. An example is autism in childhood which was originally (1952) described as schizophrenic reaction, childhood type; then as infantile autism (1980); autistic disorder or pervasive developmental disorder (1987); pervasive developmental disorder with subtypes, including autistic and Asperger's disorders (1994); and now to the current category of autism spectrum disorder (since 2013; Graham, Berman, & Bellert, 2015). It is not possible for teachers to know everything about identified disabilities as this knowledge base is vast and dynamic and the lived experience of people who have disabilities is not fully explained by the criteria that are used in diagnosis. Teachers cannot assume that because two students have the same diagnosis that their learning needs will be the same. Therefore, responsive teachers need to be aware of their assumptions about disability and about particular diagnoses and look beyond the labels to get to know each individual student as a learner. It is vital that the real learning needs of students with disabilities be explored through "ongoing discussions about cultural and education needs, preferences and aspirations" with the students and their families (Bevan-Brown, 2015, p. 7).

Assumptions about giftedness

A third of Australian educators in a recent study, when asked how they reacted on first hearing about a student being gifted were negative in their responses (Bartley, 2021). Another study from Europe revealed pre-service teachers' views were similarly negative regarding perceptions of gifted students' personalities, socio-emotional functioning, and relationships with teachers (Weyns, Preckel, & Verschueren, 2021). Analysis of the characteristics of gifted characters in movies highlighted stereotypical problems in social, emotional, and behavioural domains in contrast to cognitive functioning (Atmaca et al., 2022). Just as labels of disability can create uncertainty for teachers, so do labels of giftedness. And, yet the responsibility is the same; to get past the label, to know these students as learners, and respond to their learning needs.

A field of research anchored in conceptions of giftedness from Western antiquity focuses on what giftedness is, how to identify gifted students, and how to educate those students (Blumen & Lanao, 2006). More recent studies have traced conceptions of giftedness throughout the 20th century to the present day. The education of gifted and talented students has been influenced by the development of intellectual tests and their subsequent use to score intelligence. The field focused on students' gifts and talents in the latter 20th century, and most recently reframed to focus on high-ability students in particular domains in the 21st century (Bartley, 2021). Contemporary models of giftedness accept that high ability is the outcome of students' interaction with their environment and culture rather than solely inherent within a person.

Australian educators use a wide range of definitions of giftedness, referring to ability, knowledge, talent, and potential that is demonstrated as being above or beyond age levels, either generally or in specific domains (Bartley, 2021). None of these terms acknowledge culture, instead assuming the culture of schools as the context. In contrast, within the context of an Australian Aboriginal community, giftedness is the "ultimate enactment of culture" through cultural behaviours which are "rooted in the cultural priorities and needs of the community" with an emphasis on social and emotional domains (Thraves et al., 2021, p. 15–16). This embodiment of culture is also explicit in Māori, Pasifika, and South American Indigenous conceptions of giftedness (Blumen, 2021; Thraves et al., 2021; Webber, 2019).

Characteristics of gifted students have been compiled from Australian educators' descriptions: independence in learning, a fast rate of learning, problem solving capabilities, and maturity, self-motivation, and creativity (Bartley, 2021). The characteristics of gifted students emphasise how giftedness is influenced by the ATRiUM capabilities of active learning, relating to others, and managing self, and that it is epigenetic. Across the Pacific in Peru, a study with gifted young people from low-income households found these students to use personal reflection, initiative, and creativity; to be unconventional, insightful, and perfectionist; and to draw on sophisticated emotional resources, all tempered by low self-confidence, hypervigilance, and caution which were seen to be related to their poverty (Blumen & Lanao, 2006). This study emphasises the interaction of students with their environments.

When academic performance is the primary indicator of giftedness, it precludes any students who are underachieving, and who do not reveal their high ability. In fact, in a study in Canada, there was almost no correlation between high achievement and identification as gifted (Parekh, Brown, & Robson, 2018). Similarly, teacher nomination of gifted students in Mexico revealed confusion between high achievement and giftedness (Sánchez-Escobedo, Camelo-Lavadores, & Valdés-Cuervo, 2021). Of importance, Chaffey challenged the academic achievement assumption about giftedness in Australian and Canadian Indigenous students (Chaffey, Bailey, & Vine, 2003; Chaffey, Halliwell, & McCluskey, 2006) when he developed and implemented a dynamic assessment procedure with Aboriginal students who were not identified by traditional static assessment. Their giftedness was revealed through more culturally appropriate dynamic assessment, showing that intellectual potential was found to be hidden or invisible in the classroom when the students were assessed using conventional Western assessments. This situation is often the case for gifted students for whom other characteristics of giftedness (asynchronous development, perfectionism, overexcitabilities, loneliness, and underachievement) create a complicated situation, wherein they experience barriers to realising their learning potential (Bishop & Rinn, 2020). At the extreme, these characteristics can be disruptive in an educational setting and may be misinterpreted as being related to conditions such as behavioural, attentional, and emotional disorders (Bishop & Rinn, 2020). From this discussion, it is clear that simply relying on academic achievement to identify students who are gifted is problematic.

Rather than focusing on identification and labelling, teachers need to get to know and understand "the expression of all student abilities" and respond to those abilities with enrichment, differentiation, and acceleration (Bartley, 2021, p. 240), which is the approach of *Responsive Teaching for Sustainable Learning*. However, it is easy to underestimate student capabilities especially when some students unconsciously or deliberately hide their potential. Such situations call for very responsive teachers, who use assessment that can reveal learner capabilities more validly.

A challenge for some teachers can be the threat to their inherent authority from students who will know more and will ask deep questions about topics that a teacher may not be able to answer meaningfully. If a teacher believes that they need to know everything they are teaching, then this will be a major problem. However, teachers can facilitate learning for students (and learn with them) and utilise other resources to match the depth of learning needed (as set out in the *Layers of Responsive Teaching* model).

Activity

Pretend you are a screen writer and create a description of a student character who is gifted. Analyse your description to see the assumptions that you used.

Ask yourself what it is you see as giftedness, and how you notice characteristics and behaviours in your students. Do you notice the same characteristics across cultures? Also, consider how you react when you are told a student has been identified as gifted. Do you get excited by the possibilities for that student or feel threatened that you may not be able to respond to them? How do these reactions affect your teaching? When reflecting on your teaching, consider whether any of your students sit quietly for periods as they wait for others to finish. If so, how could you use their time as learners more fully?

Assumptions about behaviour

To continue this brief consideration of diversity, we focus on assumptions about student behaviour that influence how teachers see and respond to their students as learners. As was mentioned in the previous section about giftedness, teachers can interpret student behaviours in ways that affect their interactions and instructional planning. For example, if we see the problem as a literacy difficulty, we will aim to build the literacy skills needed. If we see it as a student not risking any errors because of a sense of perfectionism, we will approach it with that in mind. These different interpretations of behaviour can lead to widely different teacher responses to their students.

Within the situation described above there is a range of intensity of behaviours that can tell us more about the experience of the learner. For example, reluctance to write lead to a student writing the bare minimum and the teacher accepting it. Alternatively, the student may be disruptive and have externalised reactions to the writing task. Teacher frustrations can contribute to escalation of dysfunctional behaviours, which then become a matter of discipline rather than of teaching and learning.

Students have plenty of time to study teacher behaviours and to work out how to manage them. They notice how teachers engage with other students and they can make unconscious or more deliberate decisions about how to engage with teachers. Some students grow up thinking any interactions with adults are power struggles. Teachers need to take time to study student behaviours and make sense of them so that they can respond effectively, not just to reduce classroom management challenges but to increase engagement in learning. In fact, both learning and behaviour must be considered. To avoid the influence of biases, careful observation of behaviour and systematic assessment of learning can help teachers understand the function of behaviours and become better equipped to use that this valuable information in their teaching.

Observation and interpretation of behaviours can be done informally, or more systematically using functional behavioural analysis. Although more commonly associated with educational casework (Berman & Graham 2018), skills in developing a functional perspective are recommended for all teachers, particularly as school-wide positive behaviour support, and multi-tiered systems of behaviour support are increasingly embedded in schools. Thinking functionally is "an active and iterative problem-solving process that teachers can engage in to assess the dynamic interaction between student behaviour and aspects of the environment" (Fox, Sharma, & Leif, 2022, p. 23). When teachers consciously focus on what they themselves bring (RTF 2) and what students bring as learners (RTF 3), they are more likely to be able to identify the function of student behaviours, and, therefore, be able to respond most effectively to support learning and change behaviours.

Of course, some behaviours of students will raise red flags for teachers and parents about significant mental health needs. These need to be noticed and lead to appropriate discussions with families and students about specialist assessment and intervention. Behaviours in classrooms centre on students' learning, and social and emotional needs. These should be interpreted by teachers so that they understand more about their students and respond appropriately.

Activity

A challenge for teachers occurs when teachers' emotional reactions to disruptive or frustrating behaviours hinder the process of analysing student behaviour as evidence of their learning needs. It is our job to work out what the evidence means, but sometimes our assumptions, which can be very deeply embedded, get in the way. Try and catch yourself when you react emotionally to student behaviours and be mindful about your reaction. What does your reaction tell you about your assumptions and, therefore, how you interpret students' behaviour? How can you respond differently either through a change in expectations or activities, or through feedback to students?

Assumptions about learning difficulties

We have considered assumptions about disability in reference to models of disability, reliance on stereotypes of giftedness, and a functional approach to understanding the behaviours of our students. Models, stereotypes, and functions all assist teachers to make sense of the learning of their students and notice when difficulties need responses. We conclude this section on diversity with consideration of learning difficulties. How we understand and explain learning difficulties will influence how we respond to students who are experiencing problems with basic academic skills.

Learning difficulties are prevalent; differ in terms of their nature, intensity, and duration; and have many causes (NSW Department of Education, 2020a, 2021a). While the causes and nature of difficulties are important, knowing these is not a prerequisite for *Responsive Teaching for Sustainable Learning*. RTSL accepts that anyone can experience learning difficulties at times for varied reasons.

A particular subset of learning difficulties is Learning Disabilities (LD), which is the term more commonly used in the United States. Whenever anyone is diagnosed with LD in the United States, there are legislative responsibilities for schools. This system functions by using specific eligibility criteria against which the learning and development of a student is compared to diagnose LD. The usual reference for this process is the Diagnostic and Statistical Manual (DSM) of the American Psychiatric Association (APA), which clearly defines disorders of development and learning.

The DSM has been in existence for many years and has been revised considerably as knowledge of human development and learning has altered and language changed over time. The most recent version, the DSM-5 (APA, 2013), uses the term *specific learning disorder* as an overall description which covers particular academic domains, within which difficulties are experienced. Within the context of the DSM, this term has an accompanying assumption that the specific learning disorder is caused by neurodevelopmental differences (APA, 2022). While neuroscience is a fascinating field of inquiry, it is not necessarily informative for teachers who cannot consciously do anything about students' neurological structures.

On the other hand, teachers can be aware of how a specific learning disorder is defined and what this means for their teaching and monitoring of learning for students seen to be at risk. For diagnosis of a specific learning disorder to occur (1) a student has to have had difficulties with literacy or numeracy for at least six months, despite targeted help; (2) achievement must be assessed as below age level and be causing problems at school or in other contexts; (3) the difficulties had to have started at school age (for adults); and (4) the difficulties are not due to other conditions or adverse situations (APA, 2022). Terms such as dyslexia and dyscalculia are not used 'diagnosed conditions', but indicate profiles of difficulty across key academic skills that are detailed in the DSM-5 (APA, 2013).

It is common for students with specific learning disorders to have very uneven development of capabilities and to be gifted in some domains. Providing instructional support to such interesting and complex learners can be challenging for teachers, who can easily assume that their students' level of learning is the same in all domains. This assumption can be extremely frustrating for students who are not having their learning needs met. Teachers need to be open to noticing that a student has strengths or abilities that vary.

The terms learning disability, learning disorder, and learning difficulties, and others including dyslexia are used with varying nuance around the world. This can be problematic for teachers searching the research literature for evidence-based practice. The variability of specific terminology in the field of learning difficulties was highlighted by Elliot and Grigorenko (2014) in their exhaustive and cross-disciplinary investigation of research on dyslexia. At least 13 definitions were identified, revealing that the body of research evidence about dyslexia was not coherent. Inconsistencies in inclusion criteria for participants in research make it difficult to rely on findings as a body of evidence. Readers, therefore, need to ensure the definition of dyslexia – or any other term of interest – in any research paper aligns with their context.

Activity

Search for at least two research studies in Google Scholar using one of these terms:

- Severe reading difficulties
- Severe mathematics difficulties
- Severe writing difficulties
- Language disorder
- Dyslexia
- Dyscalculia
- Dysgraphia.

Find the definition of the term in each of the papers. Make a judgment about whether the two papers are talking about similar learners. Could teachers use these papers as evidence for teaching decisions for a student with that label?

Responsive Teaching for Sustainable Learning uses the term learning difficulties to refer to any experience of difficulty in learning. The difficulty can be caused by any factors including disabilities, neurodevelopmental conditions, and lack of access to education. The reality for these learners is that they are struggling, and it is our responsibility to understand their learning capabilities and respond by changing the target and intensity of teaching so that they can be more successful. As you complete this section think explicitly about how you understand learning difficulties and their causes, and how you set out to teach students who are struggling with learning. We will unpack teaching approaches and strategies in Chapter 9.

In conclusion, this chapter has considered what teachers bring to their teaching and stresses the importance of teacher reflection about who they are and how they are seen by their students. This chapter also began the examination of teacher skills and knowledge, and explored assumptions related to student diversity. While it is not possible to explicitly address all the bases of assumptions, the same reflective questions that introduce this chapter can be asked in relation to, for example, gender, socioeconomic status, and family transience (Henderson, 2008). It may be 'easy' to construct explanations for low achievement based on assumptions which may or may not be valid (Henderson, 2021). However, as responsive teachers, we need to constantly question our assumptions and our explanations for student achievement.

7 RTF 3: What do my students bring as learners?

RTF 3. What do my students bring as learners?

What prior learning and achievements, cultural contexts, experiences, interest(s), educational and developmental casework do my students bring to their learning? What is the nature of the learning group they create? What else do I need to know about the students as learners?

Introduction

The third step of the *Responsive Teaching Framework* (RTF 3) is about the influences students bring with them to their learning. The discussion in this chapter complements that of the previous two, where we focused on the frameworks within which responsive teaching happens (RTF 1) and what teachers bring to their teaching (RTF 2). Each student brings their previous learning and achievements, cultural context, experiences, interests, developing capabilities, and their families. Gathering background information about the students is the beginning of the process of assessment that continues throughout the *Responsive Teaching Framework*, and which supports all decision making in teaching. Much of the information will already be available. However, teachers will still need to carry out additional assessment when they first meet their students and as they get to know them. The outcome of finding out about what students bring to their learning, of knowing students as learners, is a description of their current learning needs. Responsive teachers need to be as clear as possible about each student's strengths and difficulties, so these can inform teaching. When knowledge of learners and their contexts is minimal, the curriculum content becomes the basis for decisions about what is to be taught, what emphases are to be used, and what is to be expected of the learners. In responsive teaching, access to the curriculum can be shaped to best meet students' needs.

Assessment of students as learners

The process of gathering information about what our students bring as learners is an assessment process, and here we refer to the decision-making

DOI: 10.4324/9781003299813-9

WHY? Purposes of assessment RTF 3

- Assessment in RTF 3 is done to determine what the students bring to their learning
- Students and teachers need this information so they can know their students as learners individually and as a group
- Students and teachers can then build on strengths and work to reduce barriers to learning

WHAT? Content of assessment RTF 3

- Content of assessment is defined curriculum, ATRiUM capabilities and influences on learning
- The focus is on prior learning and achievement, cultural contexts, experiences and interests, and casework information

HOW? Approach to assessment RTF 3

- Previous school records and reports
- Allied health reports and personal contact
- Interviews with families
- Interviews with students

Figure 7.1 The WHY, WHAT, and HOW of assessment in RTF 3.

framework introduced in Part I, that distinguishes between the WHY, WHAT, and HOW of assessment. In RTF 3 there are specific focus areas and answers to the WHY, WHAT, and HOW questions of assessment (Figure 7.1) that guide this process.

Firstly, WHY we are doing this assessment is to be responsive to students as individual learners. We need to investigate their prior learning and achievement, and then continue to get to know these learners. A clear understanding of what our students know and can do, the nature of their developing ATRiUM capabilities, and knowledge of influences on their learning, will help us determine what needs to be taught now (RTF 4) and how to teach all learners (RTF 5). The purpose of assessment at RTF 3 is relevant both to groups of students and to individual students within these groups. Responsive teachers need to know the strengths of their learners and potential difficulties in learning.

Secondly, we ask ourselves WHAT it is we need to know about our students as learners that will assist in our planning for responsive teaching. The basic information required is student prior learning and achievement in reference to the curriculum, remembering that what students bring to their learning includes their cultural contexts, prior educational and life experiences, and interests. All of these are important for teachers to be aware of, so that they design appropriate learning opportunities and build relationships with students. Some students will also bring a history of developmental, medical, social, and educational intervention, sometimes since birth. These students may have been involved in educational or health casework. Students who come with identified disabilities, recognised persistent learning difficulties, notoriety because of outstanding success, or specific transient situations such as grief and loss will bring with them considerable information that needs to be considered. This information will include insights into what supports or hinders the students' learning and development.

Strategies for HOW we access information about our students as learners starts with gathering records from previous years. Class records show achievement for class cohorts and individual records detail the achievement of students across the years (for as long as the student has been in that school or system). There may also be reports and records that come from other professionals such as specialist teachers, school psychologists, and outside agencies, plus information gathered through personal contact with other professionals, students, and their families.

It is common for teachers to say they do not want to read what previous teachers have said about their students because they want to draw their own conclusions. The justification for this stance is that it gives students a 'clean slate' if their teachers are not influenced by the opinions of previous teachers. However, such an approach can also disadvantage students. Responsive teachers, instead, keep their minds open and look for how best to support learning based on what is already known about learners and groups of learners. The experiences of previous teachers may be valuable and should be considered. However, information about students as learners accumulates and changes over time. Responsive teachers are open to constantly receiving information about learners and adapting their knowledge based on new evidence. They also reconcile contradictory information to help build nuanced understandings of each student.

Once learning groups are established, teachers can also observe how students support each other's learning and vary their teaching in response. Since responsive teachers need to know what students bring to their learning, they find out about prior learning and achievement, cultural contexts, experiences and interests, and casework information (Figure 7.2). The representation of a student as an open hexagon reminds us of the whole person who uses all ATRiUM capabilities in their learning.

Some strategies for assessment are included in the following sections. These are followed by a more detailed consideration of processes of information gathering for teachers as they get to know their students as learners.

Prior learning and achievement

Responsive teachers start with what the students already know and can do within the academic curriculum, which is matched to grades or years of schooling. Achievement levels are not always a valid indication of the potential of a student, as they only reflect what has happened before, not what may be possible. Many gifted students may be seen to be performing satisfactorily but, in fact, are not achieving in line with their potential. In other circumstances, it is possible that the levels of achievement are not revealing the difficulties experienced. In the early years of school, it is common for students to mask

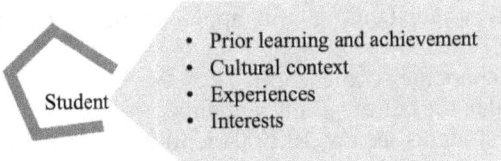

Figure 7.2 What students bring as learners.

difficulties by using other strategies to achieve. It may only be when there is more individual and literacy-intense work that their difficulties are uncovered. The situation is further complicated by phenomena such as 'stereotype threat' or 'forced-choice dilemma', which refers to how some students deliberately hide their learning ability (Chaffey, 2008; Corwin Visible Learning Plus, 2021; Gross, 1989). Responsive teachers need to keep their minds open and are aware of changing patterns of achievement.

Students have a range of expectations about learning and ways of relating to teachers that are associated with their prior learning and achievement. Students who have a history of positive and successful experiences in formal learning will tend to engage with teachers and fellow students in ways that continue to support their learning. Their expectations of learning will be affirmed, and they will generally continue to be successful. In contrast, some students with less successful learning experiences may struggle and disconnect from teachers and learning. Therefore, it is important to know what prior learning and achievement is on record, and vital to understand the complexities that may be present for individual students around achievement. It is not possible to know all the circumstances that exist; therefore, it is important for teachers to accept prior learning levels as baseline levels rather than using them to form expectations about students' future achievement.

Cultural contexts

Culture and cultural competence are significant aspects of what students bring as learners. We all embody and express our cultures through funds of knowledge (Thraves & Bannister-Tyrrell, 2017) and cultural practices which can enrich a classroom but can also be the basis of discomfort. Just as the cultural contexts that teachers bring to their teaching (RTF 2) are critical, so too are those of their students. Learning environments need to be safe and comfortable for learning to be optimised, so it is vital for teachers to incorporate cultural recognition. Cultural mismatches for students can be fundamental reasons contributing to disengagement, difficult relationships with peers or teachers, and lower levels of wellbeing, learning, and aspirations (Bates, 2018; Hilaski, 2020). It is important to not only understand the cultural contexts of ourselves as teachers and of our students, but also how these interact in educational settings.

Activity

From bicultural, multicultural, and intercultural perspectives, consider the following reflective questions about student culture. How can these questions be adapted to your context?

- What is my understanding and appreciation of the cultures of my students?
- Do I know where they come from?
- How do I value the culture of my students?
- How do my students see my cultural identity?
- How do I continue to learn about the cultures of my students and fellow teachers?

- How do I enable expression of culture (products, practice, and interactions) in the classroom?
- How do I notice and address cultural biases and prejudices?

Teachers develop their own ways of getting to know their students. In Australia, many classrooms are multicultural, and diversity can be seen and heard and explored as part of everyday interactions. Other classes are primarily bicultural, comprising European Australians and Indigenous students. Whatever the case, it is important that acknowledgement of local Aboriginal culture is part of how classrooms function. There are also classrooms within which students may look and sound culturally similar, leading to an assumption of cultural homogeneity. This may be the case since children and their families are part of the local community, or a religious community, but beneath the surface there are likely to be differences that need to be acknowledged and valued, and which can be a rich source of learning for everyone.

Activity

Try this strategy with a group of students to assist with revealing and discussing their cultural contexts. Teachers need to participate, disclosing some aspects of their experiences and interests, as well as cultural backgrounds to set appropriate expectations about revealing personal information to each other, and to build trust.

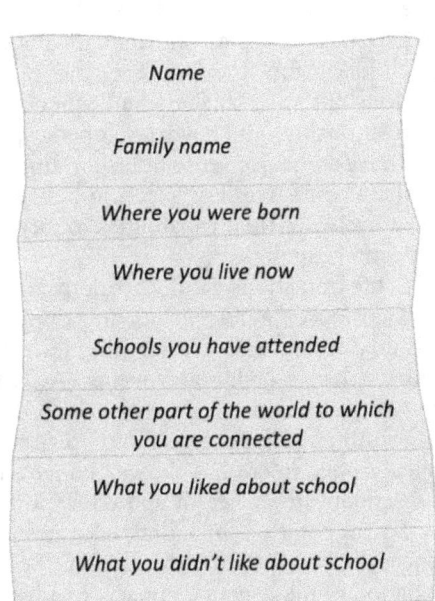

Figure 7.3 Strategy to explore cultural backgrounds.

Give each student an A4 sheet of coloured paper. Ask them to fold it in half, and then in half again, until you have eight rows (Figure 7.3). You can select any number of folds to meet your needs.

Ask students to write their first name in the top section, then their family name, and then where they were born. Ask any other questions about experiences and interests that are relevant. The students are to fill in each row in response and to fold the paper over so they can only see the blank rows.

When complete, fold the paper so only the first name can be seen, discuss these names and then move to the family name, and then through the rest in turn.

You can take as much or as little time as you like in discussion – making links to some teaching topics as you do so.

You can return to these papers at times during the school year for different purposes.

As an example, these questions were asked of students in an inclusive education subject at a regional Australian university. It was common for students to have family names that were distinctively linked to other parts of the world. Some of the students knew the derivation of their names and showed a continued connection with that part of the world (Scotland, or Poland, or Italy…) while others did not. In fact, at times students had no idea of the history of their family name, and they saw themselves to be Australian. This is a point of discussion which can raise awareness about culture and how Australia is a country populated by people from elsewhere, except for traditional owners of the land, Aboriginal and Torres Strait Islanders.

The other questions in the example (Figure 7.3) were shaped to prompt conversations about inclusion at school, and when the students felt included and when they didn't. These questions can be adapted to meet unique needs. The aim of this activity is to ensure that differences in culture are recognised and celebrated, and to contribute to the cultural competence of teachers and students.

Experiences

Each student brings their own unique lifetime of experiences with them which influences their reaction to the classroom climate, to the group of learners, to the cultural mix, and to the learning opportunities provided. Experiences include those in previous formal education settings, which are directly connected to how a student engages in those settings in the future. We have addressed some specific learning and cultural experiences in the sections above, in this section we look at other experiences that influence learning. Many students bring profound life experiences that play out dramatically or covertly in educational settings. Some children come to school each day eager to learn and set to build positive relationships with teachers and other students. They have experienced positive relationships and have developed capabilities that meet their needs. They also have a positive sense of responding to the perceived authority of teachers. Others come with less successful experiences of relationships and authority that influence their capabilities in formal education settings and, therefore, their achievements.

Experiences of stressful events such as life transitions, family breakup, acute or chronic illness, abusive parenting, sexual abuse, aggressive bullying, domestic violence, and crime can all affect child development and learning (Smith, 2018). Some of these events are termed adverse childhood events (ACEs), which can be associated, either individually or cumulatively, with conditions such as post-traumatic stress disorder (Smith, 2018). Research into how such significant life events affect physiological development has shown changes in brain structure and function, with subsequent lower health and educational outcomes in life (Soares et al., 2021). Social contexts, including educational settings, influence how these experiences are processed by children and "can contribute to the alleviation or exacerbation of the negative impacts of adversity" (Trinidad, 2021, p. 2).

Apart from ensuring safe learning environments, teacher responsiveness to such circumstances affects student engagement in academic learning and development of capabilities. There are links between childhood trauma and academic achievement and ATRiUM capabilities including attention, memory, and thinking skills (T), language skills (iU) and social (R) and emotional functioning (M; Perfect et al., 2016). The National Trauma-Aware Guidelines have been developed from professional experiences rather than research, and they stress that a trauma-informed approach will be appropriate for all students, making educational settings safer for everyone (Australian Childhood Foundation and Queensland University of Technology, 2020).

This approach to practice draws on evidence about what trauma does to developing capabilities and focuses on staged, predictable, adaptive, connected, and enabled learning (Australian Childhood Foundation, 2018). Although trauma-informed approaches to education make sense and align with responsive teaching, research is needed since there is not yet strong evidence to support widespread use in schools (Maynard et al., 2019). There is also the notion that post-traumatic growth can be a part of life journeys for some students (Tedeschi & Calhoun, 2004; Calhoun & Tedeschi, 2014). This reframing of the effects of trauma on human development and learning places a responsibility on teachers to discover how to best support those students who have experienced adverse life events.

Teachers will never be fully cognisant of all the experiences students bring with them to their learning, as many traumatic events remain hidden for decades. Teachers can, however, be sensitive to the possibilities when trying to understand patterns of student engagement, risk-taking in learning and relationships, and behaviours. When there is an observable change in patterns, it is possible that a traumatic period is in progress. Education systems and legislation provide guidelines for how teachers and allied health professionals can safely support students in schools (e.g., State Government of Victoria, Australia, 2019). Constant sensitivity to children and young people, and consideration of their privacy, are essential when getting to know about significant aspects of their lives.

Interests

Knowing the interests of students is valuable for responsive teachers. If teachers can use student interests in planning instruction, they will likely strengthen motivation to engage and learn. Teachers can deliberately use students' interests as hooks in learning. Also, some students can be resources to their teachers because of their interests and connections to networks outside the educational setting. The importance of interests is variable for learners. Some students will need their interests to be considered, while others are more open to exploring new interests. They will be curious about new knowledge and motivated to engage with new topics. Responsive teachers work out a balance so that they optimise engagement and use the richness of student interests when appropriate and extend those interests at other times.

Intensity of interest is also important, since students without strong personal interests may need to be offered "choice, novelty and links with prior experiences" (Tomlinson, 2005, p. 11). Other students will come to their learning with intense and deep interests in particular topics. In particular, some students with Autism Spectrum Disorder (ASD) will have "restricted, fixated interests that are abnormal in intensity or focus" (APA, 2013, p. 213). Such deep interests and associated bank of knowledge can be seen as a deficit that needs to be controlled, however, it can instead be used as a strength to support learning (Tansley, Parsons, & Kovshoff, 2022). Significant academic, social, and emotional benefits have been demonstrated for students with intense interests when teachers see these as strengths and the basis of learning opportunities. In this way, interests can produce a "reciprocal, enabling" influence, although there are also situations when they may create barriers to students' learning and assessment, socialisation, and inclusion in the community (Wood, 2021, p. 47).

There are formal and informal ways to find out student interests that range from administering questionnaires; asking for written lists or descriptions of what students are interested in; to incidentally noticing interests during learning activities and interactions. One of the underlying strategies in responsive teaching is to provide options for students that allow them to follow their interests as they learn specific skills within the curriculum. When any new topic is introduced, it is a suitable time to revisit this strategy in light of what students have previously experienced. This allows planning to be based on a more complete picture of students' learning needs within topics.

Activity

There will be many strategies for accessing information about student interests in professional literature. Search the internet using the phrase 'getting to know your students' experiences and interests' and draw on what you find to develop strategies that suit you and your students.

Educational and developmental casework

Some students bring with them a history of involvement in educational and developmental casework begun in response to delays or disorders in development and learning, or health conditions. The experiences of these students, and their families, with education and health professionals need to be understood, as they may influence relationships with teachers and family involvement in educational settings. There is also valuable information from within casework documentation about what students know and can do, and their responsiveness to teaching.

Casework can begin at birth for babies who have sensory or physical impairments, or genetic syndromes. These children and their families participate in assessment and intervention in "health-care clinics, hospitals, early intervention centres, rehabilitation centres, community centres, homes and schools" (WHO, 2012, p. 12). The Australian National Disability Insurance Scheme has an early childhood strategy for supporting young children with disability or developmental delay up to seven years of age (NDIS, 2022). Intervention aims to build child and family capacity to improve learning and development outcomes (Brien, Page, & Berman, 2017, p. 37). It is family centred, strengths based, culturally responsive, and inclusive (ECIA, 2016). Early childhood intervention involves assessment and therapy with allied health professionals including physiotherapists, speech and language therapists, occupational therapists, and psychologists, as well as early educators. For example, a child born with a vision impairment will be able to access specialist educators to optimise their early learning. As well, these children may be involved with health professionals who have expertise in physiology of vision, mobility and orientation, functional skills, and mental wellbeing (Raising Children Network Australia, 2021).

Other children become the focus of casework when delays or disorders in development are identified through developmental screening. Within this type of intervention, some families become home therapists in conjunction with the allied health professionals working with their child, particularly for speech, language, and physical development. At about three years of age, formal educational settings may become a part of the lives of some children who attend specialist sessions as part of their pre-school education. Support may be provided in early intervention support classes or through inclusive education support within regular childcare centre or preschool settings (NSW Department of Education, 2021b).

Parents of young children who have been the focus of casework in health and education during the first five years of their lives have engaged closely with professionals and the health, disability, and education systems. They will come to their children's school with expectations about the responsibilities they will take on in conjunction with their children's teachers. Most teachers are not familiar with the significant role families take in early childhood intervention, which is family centred, so there will need to be careful negotiation of relationships as teachers partner with these parents.

Children who have been involved in educational and developmental casework will often have a diagnostic label or labels. Labels are important for teachers to make sense of, in the context of what students bring to their learning. It is important to get to know each student as a distinctive learner. We advocate that teachers do this by using the ATRiUM capabilities to organise what is known about the students as learners (Chapter 8).

In this section we have explained WHY we want to know about students as learners and outlined WHAT we need to know about: student prior learning and achievement; cultural contexts; experiences; and interests; and any educational and developmental casework. Now we turn to HOW we are going to gather this information.

Gathering information about students as learners

We have already included some strategies for gathering information about student culture, experiences, and interests in previous sections of this chapter, noting that teachers can be as creative as possible while building teaching-learning relationships and getting to know students as learners. Other ways to gather information about students include accessing school records, other reports and verbal information from teachers and allied health professionals, and by talking with families and students.

Information from school records

Previous records within the education system contain pertinent information about students' academic achievement and characteristics of students as learners. As well as in-school data that is kept on all students, there are more extensive records that can help teachers build their understanding of individual students. Many specialist teachers in schools keep separate records of intervention and progress, as do school psychology, social work, and speech pathology professionals who work in schools. It is important to know how to access such information, since much of it is not generally available. For example, school psychology records in Australia are regarded as health records and must be kept secure. They are only available to others who are deemed to have the appropriate professional expertise to interpret them correctly and safely (Australian Psychological Society, 2016). Psychologists can provide summary reports or share information verbally. It is important to establish and maintain relationships with school psychologists to allow a mutually respectful and ethical sharing of relevant information about students as learners.

Information from allied health professionals

Information can be gleaned from educational and developmental casework records. The effectiveness of any interventions and teaching strategies should also be on record. Although families and students will be able to share their experiences of casework, the formal records will provide important details. Teachers particularly want to know what has worked for students in the past, and what has not worked. They would also be interested in who else supported the student, and how best to collaborate with the families involved. Such professional insights are helpful as teachers get to know students and their families.

Teachers should engage with allied health professionals in a respectful manner and seek their interpretation of what is held on record. Establishing a relationship with the school counsellor/psychologist/speech pathologist and asking questions that show respect for the limits of access is important. What teachers really want to know relates to the interpretation of information. Scores and diagnoses are not as useful for making good teaching decisions as analyses of students' strengths and weaknesses associated with learning. How do students use their developing ATRiUM capabilities for engaging in a learning group or formal educational setting?

Activity

Develop a set of questions to use when you discuss a student with an allied health professional. Ask questions that will help you as a teacher to know what this student brings as a learner. How would you ask about access to information useful for deciding what to teach and how to teach more effectively? How would you inquire about insights that could help guide the provision of useful feedback to students and reporting to their families? How do your allied health colleagues build relationship with students and their families? Here is a beginning script about connecting with your allied health professional colleagues for you to adapt to meet your needs.

When asking about the ATRiUM capabilities you will be able to probe the professionals' interpretation of formal test results. For example, many of the students who have been the focus of casework have formal assessments of their intellectual abilities and psychologists should be able to tell you much about what they noticed during assessments that reveal how particular students used their thinking skills.

> I am teaching Chris this year. I know you have been working with Chris over the years and I would like to be the best informed I can be so I don't make mistakes in my teaching. What can you tell me about how Chris learns?
>
> (Prompt) What are the strengths? As an active learner (A)? As a thinker (T)? in relationships with others (R)? In terms of language and symbol systems, and technology (iU)? As how they can manage themself (M)?
>
> (Prompt) What are the barriers to learning that have been shown in previous years and in your clinical assessments (ATRiUM)? How would you suggest we deal with those barriers?
>
> (Prompt) Who else has been involved in supporting this student and what have we learnt from that involvement? How could I work with these supports?
>
> (Prompt) How could I connect and partner with Chis' family? What works? What are their priorities?

Information from the family

Often family members have the most complete historical records of a child's development and learning. Indeed, when a student transfers between schools, the family may initially be the only source of information. Many education systems will not release records to another system or independent school, or if they do, this process can take a lot of time. The family is, meanwhile, available and can assist in gathering information about the student. It is important to draw on the full range of evidence about how students learn best, how they experience barriers to learning, and how to reduce those barriers. This sort of evidence can help teachers know what to do and what to *avoid* doing to make the most of their teaching.

Many families actively approach teachers, to ensure the teachers are informed about students' learning needs, while others wait to be invited. Teachers need to prioritise contact with some families since it is time-consuming process and it is best to start with those students who have history with developmental and educational intervention.

Activity

Develop your own script for talking with families about their involvement in educational and developmental casework using the script starter for teachers below.

> I am teaching Chris this year. I would like to be the best informed I can be so I teach Chris in the best possible way and don't make mistakes in my teaching that could be avoided. What can you tell me about how Chris learns?
>
> (Prompt) What are the strengths? As an active learner (A)? As a thinker (T)? in relationships with others (R)? In terms of language and symbol systems, and technology (iU)? As how they can manage themself (M)?
>
> (Prompt) What are the barriers to learning that have been shown in previous years (ATRiUM)? How would you suggest we deal with those barriers?
>
> (Prompt) Who else has been involved in supporting Chris and what has been learned from that involvement? How could I work with these supports?
>
> (Prompt) What are your priorities for Chris's learning? And what are Chris's priorities? How can I connect with Chris through interests? What works? How can I keep in contact with you as we go forward?

It is wise to harness the power of parents and families to support teaching and learning. When teachers and parents work together to support teaching, some of the most effective learning occurs. Family satisfaction with their children's schooling can be nurtured through positive and consistent home-school partnerships (Hampden-Thompson & Galindo, 2017). Teacher-family partnerships can take many forms and can be totally tacit, yet still supportive of learning. Teachers do not need to know everything about a family to support a student, and families do not need to know everything that is being taught to support learning. Communication is seen to be a minimum prerequisite for these positive relationships, but shared information and joint responsibility underpins strong parent engagement (Goodall & Montgomery, 2014).

Family involvement in schools is a dimension of school climate (Hampden-Thompson & Galindo, 2017) and is, therefore, a noteworthy influence on educational settings and on students. For example, support from whānau/family to succeed in both worlds is recognised as a key dimension of success for Māori students in Aotearoa New Zealand (Macfarlane et al., 2014). In Macfarlane et al.'s study, parents framed their children's school achievements as important alongside their cultural development at home. Effective components of parent engagement can include holding high expectations for academic achievement; providing encouragement and support rather than academic pressure; and communicating with their children regarding school (Boonk et al., 2018).

Several factors also contribute to how parents involve themselves in their children's education and with educational settings. The level of involvement is influenced by parental beliefs and self-efficacy about their role in education; general and specific invitations from schools, teachers, and students to be involved; and parent resources and skills (Whitaker, 2019). Some families see education as the professional responsibility of the teacher and the school, so they withdraw. Others like to be kept informed and will approach the school if necessary. Some like to be engaged in not only their child's learning but in the life of the educational setting.

There will be some students whose families have had negative experiences with formal education and government departments, sometimes over generations. These families actively avoid contact with schools. Schools can also be seen as hard-to-reach (Harris & Goodall, 2008) by other families. In such situations it is easy for teachers to imagine reasons that may or may not be valid. Teachers need to check their biases and assumptions when trying to explain the distance some families like to maintain. Teachers can then take active roles in breaking down the barriers and facilitating partnerships with families.

Information from the student

As well as evidence from previous teachers, allied health professionals and families, the students themselves provide evidence that can be informative for teachers. Responsive teachers need to access information, and establish a relationship with all students, particularly with those who have experienced barriers to engagement and learning, and who may be discouraged.

Student-teacher dialogue with a particular focus on inclusion has been developing in Europe (Messiou & Ainscow, 2020). This work is derived from research that sought to capture the voices of students who are marginalised (Messiou, 2012, 2019). Student voice is an often-sidelined dimension in teaching, but it is essential in responsive teaching. The voices of students provide input into two of the four types of evidence that teachers need to consider – evidence from the learner and family experience and evidence of learning within teaching.

Accessing student voice is a sensible approach for teachers who want to know about their students and their learning. It is also something teachers are bound to do according to the Convention on the Rights of the Child, which states that "children have the right to say what they think should happen when adults are making decisions that affect them and to have their opinions taken into account" (UN, 1989, Article 12). Not only are children to be given opportunity and to be assisted to express their opinions, but they must also be listened to and have their views acted on as appropriate (MacArthur, Berman, & Carroll-Lind, 2018). Therefore, it is important for responsive teachers to not only ask students about their prior learning, their culture, experiences, and interests but also to ask them what works for them as learners. Many students are perceptive about what it is that teachers do that works for them. This is not to say that teaching can be everything students think they would like, but teachers can certainly consider student insights about what they judge as effective teaching.

What other information is needed?

Once teachers have gathered the kind of information already discussed, they can consider what else they need to know to make good decisions about teaching and put a plan in place. In relation to academic learning, teachers can check on current knowledge and skills so that there is a baseline for teaching. These assessments complement what is already on record and give teachers and students up-to-date information about what they know and can do, and what is to be learned next.

It might also be appropriate to seek specialist assessment. For example, there are times when a student's capabilities are difficult to interpret. Specialist assessment expertise is not always accessible or appropriate, but at times it can be just what is needed. The process of finding out more about students as learners continues throughout teaching, and the need to seek specialist assessment can arise at any time. Families are the best allies in this process, as it is often the case that they have been contemplating the same questions about their child's learning and are interested in finding out more.

What is the nature of the learning group?

Although the information gathering discussed so far is in reference to individuals, teachers are also interested in the nature of the learning group that is created by the combination of students in a group. In terms of academic achievement, the previous records of the students can be collated into a class profile. All teachers know that any grouping of students creates complex social contexts and that classroom management of social behaviour may become the focus for teachers, detracting from time available for teaching and learning.

The basic relationship in teaching is that of the teacher with one student (Figure 7.4). This occurs when there are interactions around a learning activity, when the teacher uses teaching strategies and when the learner uses their capabilities to engage with the activity and the teacher. In the representation of the interactions between a teacher and learner in Figure 7.4, the shapes of the two people are based on the ATRiUM pentagon with one open side showing the direction of focus. The two arrows indicate contributions to the interactions from each person.

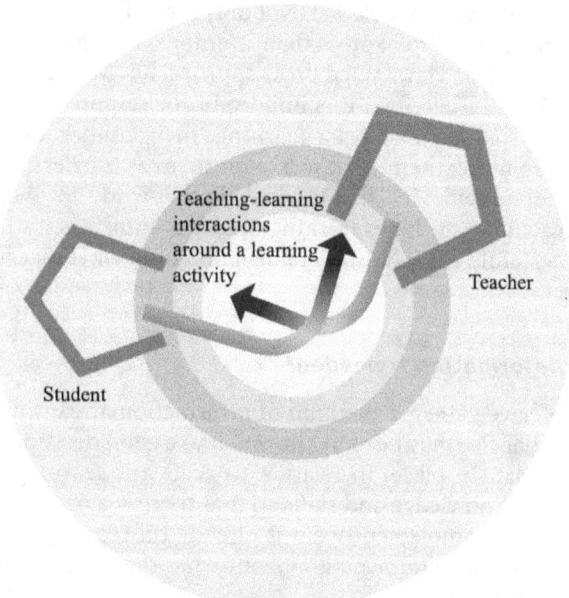

Figure 7.4 Teaching-learning interactions around a learning activity.

Adapted from Berman & Graham, 2018.

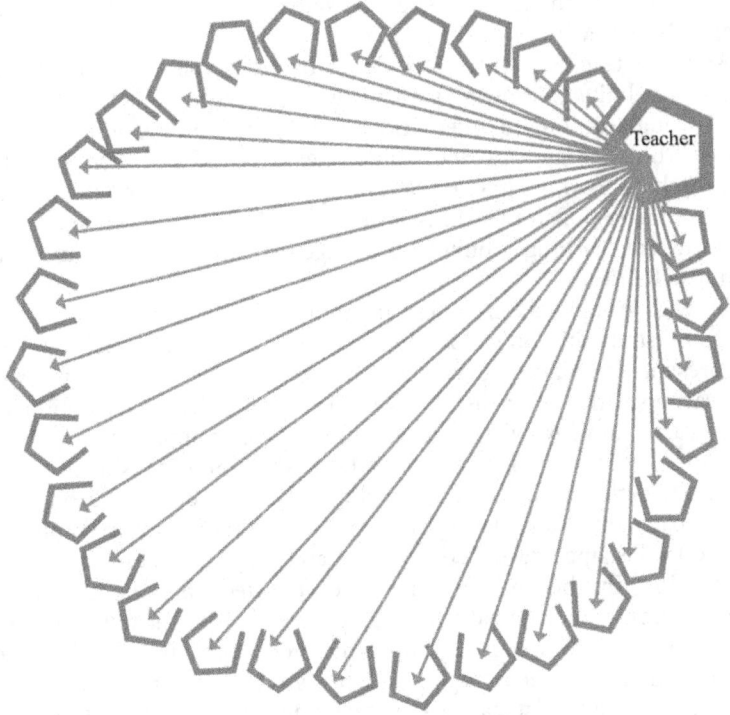

Figure 7.5 One teacher's dyadic relationships with each of 30 students.

It follows that the number of relationships in a group of two is one, as in Figure 7.4, but in a class of 30, for example (Figure 7.5), the teacher has 30 relationships to manage, one with each student.

The representation in Figure 7.5 is what teaching and student relationships are like when students are passive and do not interact with each other. It is what happens when teachers use an expository teaching strategy, and the connection is between the teacher and each of the students. However, when students are active and interacting learners, the relationships in the group are more complex. The number of dyadic relationships in a group of 30 students (and one teacher) will be 465. Each student has to navigate this kind of complexity every day, while they are trying to learn. So, does the teacher!

There has been research looking at class sizes and how they relate to student achievement. Results have not been supportive of reducing class sizes, while traditional teaching approaches are used. Expository teaching and individual written work can be just as effective with large groups. While teachers spend much time organising and managing larger numbers of students, they have less time and space to be responsive. However, if teaching approaches alter to take advantage of a smaller number of students and relationships within a group, the size of the group really does matter. Current research suggests that smaller class sizes are likely to have a small positive impact (Corwin Visible Learning Plus, 2021). Reducing class size is most effective in the first four years of schooling when the class consists of disadvantaged learners and teaching is evidence-based (Mitchell, 2018).

Responsive teaching, which is evidence-based, advocates smaller groups so that the possibility of knowing students well and responding to their learning needs through responsive differentiation and *Layers of Responsive Teaching* is possible. The teaching approaches that we explore in Part II Chapter 9 expect active teaching-learning interactions. In the experience of the authors, an optimum size for responsive teaching is between 15 and 20, which allows for the flexible use of learning groups and engagement in interactive and exciting learning activities.

Even with groups this size, there are enormous numbers of relationships at play. To illustrate this, only a fraction of those dyadic relationships in a group are represented in Figure 7.6, which shows the potential complexity in a group of 20 learners with one teacher. In many classrooms, there are additional adult teaching assistants involved, which compounds the complexity.

The social connections, patterns of relationships, and cohesion in any group influence the effectiveness of learning for individual students. Each individual student's capabilities for relating to others (R) and their social communication skills (iU) will shape how effectively they can engage in relationships that support learning. This becomes even more complicated when the focus for some students becomes their social relationships, rather than learning. It is useful to analyse the relationships in a group of learners, to begin to understand the dynamics and how the learning of students is supported or hindered.

A sociogram can assist teachers to understand the relationships in groups of students. Usually, a set of questions is asked of students and their responses mapped so that clusters of connections or isolated students can be identified.

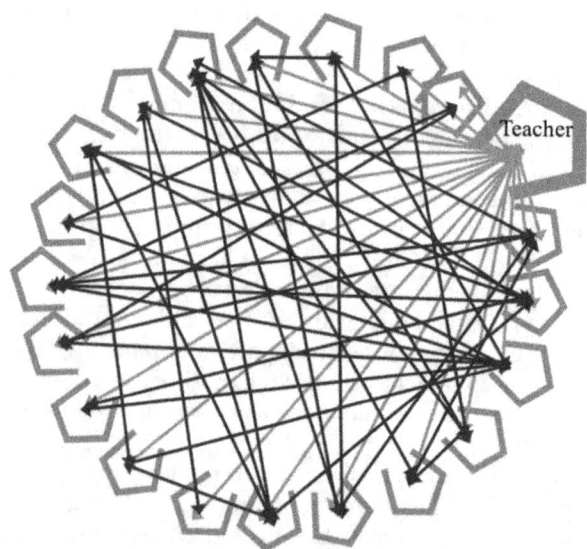

Figure 7.6 Some of the 210 relationships in a group of 20 students and one teacher.

RTF 3: What do my students bring as learners? 101

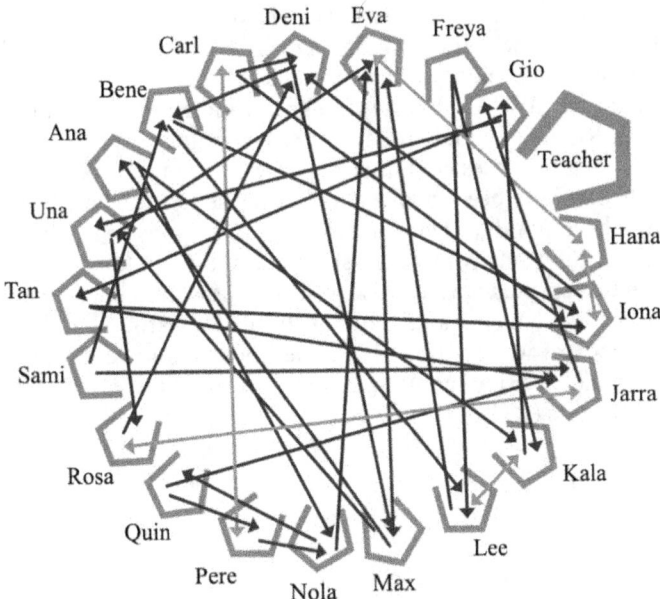

Figure 7.7 A sociogram showing student preferences for group work.

The questions depend on the purpose of the assessment activity. For example, if a teacher wants to see if anyone is isolated then questions about who each student would like to sit with, or do a project with, or play a sport with, the teacher will provide the data for a sociogram. In the following example (Figure 7.7), students were asked to identify two people with whom they would like to work. The lines with one arrow to the selected students, and the lines with double arrows mean mutual selection (Kala and Lee; Pere and Carl; Jarra and Rosa; Eva and Hana). Two students, Freya and Sami, stand out as not being selected by anyone although they each identified two people.

Sociograms assist teachers to understand the complexities of relationships within a group of students. Teachers can then sensitively use this information to engineer groupings that will meet the needs of isolated students and create flexible functional learning groups. It is important not to reveal the mapping to students as the analysis could be unhelpful for how they see themselves socially and relate to others (R). Responsive teachers need to notice the social dynamics of their classes and actively organise and manage the group to optimise learning engagement. In practice, this can mean that teachers use flexible groupings not only to target explicit teaching, but also to support social connection between students.

Activity

Create a sociogram to map the relationships of the students in your class. Ask the students to select four students with whom they would like to do group work and map the data so that clusters and isolated students are identified.

In conclusion, in this chapter we have considered what responsive teachers need to know about what their students bring to their learning (RTF 3). The assessment decision-making framework has helped by defining WHY teachers need to do this, WHAT they need to know, and HOW they can gather this information. Knowing about students' prior learning and achievement, cultural contexts, experiences, and interests, as well as any educational casework the students may have been involved in, helps teachers to know their students well enough to respond to their learning needs. Responsive teachers can then build on their knowledge of student strengths and work to reduce barriers to learning. In this chapter, we have also looked at how individual students come together to create dynamic and complex groups of learners. In the following chapter, we look at ways of organising the information we have gathered so that we can make decisions about what to teach now (RTF 4) and how to teach for all our students (RTF 5).

8 RTF 4: What do I need to teach now?

RTF 4. What do I need to teach now?

What are the current learning needs of this group and individual students? What learner readiness and interests need to be taken into account? What ecological influences and ATRiUM capabilities support and hinder learning? What are the priorities for Sustainable Learning at this time? What are the intended learning outcomes?

Introduction

The fourth step in the *Responsive Teaching Framework* requires teachers to make decisions about what to teach, at a particular time to their students. This question follows on from the articulation of what students bring to their learning (RTF 3) and requires professional decision making that is responsive to the learning needs that have been identified. We take the information we have gathered about students and organise it in terms of readiness, interests, and develop a *Sustainable Learning Profile*. We then consider curriculum expectations and develop intended learning outcomes for groups of learners and individual students.

Learner readiness, interests, and learning profile

A focus on student readiness for learning, interest in learning, and a *Sustainable Learning Profile* assist responsive teachers to make explicit determinations about what to teach now. When we look at how to teach for all our students (RTF 5), we need to have organised what we know about our students as learners (RTF 3) in terms of their readiness, interests, and profiles as learners, which are key to differentiated instruction (Tomlinson et al., 2003).

Readiness

Readiness for learning was initially described in the context of differentiated instruction by Tomlinson et al. (2003) with reference to Vygotskian learning theory and associated research evidence that learning tasks need to be at an

DOI: 10.4324/9781003299813-10

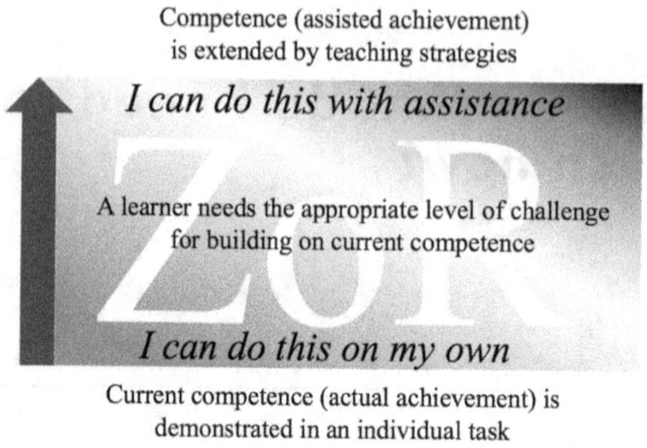

Competence (assisted achievement)
is extended by teaching strategies

I can do this with assistance

A learner needs the appropriate level of challenge
for building on current competence

I can do this on my own

Current competence (actual achievement) is
demonstrated in an individual task

Figure 8.1 Zone of Readiness.

Adapted from Berman & Graham, 2018.

appropriate level of challenge to maintain students' motivation and engagement. The idea that any instructional task should be in the zone of proximal development (ZPD) came from Vygotsky's use of intelligence tests, to which he added mediation (teaching) to facilitate assisted achievement (Vygotsky, 1978). He was thus able to make more sense of differences in readiness for learning through analysing the differences in zones of potential or proximal learning that he observed.

An appropriate level of challenge in learning lies within a student's zone of proximal development or zone of readiness for learning, their ZoR (Figure 8.1). If a task is too hard, even with teaching support, or too easy, then it is not a learning opportunity. Instead, it is a task that can only be done with assistance from a teacher (or other more knowledgeable other). To be successful, the learner must practice skills before being able to do the task independently in the near future.

Determining the size of the ZoR, that is, the extent of students' readiness for learning and identifying how much challenge to provide for individual students is one of the most difficult aspects of teaching. Even adept teachers do not always get it right. It is not unusual for teachers to plan a great lesson but find that it does not hit the mark for some of the students in the class as they either finish very quickly, or they find it difficult to interpret or manage the activity. It is also important for teachers to constantly reflect on whether the activities assigned to students are really learning opportunities or just keeping them busy. All the responsive teaching approaches we advocate, from knowing what students bring to their learning (RTF 3), to relying on robust learning progressions, and using *Universal Design for Learning* and responsive differentiation, aim to increase the chance of getting the 'level' of challenge right for our students.

Interest

The second dimension of what students bring to their learning was defined by Tomlinson et al. (2003) as being interested in learning that is linked to competence and self-determination, engagement and motivation, satisfaction, and achievement. Students who are interested in learning new things are set up to be active learners (A). These students are curious, they want to make sense of the world and to know more "for the sake of knowing" (Schutte & Malouff, 2020). Teachers can instigate and nurture interest in topics not yet known. Interest in learning involves curiosity which has a strong link to creativity (Schutte & Malouff, 2020). It is also influenced by ATRiUM capabilities that support participation and cooperation in completing the activities organised by teachers.

Early research into human interest made a distinction between individual interests (which are relatively enduring) and situational interest (Schiefele, 1991) which can be stimulated by teachers. All students "will be more motivated, independent and focused if the activity is intrinsically interesting to them" (Wood, 2021, p. 47), therefore when student interests are used in designing learning opportunities, this can increase access to learning, learning-activity completion, and consolidation of ATRiUM capabilities. Interest in learning is, therefore, not a fixed trait of individual students. It is something that can be activated and nurtured by teachers who set expectations, model the excitement of learning new things, and who use questioning to prompt interest. Responsive teachers also see their students' interests as a resource to be utilised, so that students are more likely to become engaged in learning. This depends on whether teachers know about the interests of their students so that this knowledge can be used in task design. Responsiveness involves not only engaging learners through their interests but also extending their interests and facilitating active learning.

Learning profile

A learning profile is the third dimension of what students bring to their learning and is inherent to the Tomlinson model of differentiated instruction. This notion initially referred to "learning style, intelligence preference, gender and culture" (Tomlinson et al., 2003, p. 129) and drew on research conducted up to the end of the 20th century that attempted to define thinking styles according to gender, culture, and race. This research was firmly anchored in the US educational and legislative frameworks. However, the practice of classifying learners according to learning styles has not been supported by research findings (Cuevas, 2015; Kirschner, 2017; Willingham, Hughes, & Dobolyi, 2015). Responsive teachers do not sort students according to particular types of learning styles or intelligences. Responsive teachers, instead, accept that learners draw on all their ATRiUM capabilities and use dynamic ways of learning that change as they build their repertoire of strategies. Responsive teachers also know that is not appropriate for students to be dependent on one way of learning. Over-reliance on particular ways of learning and thinking can become barriers. Therefore, it is important for students to build multiple skills and capabilities that they can use flexibly and adapt to new learning situations.

For the purposes of *Responsive Teaching for Sustainable Learning*, we use a learning profile or description of students' learning needs defined by the five capabilities that comprise ATRiUM coupled with known influences on learning. The *Sustainable Learning Profile* requires two processes that start with a mapping of ecological influences on learning.

Ecological map of influences on learners

We will now provide a way to organise what is known about our students as learners (from RTF 3) using the ATRiUM capabilities (i.e., processes of learning) and the ecological framework to help clarify student learning needs. Knowing what our students bring as learners is central to being responsive and able to differentiate meaningfully. We do this by understanding how students function as learners both independently and in a group. Responsive teachers consider how students learn actively (A), how they draw on and use thinking skills (T), how they relate to others while learning (R), how they use the cultural tools of language and other symbol systems (iU), and how they manage their learning (M). Teachers want *all* these capabilities to develop in depth and breadth as our students learn. Additionally, teachers are conscious of the influences that affect learning and need to incorporate these understandings into this profile. Figure 8.2 is the basis of this process.

This process of organising what is known about students as learners, within an ecological framework and according to ATRiUM, has been carried out by

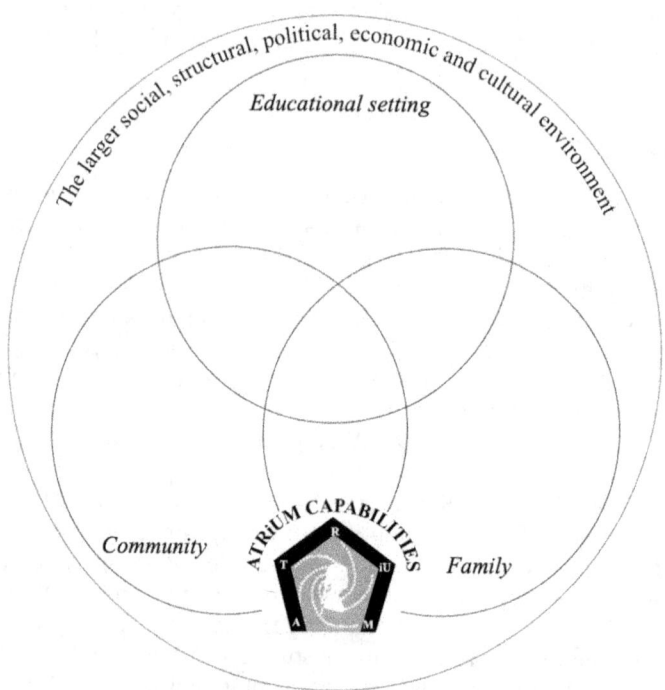

Figure 8.2 Student use of ATRiUM capabilities happens within this ecology.
Adapted from Graham, Berman, & Bellert, 2015.

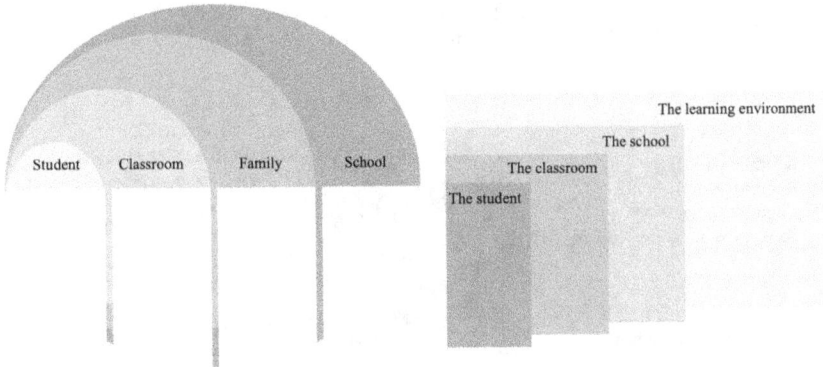

Figure 8.3 Other examples of ecological map structures.

many university students in subjects about *Sustainable Learning* and responsive teaching, and by practising teachers enrolled in professional learning courses in Australia and Latin America. Our work has shown that this model resonates with teachers, helping them to manage the enormous body of information about students that informs their decision-making about what needs to be taught now (RTF 4) and how it can best be taught (RTF 5). These frameworks also provide a visual representation of the key information within an ecological map which enables teachers to see the main influences on their students. Many teachers have carried out this task, generating a variety of ecological maps with different structures. Some teachers preferred using a table instead of a map, while others used nested representations as in Figure 8.3.

These maps can be populated with information relative to each layer of influence, effectively highlighting aspects of these contexts that are pertinent at the time. As is evident, teachers can adapt the layers and the structure to suit. Alongside this mapping, it is also important to consider ATRiUM to describe students' capabilities.

Elaborations of ATRiUM such as in Figure 8.4 which lists terms associated with each capability can help unpack students' profiles. Many of these terms are used by educational and other professionals and found in reports about students. This figure helps to organise terms according to ATRiUM capabilities and prompts teachers to consider students' strengths and difficulties within each capability. Further elaboration is included in Chapter 10.

Everything teachers know about their students as learners can be organised according to the ATRiUM model. This model provides a framework for asking the right questions about learners and provides a common language that can be used by teachers, students, and families to share their understandings of learning needs. As an example, ADHD is typically about a student paying attention to everything (i.e., being easily distracted), tending towards impulsivity and getting frustrated easily. These behaviours are aspects of engagement (A), attention (T), social skills (R), and managing impulsivity and having persistence (M). There could also be difficulties with confidence (M) and

108 Using the responsive teaching framework

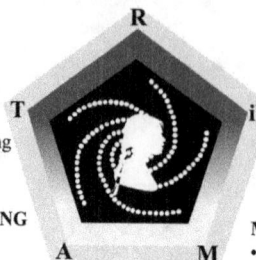

RELATING TO OTHERS
- Cultural practices
- Social communication
- Social skills

THINKING
- Information-gathering
- Building understanding
- Cognitive processing
- Strategic & reflective thinking

USING LANGUAGE, SYMBOL SYSTEMS & ICT
- Receptive & expressive language
- Literacy & numeracy
- ICT skills

ACTIVE LEARNING
- Engagement
- Motivation
- Interest

MANAGING SELF
- Self-regulation
- Metacognition
- Emotion and mood regulation

Figure 8.4 ATRiUM capabilities.
Adapted from Berman & Graham, 2018.

growth mindset (A). Profiles will be different for individual students and are understood through considering individual ways of functioning.

Activity

Search the internet using this question: How does attention affect learning?

You can do this for all terms in Figure 8.4 to see how the ATRiUM capabilities support learning and how difficulties related to them can be barriers to learning.

Notice that we are asking about 'attention' and not 'attention difficulties'. It is important to access a wider perspective on this aspect of learning and how it works to support learning for most students. First explore how learning is facilitated by the ATRiUM capabilities, then explore how skills related to each capability may hinder learning for some students.

An example of an ecological map

The example in Figure 8.5 uses the ecological map developed for this book and refers to influences and ATRiUM capabilities that are pertinent at this time for the target student, Anders.

Clarifying the layers of influence helps teachers identify the factors that support and/or hinder learning and organise information according to ATRiUM capabilities. In this example, the student has well established routines for learning within an open plan classroom. Expectations for relating to others (R) and managing self (M) in flexible groupings have been established, and so the setting is organised and predictable. This should support learning for Anders because the routines are familiar. The teacher has noted some issues that Anders has in relating to teachers and peers (R) and how he sees himself as a learner, with a fixed mindset and low self-belief identified (A & M). These are significant issues for Anders and are hindering learning. Aspects of the

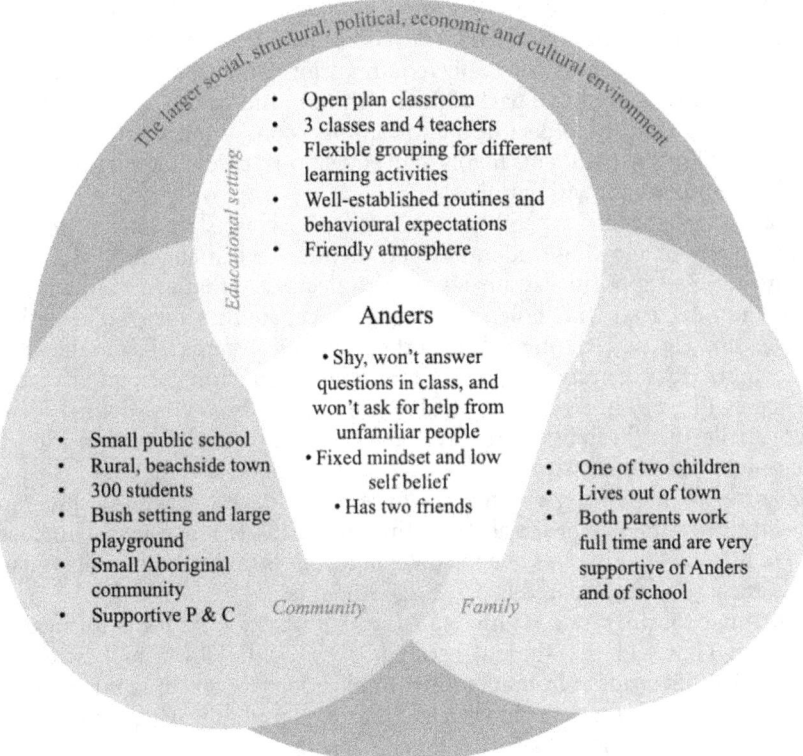

Figure 8.5 Example of an ecological map around a fictional student, Anders.

educational setting, and of the family and community within which Anders is learning, have also been identified. He is in a small community which is likely to support his sense of comfort with others and reduce his shyness, but this may need to be investigated further.

While it is understandable that students rely on their strengths as they continue to develop, it is important that strengths are not used to compensate entirely for difficulties. Ideally, all capabilities need to be used and developed.

Sustainable learning profile

When we organise information about what environmental influences and ATRiUM capabilities students bring to their learning, and specifically consider how these support and hinder learning, we create a *Sustainable Learning Profile*. Within this profile, priority areas can be examined and understood, and implications for teaching developed. The time and energy needed to create this profile is invaluable when a student presents with difficulties and teachers need to make sense of individual learning needs. It is also possible to create profiles for all students when a teacher has one group for a lengthy period. For teachers who teach a number of groups, this process needs to be more selective.

A *Sustainable Learning Profile* starts with a description of the aspect of the learning environment or student's ATRiUM capabilities that needs to be better understood. This process inevitably requires prioritising. Teachers can identify these priorities as a normal part of their planning, and/or can collaborate with students and families to decide. Significant decisions about what needs to be learnt next for those students involved in educational casework must always be made in conjunction with families.

Sometimes specific capabilities, for example social skills, are prioritised with the aim of allowing students to become more self-managing (M), but in the meantime supportive strategies are also needed so that access to curriculum is not deferred. This holds true for many capabilities such as: using language, literacy and numeracy, or other coding systems (iU); interactive behaviours (R); frustration tolerance and mood regulation (M); and thinking strategies (T). Specific capabilities also need to be the focus when students with intellectual disabilities are developing the skills needed to transition to their next educational setting or life after school. This is also the case for gifted students who may struggle with lower-order knowledge and skills despite proficiently using higher-order abstract thinking. This is not unusual in cases where literacy learning has been problematic, but thinking and oral language skills are superior compared to same-age students.

The final consideration within a *Sustainable Learning Profile* is focused on teaching: How can the student's strengths be used? How can barriers be reduced? What needs to be taught now? Implications for teaching can be based on teacher experience to begin with and then explored fully using professional and research-based sources.

The following Table 8.1 is an example of a *Sustainable Learning Profile* developed for a fictional student, Bela. It is not possible to include everything about a student in a *Sustainable Learning Profile*, so instead it focuses on a few prominent issues. For Bela (Table 8.1), three factors (social connections, reluctance to write, and openness to feedback) are identified. The first factor indicates a need to know more about Bela's writing skills, and the possibility that there is need for intensive literacy teaching to build her competence. The other factors illustrate the influence of social relationships on Bela's engagement with learning, and her dependence on interactions to support her learning, as well as her responsiveness to feedback. The profile suggests a possible over-dependence on others (both teacher and peers) that hinders Bela's independence and self-management of learning.

In developing Bela's profile, the evidence has come from her teacher's observations and conversations with Bela about her learning. Bela's teacher has also observed how she has interacted with and responded to her peers. Implications for teaching and learning that follow from the profile are concerned with further exploration of Bela's written literacy skills; explicit teaching and acknowledgment of on-task behaviours; and ensuring an emphasis on judgement about feedback within writing conferences. As well as a focus on the development of literacy skills and possible intervention, there is also a suggestion about a work-around which will allow Bela to continue to learn how to generate conceptual and creative writing using a scribe so that her reluctance to write is avoided. Reluctance to write is common when delayed literacy has

Table 8.1 Sustainable Learning Profile

Description of what the student brings to their learning or an influence within the learning environment	Explanation of how it is supporting learning	Explanation of how it is hindering learning	Evidence – how do I know this?	Generation of implications for teaching and learning
Reluctance to write	–	Bela uses her social interests to avoid writing tasks (R, iU, M)	Observations; Report from parents; Incomplete written tasks	Investigate writing skills and plan for systematic teaching of writing; provide some tasks with scribes so she can contribute verbally
Social connections	Bela engages with groups on learning activities and interacts effectively when problem solving (R, iU)	Bela can be distracted by social relationships (R, M)	Teacher observations; Incomplete tasks	Be in proximity of Bela's group to cue her to stay on task; Explicitly teach group skills for staying on task
Open to feedback	Bela likes to receive feedback, then to revise her work and show the changes she has made (A, T, R, M)	Bela takes any feedback and is not yet able to judge feedback; pleasing friends who give feedback is very important (A, T, R)	Was observed making changes to work; Conferences about work – seeking feedback and explaining how she made changes	Provide regular conferencing and teach Bela to make judgements about feedback

been a barrier to learning new concepts and developing thinking skills. Students like Bela require continued access to high-level curriculum as well as appropriate literacy teaching. Teachers may assume that both dimensions of learning are aligned, when they could be grossly mis-aligned, causing considerable challenges. The saying *learn to read, so you can read to learn* is absurd and also true. Young children learn many things both while they are learning to read and when they can use reading as a tool for learning. Curriculum has managed to combine these two emphases, but at times, such as in Bela's case, this needs to be unpacked.

In an ideal world, a *Sustainable Learning Profile* would be used to organise information for all students. In practice, it can only be done for a few targeted students in a group, particularly those who are the focus of casework. It can be helpful to explore the similarities and differences in learning needs by examining the learning needs of two students with similar diagnoses. One teacher at an in-service course in Australia focused on two students with diagnoses of dyslexia, examining issues around active learning (A: motivation, curiosity, risk taking), relating to others (R: social skills), and managing self (M: persistence, confidence, and self-esteem). These were identified differently for each student, and then linked to how the students saw themselves with this label. One student felt relieved, while the other interpreted this to mean that she could not ever learn effectively. The teacher was then able to respond differently to each student to better support their identities as learners, and thus their learning.

Other teachers who have used this process reflected:

> *on characteristics of my learning and work environment and on the capabilities of my two students. ... My mindset has changed, and I am able to see the influence of these characteristics through the lens of the ATRiUM capabilities.*
>
> *By explicitly naming the myriad of capabilities these students bring to their learning, I was regularly making connections between strategies or implications for teaching that would not only affect Rhys's learning, but also Sil's, and quite possibly other students in my classroom. By aligning the characteristics that these two students brought to their learning with the ATRiUM framework, I was able to make insights into my students' learning that I had not previously.*

Another teacher's comment shows how this process can be enlightening when completed for students who are a bit of a mystery as learners.

> *Upon reflecting over Mika's struggles to manage his emotions when presented with a change in his routine, I had not considered how actively he was trying to solve his problems. I had not considered that his 'meltdowns' were actually his way of trying to communicate and cope with something he found immensely difficult.*

This reflection emphasises an understanding of the function of behaviour as part of knowing a student as learner (see Chapter 7). The next comment reminds us that sometimes students slip under the radar.

> *I know that as a teacher I have been content with the higher students completing their work and not thinking hard enough about their actual needs and how to extend them. The completing of this process has really confirmed to me that the learning needs of every child are different but are all equally important. Every child within our classrooms deserves to be taught what their learning needs dictate.*

There have been many attempts at collating information and defining individual student learning needs through individual (or personal) education (or learning) plans (IEPs, ILPs, PLPs) usually for students with disabilities, difficulties, or disadvantage (OECD, 2008). This process can be overwhelming and often, instead, became the production of a document placed in a file for accountability purposes. Responsive teachers need to organise what is known about their students so they can respond to their current learning needs. The *Sustainable Learning Profile* allows them to highlight key aspects of individual learning needs and consider how best to teach in light of this information. Even knowing more about one or two students can make a big difference for teachers, who need to respond to all. For instance, one teacher reported that the experience of focusing on two students had "deepened my understanding of all of my students and helped me use more effective strategies to promote their learning and understanding", which is testimony to the usefulness of the process as a structure for professional reflection. This also reminds us that understanding the teaching and strategies that are effective for one student can have implications for others, thus making teaching more effective for all learners.

Intended learning outcomes

Teachers determine what is to be taught now (RTF 4) in reference to the curriculum and the expectations of the school or system (RTF 1), and with regard to *Sustainable Learning Profiles*, which focus on particular aspects of the curriculum and the development of capabilities and strategies for reducing barriers to learning. Responsive teachers need to reconcile teaching expectations with the learning needs of students in order to define intended learning outcomes.

Curriculum is organised sequentially, and most decisions about what to teach are based on what has already been taught. Many schools have mapped the curriculum and have planned topics across grades as part of their organisation. Since teaching does not always result in learning, however, it is important to check what the students have learnt so that valid assessment information can be the basis for the next phase of teaching. Responsive teachers need to know what the students know and can do – not only what they have been taught.

Intended learning within any curriculum content area is usually defined with the assistance of research-based learning trajectories and hierarchically organised progressions. That means it is possible to move within the curriculum to determine what to teach. It also means teachers can draw on a range of content and objectives to map and match the range of learning needs across a class. It is also important for teachers to make a distinction between the curriculum content and the processes that students use in learning and in demonstrating their learning (i.e., the ATRiUM capabilities). The Australian Curriculum documentation has an explicit mapping of capabilities across the learning areas so that it is possible to identify the learning processes underpinning the content described for each level (ACARA, 2022b).

Curricula have always been developmental, containing progressively more complex and higher-order learning from the early to final years of school. Curricula have been variously prescriptive with more systematic and explicit details of learning progressions developed recently to complement the defined skills and knowledge content. The learning areas detail the knowledge and skills that are to be learnt, but the learning progressions provide more explicit information about typical pathways of development and, therefore, more guidance about what to teach next. Once the assessment of prior learning and achievement has determined what a student knows and can do, progressions indicate what needs to be learnt next. These evidence-based developmental pathways, learning progressions and theoretical frameworks support teacher decision-making about what to teach next.

Developmental pathways

Developmental and learning pathways, or trajectories, are derived from research about typical development in specific domains of learning (Duchesne & McMaugh, 2019). Any textbook on human development and learning will contain developmental progressions for physical development (gross and fine motor) and more focused sets of skills within that domain, such as handwriting or ball throwing. There will also be progressions for psychosocial (personal and social) development, language development, cognitive development, and other aspects such as moral development (e.g., Hoffnung et al., 2018; Peterson, 2013). The typical pathways of development of all these domains of human learning are now known and encompass the whole of life. These well-evidenced pathways are used in assessment by professionals who are involved in developmental and educational casework and who can ascribe 'age equivalents' to every aspect of development from gross motor skills to handwriting, language, cognition, and social and emotional capabilities.

Developmental science has also defined development for particular groups of children. For example, a detailed analysis of the development of children who have Down Syndrome can provide information about potential pathways of development. However, much of this research has been carried out within a very medical model of developmental disability and, therefore, is to be viewed critically by educators. Recent examples of such research provide more detail about learning trajectories for children with Down Syndrome (Faragher & Clarke, 2013) and conclude that, for example, their physical development is typical but delayed (Locatelli et al., 2021). Importantly, this research also provides direction for teachers by acknowledging the responsiveness of students with Down Syndrome to teaching (Faragher & Clarke, 2020; Faragher, Stratford, & Clarke, 2017). Remembering that we need to use any diagnostic label as a starting point, and not a formula for teaching, teachers can explore the research evidence about development that assists in understanding what can be taught next.

Activity

Developmental pathways are integral to the Early Childhood curriculum in Australia in the form of milestones within physical, social, emotional, cognitive, and language developmental domains (ACECQA, 2017). Additionally, there are indicators which are used to encourage early childhood educators to note and if not met to seek specialist advice about children's development.

Carry out an internet search for young children's developmental milestones in a domain of development, e.g., 'developmental milestones fine motor'. Explore the resources that are available. You will find health websites with detailed charts of development, parent sites with checklists, and educational-system websites for parents. You will also find sites that focus on processes for early childhood screening which may provide the first indicators of any potential developmental delays or disorders.

You can also explore differences in development for groups of children by including a named disability or situation (e.g., gifted, intellectual disability, Down Syndrome, Fragile X Syndrome, Spina Bifida, premature babies, poverty) in your search.

Learning progressions

Recently, two explicit developmental pathways, or learning progressions, were included in the Australian curriculum for schools (ACARA, 2020a). These provide a reference for assessment and for determining what students need to learn next. The creation of explicit learning progressions for strands within learning areas has been happening in science and mathematics for more than ten years, with a focus on the development of conceptual understanding (Duschl et al., 2011). Considerable research has been revitalised by the introduction of learning progressions in the Australian Curriculum, with advocacy for curriculum to be reframed from a scope and sequence of content to be brought into alignment with learning progressions that describe the pathway from "current identified knowledge of key concepts to a deeper knowledge" (Callingham et al., 2021, p. 339).

The use of learning progressions is also occurring internationally. In fact, the impetus at least in part originates with the United Nations' requirement to have consistency in the measurement of reading and mathematics learning across countries in order to judge performance relative to the Sustainable Development Goals (Adams, Jackson, & Turner, 2018). Learning progressions, which "represent the complex ways in which learners actually build upon their prior learning, recognising that those descriptions of learning are only approximations as far as individual learners are concerned" (IEAN, 2020, p. 3) are being explored around the world. As "learning progressions provide discipline-specific models for attending to student thinking and for appreciating how detailed aspects of partial understandings might mature into more sophisticated conceptions", they have built in support for teaching (Shepard, 2018, p. 170).

In a project carried out by one of the authors of *Responsive Teaching for Sustainable Learning*, school psychologist success with dynamic assessment of mathematical learning was found to have been influenced strongly by the assessors' conceptual knowledge of the learning they were assessing (Berman & Graham, 2002). Depth of knowledge of the conceptual learning progression supported spontaneous mediation (teaching) within the assessment. This aspect of teacher knowledge of learning progressions supports teaching, from planning, to determining what to teach next, and through the provision of on-the-spot feedback for learners. Teachers informally develop learning progressions from their professional experience, which becomes internalised and can be drawn on while teaching, both to assess student learning and to plan what is to be taught next.

A change in mindset from curriculum scope and sequence to learning progressions has implications, not only for curriculum development and teacher professional learning, but also for assessment. The inclusion of descriptions of what learning looks like at a particular point on a learning progression provides learners with meaningful references for self-assessment, a key process for developing self-regulated learning (Goral & Bailey, 2019). These descriptions of learning are more helpful in defining what has been learned, or what a student is ready to learn next, than conventional quantification of learning through scores (IEAN, 2020; Shepard, 2018). Learning progressions should be "based firmly on research evidence" about learning in specific domains (IEAN, 2020, p. 3). Such research evidence comes from observation, assessment of student learning and development, and the validation of progressions for large scale use. When teachers use learning progressions, they draw on their professional problem-solving skills to make sense of student learning and make decisions about what to teach next.

Theoretical frameworks

Theoretical frameworks can also help teachers decide what to teach next, by providing principles for decision-making. Two useful theoretical frameworks are the SOLO (Structure of the Observed Learning Outcome) Taxonomy (Biggs & Collis, 1982), which focuses on the development of conceptual understanding and Dreyfus' (2004) model of skills acquisition.

SOLO provides principles for understanding the increasing progression of conceptual learning within specific domains. It has been applied in many curriculum areas, including computer programming (Malik, Tawafak, & Shakir, 2021), mathematics (Afriyani, Sa'dijah, & Muksar, 2018), physics (Nunaki et al., 2019), cryptography (Patterson, 2021), and science (Davies & Mansour, 2022). The structure of SOLO's explanation of conceptual learning is represented in Table 8.2.

Initial learning involves acquiring facts, which is surface learning; the building of a body of knowledge about aspects of a topic. When enough facts are known, learners can connect them in relational ways, creating meaning at higher levels. Deeper thinking extends relational knowledge. This structure of

Table 8.2 SOLO taxonomy

Quantity of learning (surface)			Quality of learning (deep or higher thinking)	
Not knowing	Knowing one aspect	Knowing multiple aspects	Knowing how the multiple aspects relate to each other	Knowing how these aspects can be extended into different ideas or contexts

Biggs & Collis, 1982.

Table 8.3 Model of skill acquisition

Skill development				
Focus is on mechanisms of context-free skills or sub-skills (Novice)	Beginning of matching to relevant context for use of skills (Advanced beginner)	Seeks rules and reasoning to assist with selection and planful use of skills (Competence)	Rules and principles for using skills are gradually replaced by situational discriminations (Proficiency)	Increasingly nuanced discriminations (Expertise)
	Emotional component			
	Satisfaction of skill use, as well as reaction to errors, allows extension from being rule bound	Continued optimal level of anxiety related to situational use of skills; involved, experienced performer	Immediate intuitive situational response	

Dreyfus, 2004.

learning outcomes developed from the analysis of students' written explanations (Biggs & Collis, 1982) and assists teachers to decide what to teach next. This may be in the form of more information about a topic (multi-structural), opportunities to make connections and see patterns based on those facts (relational), or the opportunity to apply the ideas in another context (extended abstract).

To complement the conceptual learning progression theory of SOLO, a model of skills acquisition is helpful, such as that proposed by Dreyfus (2004; Table 8.3). In this model skills are decomposed and decontextualised into sub-skills, then matched to context and rules and reasoning are subsequently applied to assist the strategic use of the skills. This is followed by the development of situational discrimination for the use of the skills in question. Alongside this progression is an emotional component, which seeks to articulate the risk-taking involved in learning new skills, and how these build towards proficiency and finally expert application.

Together these theoretical frameworks define progressions of learning that include both knowledge and skills and can be used within curriculum discipline areas. They provide principles to help organise content according to the quality of knowledge and skills required.

Defining intended learning outcomes

Responsive teachers explicitly define intended learning outcomes as goals for learning, in reference to curriculum, developmental and learning progressions, and *Sustainable Learning Profiles*. The structure of the goals depends on the context for teaching, since different curricula and systems require distinct methods of detailing what students will learn. Within these varying contexts, teachers need to be explicit about learning intentions, and to set up processes for monitoring learning and determining when the goals have been achieved.

Intended learning outcomes need to be appropriate for all learners. Responsive teaching uses both teacher and student-designed learning goals, and an explicit approach to clarifying what students need to KNOW, UNDERSTAND, and be able to DO (Tomlinson & Moon, 2013, 2014). By specifying what learning looks like across these three dimensions, teachers can share information about the target of teaching, what their students will learn, and what success will look like. Within a Universal Design for Learning (UDL) approach to differentiation, goal setting is part of the executive functions domain and a process that needs to be explicitly taught (CAST, 2018). Student commitment to goals affects their approach to learning, with a greater commitment to self-set goals recommended as students feel more in control of their learning (Nordengren, 2019). However, teachers need to mediate the intentions of students so that they are not only realistic but challenging and potentially open up new learning. Students involved in setting their own learning goals appear to grow to understand their learning needs, generate their drive to learn, and be able to reflect on their own learning (Nordengren, 2019). Furthermore, the negotiation of intended learning goals supports students' achievement motivation (Locke & Latham, 2019).

A structured approach to defining explicit intended learning outcomes is derived from the SOLO taxonomy (Biggs & Collis, 1982). SOLO defines intended learning using facts, ideas, and concepts which are grouped, classified, and contextualised, and then described in terms of actions within learning activities and assessment tasks (Biggs & Tang, 2022; Martin, 2011). As an example, this process of 'constructive alignment' can be applied in a science class using the following steps: identify all facts, ideas, and concepts in the topic; classify these according to the SOLO taxonomy; identify possible contexts for extension to the highest level of thinking; group and make connections between ideas, concepts, and contexts; and then assign SOLO verbs (Table 8.4) to learning activities and assessment tasks (Martin, 2011). This process recognises both the varying depth of concepts and ideas, and the activities that students can apply to learn those concepts. Both dimensions can be varied as part of differentiation, according to students' needs, and in reference to conceptual activity associated with SOLO levels.

Teachers and students can select appropriate verbs to use for intended learning outcomes, indicating the inherent difficulty of the activity, and the associated quality of the anticipated learning. In the following example (Table 8.5), the topic has been organised according to SOLO levels, with selected verbs for each level. This allows teachers and students to be cognisant of what the next level of learning looks like and to set appropriate learning goals.

By drawing on the key concepts and related verbs, it is possible to clearly define exactly what is to be taught and what it will look like in an assessed activity. Using SOLO has been shown to strengthen the teaching of those who teach outside their discipline, and who teach across multiple disciplines (Davies & Mansour, 2022). It is helpful for both learners and teachers to

Table 8.4 Verbs according to SOLO levels of quantity and quality of learning

Quantity of learning (surface)		Quality of learning (deep or higher thinking)	
Knowing one aspect (Unistructural)	Knowing multiple aspects (Multistructural)	Knowing how the multiple aspects relate to each other (Relational)	Knowing how these aspects can be extended into different ideas or contexts (Extended abstract)
Memorise, identify, recognise, count, define, draw, find, label, match, name, quote, recall, recite, order, tell, write, imitate	Classify, describe, list, report, discuss, illustrate, select, narrate, compute, sequence, outline, separate,	Apply, integrate, analyse, explain, predict, conclude, summarise, review, argue, transfer, make a plan, characterise, compare, contrast, differentiate, organise, debate, make a case, construct, review and rewrite, examine, translate, paraphrase, solve a problem	Theorise, hypothesise, generalise, reflect, generate, create, compose, invent, originate, prove from first principles, make an original case, solve from first principles

Verbs from Biggs & Tang, 2011.

Table 8.5 SOLO analysis of a topic in science education for a primary class

SOLO level	Uni- or multi-structural		Relational	Extended abstract
Content	Energy Electrical Chemical Nuclear	Sound Light Kinetic Potential	Transfer Transformation	Energy and fossil fuels Saving energy Alternative energy
Verbs	Identify List	Define Describe	Compare and contrast	Reflect Predict

Martin, 2011, p. 13.

organise the progression of learning activities according to SOLO verbs. As an example, from practice, sets of intended learning outcomes, defined using SOLO in the context of early childhood education are provided in Table 8.6. These examples are aligned with the New Zealand Key Competences, and hence with ATRiUM capabilities, and are selected from a rich body of similarly organised ILOs in early childhood education (Hook & Cassé, 2013).

The developmental nature of this table allows students to match descriptions to their current learning and also describes what the next outcome for

Table 8.6 Examples of levels of ATRiUM capabilities expressed as intended learning outcomes according to SOLO for pre-schoolers

ILO and ATRiUM capability	Pre-structural	Uni-structural	Multi-structural	Relational	Extended abstract
Active learning (A) I am learning to take part in a group discussion by: … sharing … listening … responding … summarising	I might agree with someone else's ideas, but I can't yet share my own.	I can contribute my ideas if I'm encouraged.	I can contribute my ideas voluntarily.	…and I can listen to and respond to the ideas of others.	… and I can summarise the ideas from a small group discussion. I can create questions to learn more.
Thinking (T) I am learning to think creatively.	I need help to think of a new idea about [x].	I can think of many ideas about [x].	I can think of many ideas about [x] from different points of view.	… and I can explain these ideas.	… and I can evaluate the 'newness' of the ideas.
Relating to others (R) I am learning to work with others.	I behave in a way that suits me.	I behave in a way that suits me. I need to be reminded that this may not suit others.	I behave in a way that suits me. I know this may not suit others.	I behave in a way that suits me and the people I am with. I expect others to do the same.	…and I check the way I behave when I work with others to see if I can improve.
Using language, symbol systems and ICT (iU) I am learning to use symbols or hand signs to represent the SOLO level of my learning outcome.	I need help to identify the SOLO level of what I am going to learn.	I can identify the SOLO level if prompted.	I can independently suggest a SOLO level.	… and I can explain why I have chosen that SOLO level for my learning outcome.	…and I can identify my next learning steps.
Managing self (M) I am learning to take personal responsibility.	I find it hard to take responsibility for my response to others.	I need to be reminded that I own what I do.	I take ownership of what I do.	… and I can explain why it is important to own my actions.	… and I can help others learn to be responsible.

Selected examples from Hook & Cassé, 2013, pp. 29–39.

Table 8.7 SMART goal structures

S	Specific or strategic	S	Specific	S	Specific
M	Measurable	M	Measurable	M	Measurable
A	Attainable or achievable	A	Ambitious	A	Action verbs
R	Relevant	R	Realistic	R	Realistic
T	Time-bound or time-based or tied to routines	T	Time-bound	T	Time-limited
		I	Inspiring		
	After Doran, Miller, & Cunningham (1981)		Pameijer (2016)		Hedin & DeSpain (2019)

Adapted from Berman & Graham, 2018.

them looks like. The structure of intended learning outcomes can also be shaped by other approaches, including SMART goals.

SMART goals are common in education, having come from within the context of management and originally standing for Specific, Measurable, Assignable, Realistic, and Time-related aspects of performance outcomes (Doran, Miller, & Cunningham, 1981). The meaning for each letter in SMART has been variously altered since then and the usual wording in educational contexts is the first version shown in Table 8.7.

SMARTI (Pameijer, 2016) was developed within the context of school psychology in Europe and emphasises ambition (for A) and inspiration (I). The more recent version of SMART (Hedin & DeSpain, 2019) has reframed the A to be action verbs, which takes us back to a key dimension of SOLO, with verbs that distinguish between different levels of thinking. When action verbs are included in intended learning outcomes in other domains, they are drawn from a wider field and will refer to other activities that students engage in while learning. A comprehensive list of verbs referring to student behaviour in learning (Adelman, 2015), however, can be used in intended learning goals. Examples from this list are shown below in Table 8.8.

Table 8.8 Verbs related to activities of students

Verbs describing what students do when they *inquire*	Examine, experiment, explore, hypothesise, investigate, research, test
Verbs describing what students do when they combine ideas, materials, observations	Assimilate, consolidate, merge, connect, integrate, link, synthesise, summarise
Verbs that describe what students do in various forms of *making*	Build, compose, construct, craft, create, design, develop, generate, model, shape, simulate
Verbs that describe the various ways in which students utilise the materials of learning	Apply, carry out, conduct, demonstrate, employ, implement, perform, produce, use
Verbs that describe what students do in rethinking or reconstructing	Accommodate, adapt, adjust, improve, modify, refine, reflect, review

Adelman, 2015.

122 Using the responsive teaching framework

Table 8.9 Verbs for cognitive processes from the revised Bloom's taxonomy

Remember	Understand	Apply	Analyse	Evaluate	Create
Recognise Recall	Interpret Exemplify Classify Summarise Infer Compare Explain	Execute Implement	Differentiate Organise Attribute	Check Critique	Generate Plan Produce

Krathwohl, 2002.

Another source of verbs for intended learning outcomes is Bloom's taxonomy which was developed by tertiary educators as a way to write intended learning outcomes (Moseley et al., 2005). The revised Bloom's taxonomy distinguishes between four types of knowledge (factual, conceptual, procedural, and metacognitive) and contains six sets of verbs that can be used by teachers and students (Anderson et al., 2001; Krathwohl, 2002). Examples of these verbs are shown in Table 8.9.

These examples demonstrate that it is possible to write explicit intended learning outcomes, including the action that is required of students, by arranging a set of outcomes so that students know what they can do to build on their current levels of achievement. These intended learning outcomes guide not only the learning activities (RTF 5) but also the assessment activities (RTF 6) and feedback processes (RTF 7) of *Responsive Teaching for Sustainable Learning*. If the aim is to teach particular thinking skills, then these need to be incorporated within both the learning and assessment opportunities, in what Biggs and Tang (2011) term 'constructive alignment' (Biggs & Tang, 2011).

Activity

Search the internet for Bloom's taxonomy and see how it has been used by teachers to develop intended learning outcomes.

In summary, once teachers are conscious of curriculum expectations (RTF 1) and understand what their students bring as learners (RTF 3), they decide what the students need to learn now, and consequently what is to be taught (RTF 4). This requires being informed by the broad expectations of the education system and using information about student readiness and interests, and what may be supporting and hindering learning. This information can be consolidated into a *Sustainable Learning Profile*. Teachers use professional decision-making to decide what needs to be taught so that learners access the curriculum in ways that will best meet their learning needs. Developmental pathways and learning progressions are useful for responsive teachers who use them to define learning outcomes, in terms of both the curriculum and ATRiUM capabilities. The structure of intended learning outcomes decided on for students depends on the requirements of educational settings, the approach of teachers, and can be supported by theoretical models which define increasing quality of learning. Responsive teachers include student input into the development of learning goals so that students have a sense of control over their learning, and clarity about the intention of the teaching and learning interaction. Within the *Responsive Teaching Framework* teachers are now ready to make decisions about how best to teach all their students (RTF 5).

9 RTF 5: How do I teach for all my learners?

RTF 5. How do I teach for all my learners?

How do I establish teaching-learning relationships? How do I set up an inclusive learning environment? What teaching approaches, teaching strategies, and learning opportunities should I use? How do I teach ATRiUM capabilities? How do I collaborate with others in teaching?

Teaching to meet the learning needs of all students is both an obligation and a challenge. Responsive teachers focus on the whole learner and deliberately teach ATRiUM capabilities. They utilise personal and professional capabilities to establish teaching-learning relationships, set up inclusive learning environments, and plan teaching approaches and learning opportunities that contribute to the effective teaching of all students, including those who are reluctant to engage or are slow to make progress. Planning for effective teaching that engages students in authentic learning is essential. This has been emphasised in previous chapters, within which the reflective questions of the *Responsive Teaching Framework* lead to an awareness of the many influences on students as learners. Information about learners is then organised into *Sustainable Learning Profiles* which provide direction for what needs to be taught with reference to curriculum learning outcomes and a focus on ATRiUM capabilities. *Responsive Teaching* happens in a learning environment that is designed to include everyone, and to be safe for sharing the vulnerability that comes with learning.

The nature of the relationship between teachers and learners is important to consider in the inclusive learning environment. It sits alongside the *Deliberate Actions of Responsive Teachers* (DARTs) as a foundation for the selection of teaching approaches and learning opportunities that are organised according to how they will best support the learning of all students.

Teacher-student relationships

At the centre of Figure 9.1 are teacher-student relationships, within which teacher activity is framed as a set of *Deliberate Actions of Responsive Teachers* (DARTs; Berman & Graham, 2018). These actions are derived from research and theoretical work focused on the interactions between effective teachers

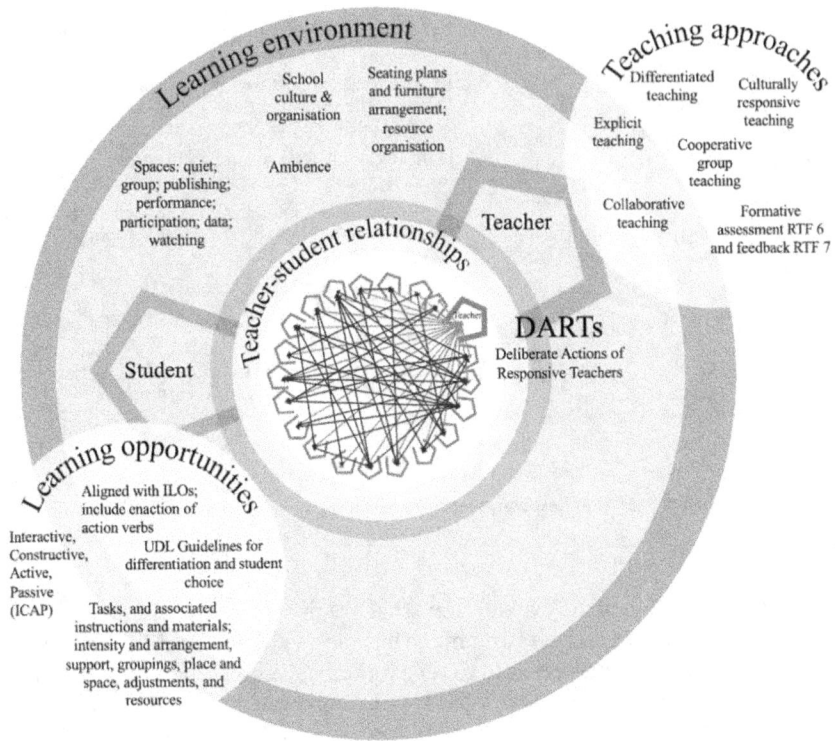

Figure 9.1 Responsive Teaching.

and successful learners through mediated learning (Skuy, 1997) and direct instruction (Liem & Martin, 2013). DARTs also align with the key components of effective teaching highlighted by Mitchell (2014, 2018, 2020) and Hattie (2017, 2018) and emphasise the social connections that support learning. There are multiple relationships occurring simultaneously in any classroom, and each student's interaction with the teacher, either direct or indirect, is uniquely important. DARTs define what responsive teachers consider in establishing effective teacher-student relationships Figure 9.2.

DART 1 establishes the relationships between teachers and learners and their expectations of each other. This requires a philosophical consideration of the purpose of education and of the roles of teachers and students. It also can be an opportunity to check teachers' and students' assumptions about instructional relationships. Teachers set expectations for the growth of each student considering their ability to learn and manage their own learning. The expectations are of active learning (A), relating to others (R), managing self (M), growth in thinking (T), and using language and symbols systems (iU). How teachers and learners work together to achieve the intended learning outcomes is based on credibility and responsibility (Berman & Graham, 2018).

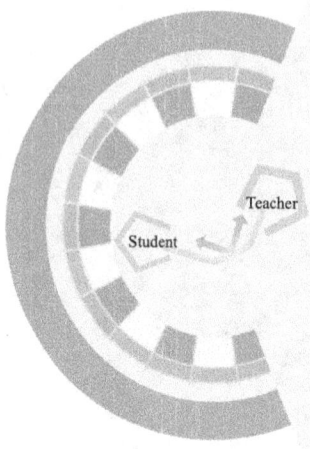

1. Setting and maintaining expectations about the intention of the teaching
2. Establishing expectations of the sharing needed to reveal the unique differences of the learner and make learning explicit or evident
3. Defining goals for learning and processes for noticing growth and change through learning
4. Explicitly tuning into current competence as well as providing challenge for developing competence
5. Interpreting and sharing meaning
6. Highlighting the relevance of the learning for other times and in other situations
7. Developing consciousness and self-regulation of thinking and behaviour in learning

Figure 9.2 Deliberate Actions of Responsive Teachers (DARTs).
Berman & Graham, 2018.

DART 2 establishes the expectations that are necessary to acknowledge the unique differences of learners and make learning evident. DART 2 has a basis in trust so that students feel able to reveal themselves as learners. It depends on the establishment of a "safe, positive and motivating classroom environment" (Mitchell & Sutherland, 2020) within which teacher availability is communicated both verbally and non-verbally (Witt, Wheeless, & Allen, 2004) and teachers follow through when help is sought (Qayyum, 2018). There are many strategies that teachers use so that their students can discretely request assistance. Professional teachers make decisions about how much of their lives they share and ensure that classrooms are safe for their students. Teachers model the expectation that everyone will make mistakes and learn as a result.

DART 3 occurs when teachers partner with students to set expectations, determine intended learning goals, and set up monitoring processes. This third deliberate teacher action is explored in detail in RTF 4. Teachers' ongoing incidental conversations about the growth of knowledge, understanding, and skills also relate to DART 3. Strategies useful for monitoring learning, including graphing practice scores, collating facts and terms in a glossary, and the use of 'exit tickets'.

DART 4 is enacted when teachers explicitly tune into their students' current skill level and provide challenges to increase their performance. Current and developing competence are the two boundaries of the Zone of Readiness (RTF 4). These can be a focus of ongoing conversations between students and teachers that are supported by evidence of both independent and assisted achievement. This approach to understanding learning comes from a developmental perspective. Both teachers and students recognise when assistance as needed and celebrate achievement when it is no longer needed. Responsibility for learning is shared. Teachers make decisions about how much direct teaching or guidance is needed, and students make decisions about seeking help. There is a graduated release of responsibility (Fisher & Frey, 2008) with both students and teachers assuming different amounts of responsibility over time.

DART 5 focuses on interpreting and sharing meaning. Teachers and learners make meaning together, as intended in the curriculum, and as shaped by the cultural contexts of learning. Through dialogic talk, teachers use their skills to ask questions that help their students by "activating previous knowledge and guiding the integration of new knowledge" (Craig, 2013, p. 414). As language and social communication are cultural tools (Zhu & Edwards, 2019), cultural dissonance can occur within classroom discussions. Responsive teachers need to be conscious of this and sensitive to any student behaviours that might indicate difficulties. In actions related to this DART, teachers design their classrooms as interactive settings where talk is the primary tool used for teaching and learning. The more formal interactions of 'teaching talk' and 'learning talk' in classrooms build on 'everyday talk' that is used by all of us as part of social engagement (Alexander, 2018). Alexander (2018) has also outlined the practical nature of dialogue and described how teachers can set up their classrooms so that deliberate conversations foster the interpretation and sharing of meaning.

DART 6 highlights the relevance of learning to other times and situations. It is important for all learning to be contextualised, and for students to understand where and when they can use their learning. This transfer of learning to new contexts or situations is an extension of the meaning negotiated in DART 5 and is about establishing the utility of learning. Transfer as a topic has been well researched (Hattie & Donoghue, 2016). The allied notion of generative learning (Marton, 2006), where learning something prepares students to learn more in the future, sits well with *Sustainable Learning*.

DART 7 refers to students' development of students' consciousness and self-regulation in order to foster their awareness of the processes of learning. Through self-regulation students can increase their agency (A) and become self-regulated learners (M). Responsive teachers ask students to reflect on and discuss how they did a task, how they planned it, what they thought about, and what influenced their decisions about the strategies they used. Specific teacher promotion of planning and strategic learning is discussed later in this chapter when focusing on teaching for managing the self (M).

The seven DARTs allow responsive teachers to set expectations for how they will relate to their students as a group and as individuals. Within these relationships, they establish basic expectations for how the teaching and learning will happen and what responsibilities teachers and learners have. The learning environment within which learning relationships are established and maintained is the next consideration in this chapter.

Activity

How do the *Deliberate Actions of Responsive Teachers* fit with other suggestions about what teachers should know and do? Specifically, how compatible are the DARTs with Rosenshine's (2012) principles of instruction?

Rosenshine argued that the following teacher actions underpin any effective approach to instruction:

- Perform daily review.
- Present new material using small steps.
- Ask questions.
- Provide models.
- Guide student practice.
- Check for student understanding.
- Obtain a high success rate.
- Provide scaffolds for difficult tasks.
- Allow independent practice.
- Perform weekly and monthly reviews.

Could you create a model that combined DARTs with Rosenshine's Principles?

The learning environment

Within positive school and classroom cultures, optimal learning environments are culturally sensitive, and have adequate physical resources so that differentiation and multi-tiered systems of support for learning and behaviour can function effectively (CAST, 2018; Hattie, 2017; Mitchell, 2018; Mitchell & Sutherland, 2020; Corwin Visible Learning Plus, 2021). The Universal Design for Learning (UDL) principle of engagement is derived from the notion of *invitation to learn* which is operationalised through teachers' responses to students' interests and how they support students' efforts, persistence, and self-regulation. The aim is for students to participate within learning environments that are inviting and flexibly led (Tomlinson, 2017a) so that they grow into learners who are purposeful, motivated, resourceful, knowledgeable, strategic, and goal-directed (CAST, 2018; Tomlinson, 2001). Within the classroom, individuals are expected to listen and think about what is heard, give others time to think, and respect alternative viewpoints as a basis to encouraging the dialogue that is fundamental in interactive settings (Alexander, 2018). The interactions between teachers and students need to meet the principles of being collective, reciprocal, supportive, cumulative, and purposeful. In this way, students and teachers contribute together to a constructive and respectful social group (Alexander, 2018, p. 566).

Classroom climate is a term referred to when discussing the range of provisions made for students within the learning environment. Classroom climate does not yet have a universal definition (Wang et al., 2020). It is referred to in a range of ways including classroom environment, ecology, milieu, and psychosocial environment (Adelman & Taylor, 2005). The 'classroom climate' term is related to school climate which can be defined as the "pattern of students', parents', and school personnel's experience of school life [that] reflects norms, goals, values, interpersonal relationships, teaching and learning practices, and organisational structures" (Cohen et al., 2009, p. 182). Researchers generally agree, however, that classroom climate includes the following dimensions: safety; teaching and learning opportunities; relationships; and the institutional environment (Cohen et al., 2009).

Safety is supported by shared whole school expectations, consistent responses to behaviours of concern, and policies that support violence prevention (Cohen et al., 2009). Teachers must ensure they have explicitly developed, taught, and practised shared expectations in the classroom and have a considered range of responses to behaviours of concern. Interpreting behaviour as a form of communication and providing consistent, timely, and responsive interactions contributes to a positive learning environment (Pianta, Hamre, & Allen, 2012). The social-emotional element of classroom climate includes attitudes to inclusion and the enactment of violence prevention policies. In the Australian context, The Australian Student Wellbeing Framework has been developed as a national initiative to support schools to develop learning communities that "promote student wellbeing, safety and positive relationships" (Education Services Australia, 2020, para 2).

The physical set up of classrooms plays an integral role in creating a positive classroom climate. Physical settings have a powerful influence on expectations, attitudes, and behaviour (De Nobile, Lyons, & Arthur-Kelly, 2017) and contribute to students feeling safe and secure. Physical settings can also support instructional practice through the considered use of activity spaces, seating plans, movement corridors, resource placement, and displays.

Responsive differentiation requires spaces for different types of interactive learning activities which can be accessed as needed. Flexible learning groups and multiple ways of engaging in learning require a range of learning spaces, often at the same time. Teachers need to access the spaces that match the teaching and the learning opportunities the students are to engage in. Spaces are required for quiet work, watching demonstrations, group activities, publishing, participation, performing, and collecting and analysing data (Whyalla Secondary College, 2019).

Banks (2014) highlights ways that the physical arrangement of the classroom can support student learning. These include having designated places for materials, and routines for distributing, using, and returning resources. As per UDL guidelines, the use of materials with a diversity of learners needs to be considered. The placement of furniture, for example, needs to allow for safe movement around the classroom, and the use of displays or other learning stimuli should not be distracting for students (Banks, 2014). Seating plans and furniture arrangements are used to position students in ways that match the learning focus of sessions. For example, furniture placed in rows directs students to the front of the room and is used when the pedagogy is teacher-centred and student work is individual (De Nobile et al., 2017). U-shaped arrangements are for when the pedagogy is teacher-centred but requires student-student interaction. This arrangement is also useful for whole-class discussions or debates. Arrangements of three or more chairs and desks grouped together are used when activities are student-centred and involve interaction. Cooperative group learning encourages fluid movement and requires workstations (De Nobile et al., 2017) that allow groups to function more independently and access different resources.

The physical environment also includes ambience, which refers to how the classroom feels, looks, smells, and sounds to students (De Nobile et al., 2017). Morrow and Kanakri (2018) found that bright LED lighting increased the

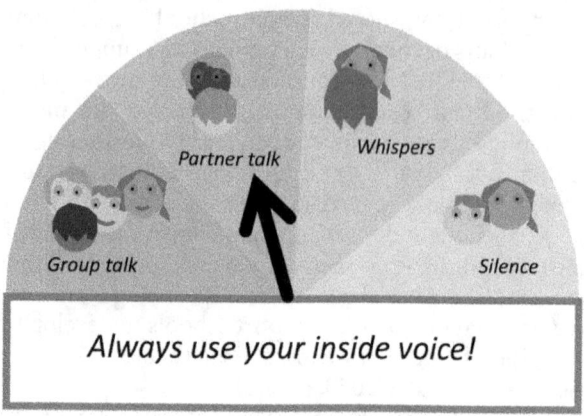

Figure 9.3 An example of a classroom visual support for managing noise levels.

alertness, focus, and performance of students. While teachers are generally not able to choose classroom colours, light tones reduce the need for artificial lighting and make the room appear open and fresh (De Nobile et al., 2017). It is also important to consider light in the classroom, as it can impact student access to reading and writing tasks, as well as affect student behaviour. It is important in an inclusive classroom to have an awareness of light sources, particularly for students who need a clear view of teachers' faces, including their mouths, to help them understand verbal instructions. Teachers should attempt to place themselves in the room where there is not too much shadow or glare on their faces.

The level of noise needs to be monitored in classrooms as well. Teachers soon learn which noise is work-related and which is not and develop procedures to regain and control class attention (De Nobile et al., 2017). Using visual aids for this can work well. For example, a teacher might use a visual with a dial that can be set to the noise level that they prefer for an activity (Figure 9.3). They can indicate on the dial when the noise is getting beyond what is acceptable and use the visual to cue students back to the level expected. There are also software applications that can be used in classrooms for noise tracking.

Finally, managing temperature in the classroom is dependent on whether there is heating/cooling, ventilation, and blinds or curtains. While teachers may not have control over temperature, they can think about the best times of the day to plan focused work versus work that requires less concentration, particularly if classrooms get particularly hot or cold at certain times. Having considered teacher-student relationships and the importance of the learning environment, this discussion now turns to evidence-based approaches that are used in responsive teaching.

Teaching approaches

Responsive teachers need to use various approaches at different times, depending on the learning needs of their students and the curriculum that is being taught. Differentiated and culturally responsive approaches are fundamental, and are complemented by collaborative, explicit, and cooperative group teaching.

Differentiated teaching

In contrast to the 'chalk and talk' model of teaching that has been the default in classrooms since the development of formal schooling, it is now accepted that not all students in a classroom need to be doing the same thing at the same time with the teacher as centre of proceedings. This is a natural consequence of a differentiated approach to teaching and often provides challenges for teachers in how to organise and manage multiple activities. Ways to accomplish differentiation include establishing learning centres or interest centres and providing students with activity choices and contracts. Such classroom organisation presents a variety of modes for learning activities and options for the expression of learning, which means that students in the same class can be doing many different things for significant parts of the school day. These strategies emphasise a sharing of responsibility for what students do as they learn and where they choose to be as they learn. The teacher's role in this scenario begins with planning to set up learning possibilities, and then moves to facilitating students' access to well-designed activities and opportunities.

Activity

Search the internet for professional resources and practice advice on how to implement some of the strategies that can help organise a differentiated classroom. You will find many teacher conversations sharing what works on social media and blogs and in professional publications. In addition, many education systems provide details for teachers. Here are some to explore:

- learning centres or interest centres
- learning contracts
- selections of activities through menus, tic-tac-toe choice boards
- tiered assignments or rich tasks.

The materials or resources that teachers draw on when providing learning activities in a differentiated classroom are important. The UDL framework emphasises the importance of both materials and methods, that is, the resources and the strategies used in teaching. A focus on materials or resources starts with the consideration of barriers which can inadvertently be created by resources or materials. This point is illustrated by the three examples provided in Table 9.1.

While the resources in Table 9.1 can still be used, it is important to consider the barriers inherent in what students are required to do to engage with them. If there are learners who cannot access these materials, teachers must provide alternatives as part of their planning. For example, if using a textbook, teachers can find an accessible version that has an audio component or select parts of

Table 9.1 Traditional classroom materials and the barriers that they can create for learners

Text-based materials (textbook/handouts)	Audio-based materials (lectures/video)	Image/graphic-based materials (video/handouts)
Require students to: • See • Decode and comprehend written text • Process visual information	Require students to: • Hear • Identify key points • Process aural information • Be physically or cognitively able to take notes	Require students to: • See • Process visual information

Adapted from IRIS Centre, 2021.

the text to be simplified with visuals. When using video, ensure that captioning is provided to make this media more accessible. When using graphics, include an accessible description to support those who may not be able to see or process the information contained in it. Previously, such planning was only considered when there was a student with an identified disability in the classroom. In contrast, UDL sets the expectation that all students will have options for how they access the curriculum.

As already stated, the aim of school is to create expert learners who are purposeful, motivated, resourceful, knowledgeable, strategic, and goal directed. Guidelines for opportunities to provide purposeful and motivating learning delineate the principle of engagement across three phases of learning: access to learning; the building of that learning; and the internalisation of learning (CAST, 2018b). These phases involve providing opportunities for recruiting interest and sustaining effort, persistence, and self-regulation (CAST, 2018b). This same process is detailed for resourceful and knowledgeable learning (action and expression) and strategic and goal-directed learning (representation; CAST, 2018b). Effective teaching methods are strategies that can be continually adjusted to meet learners' needs and which endeavour to reach all students within a collaborative environment (Meyer, Rose, & Gordon, 2014, p. 78).

Providing options for students means that teachers need to be creative about what they offer. Discipline-based intended learning outcomes and content are defined by the curriculum, but how these are taught is full of possibilities. When generating learning activities, teachers can draw on the whole curriculum that includes languages, physical activities, creative arts, technologies, sciences, as well as spoken and written words, and discipline-based symbol systems. The school and community also contribute possibilities through offering relevant real-life problems, and the internet and associated information and communication technologies make national and international issues and current events accessible as a basis for learning opportunities.

Activity

Search for *differentiation* on the website of your local education system and see what resources you can find that help frame this approach to teaching. Consider the language being used in your system and find examples of how to put differentiation into practice. Carry out some professional reflection about what aspects of differentiated instruction you already use in your teaching.

Culturally responsive teaching

The importance of culturally responsive teaching grew out of the North American context, within which an "ethic of caring is the *ideological grounding*, cultural communication is the *tool*, curriculum content about ethnic and cultural diversity is the *resource*, and instruction is the *praxis* of culturally responsive teaching" (Gay, 2018, p. 203). Ways of learning are culturally inculcated in early childhood (Gay, 2018) and children, therefore, come to school with expectations of how they will function as learners and how teachers will teach that may or may not be aligned with cultural protocols. In the context of colonised countries, it is vital to aim for both a strong Indigenous identity grounded in community PLUS academic success (Sarra, 2011; Macfarlane et al., 2014).

What needs to happen, but will take time to achieve, is for teachers to question the expectations they hold for their students and interrogate limiting perceptions (RTF 2). This is particularly important in the context of classroom culture. From this perspective, teachers are culturally responsive if they recognise and appreciate cultural variance among students, learn about and become aware of culturally-influenced learning patterns, look beyond cultural patterns to see individuals, and plan inviting instruction that is responsive to cultural differences and individual interests (Dack & Tomlinson, 2015).

Pedagogy that can "embrace and build on students' identities and backgrounds as assets for learning" is needed in Australia (Morrison et al., 2019, p. 58). To date, culturally responsive teaching in Australia has been diverted by attempts to define Indigenous learning styles. Just as learning styles have been found unsupported in Western psychology, so too they are not helpful in the context of Indigenous learners (Vass, 2018). Empirical research to help define a culturally responsive approach for Australian schools has started by asking Aboriginal students and families and their teachers about quality teaching (Lloyd et al., 2015). It is essential that teachers accept responsibility for providing all students with effective responsive teaching supported by cultural competence and deliberate cultural inclusion.

Collaborative teaching

Collaborative teaching allows teachers to reduce their professional isolation, build knowledge and skills, and share responsibility and expertise. It strengthens their teaching, particularly for students with disabilities (Mitchell & Sutherland, 2020). Working collaboratively requires a change in mindset away from the expectation that one teacher remains responsible for a group of students. Co-teaching or team-teaching allows teachers to bring more than one set of expertise to the activities in classrooms. Sometimes two or more teachers have responsibility for a larger group, or they job share, or a classroom teacher may work with a specialist educator intermittently. Such partnerships require planning time during work hours to set goals, design learning opportunities, agree on strategies for managing behavioural issues, and settle on ways of providing feedback to students (Mitchell & Sutherland, 2020).

Other models of collaboration in teaching are related to educational casework and layers 2 or 3 of responsive teaching. For classroom teachers, this means consultation with specialist teachers or allied health professionals and their regular or intermittent presence in the class for observation or support. Multiple perspectives enrich shared understandings of students as learners and support subsequent decision-making. This creates a shared responsibility for teaching and learning, which needs to be suitably resourced (Berman & Graham, 2018).

Another common situation occurs with assistants to teachers who are variously known as teacher aides, learning support officers, or paraprofessionals. How teachers work with teaching assistants is variable. When well-planned, their collaboration can strengthen teaching and learning by allowing the teacher to focus intently on teaching. Teaching by assistants is often transmissive rather than constructive (Vogt et al., 2021), and although there can be social and emotional benefits, it can distance vulnerable students from their teachers (Pinkard, 2021). Teachers must ensure that students who need the best possible teaching are not taught by proxy (Berman & Graham, 2018), that is, by the "lowest-paid, least qualified and insufficiently supervised personnel" (Giangreco, 2021, p. 280). The learning and independence of students with low achievement levels and special education needs are not enhanced by this resourcing, unless it is well deployed (Webster, Blatchford, & Russell, 2013).

Principles for rethinking the roles of teaching assistants include questioning the assumptions underlying teaching assistants' contribution to education; ensuring the continuation of structures for teaching such as *Layers of Responsive Teaching*, and individually-appropriate intended learning outcomes; selecting or designing supports that match students' learning needs rather than seeing teaching assistants as the solution; taking note of student voice and self-determination; attaching teaching assistants to teachers (not to students); and determining the role of teachers before adding teaching assistants' efforts to classrooms (Giangreco, 2021).

In terms of the whole school, most educational settings have structures that include schoolwide teams who work together to make decisions and allocate resourcing. These teams are variable in how they support collaboration and can often be purely administrative. Leadership can support the effectiveness of all collaborations through the allocation of time for joint planning that builds shared understanding of responsiveness, processes for assessment, use of intended learning outcomes, preferred teaching strategies, and the importance of connections with families (Scruggs, Mastropieri, & McDuffie, 2007).

Research about collective efficacy provides further evidence of the potential of teacher collaboration to accelerate learning (Corwin Visible Learning Plus, 2021; Moosa, 2021). Collective self-efficacy is stronger when teachers themselves are engaged in cooperative or collaborative learning and when efficacious individuals get together (Moosa, 2021).

Explicit teaching

Explicit, systematic teaching is key to effective learning, particularly for students who are at risk of experiencing learning difficulties (Gauthier et al., 2004; Hempenstall & Buckingham, 2016; Rosenshine, 1986). While explicit teaching reflects traditional instruction in many ways, it is an integral part of a much richer educational experience (Mitchell, 2018). Some aspects of learning will always need a mastery learning approach (Guskey, 2010) and students will need to be repeatedly exposed to the same domain of learning and engage in spaced and interleaved practice (Rohrer et al., 2020) in order to establish conceptual knowledge and skill competence (Hattie, 2017).

Explicit teaching is most important when the topic contains "well-defined knowledge and skills" (Rosenshine, 1986, p. 152). It is vitally important when teaching the main symbol systems (language, literacy, and mathematical) that it also needs to be systematic so that the complexity of the learning is built up over time. For example, literacy learning for many students depends on explicit and systematic teaching of the five key aspects of reading: phonemic awareness, decoding, vocabulary, comprehension, and fluency (Hempenstall & Buckingham, 2016; National Reading Panel [US], 2000). Students who are struggling have often not experienced explicit teaching of phonemic awareness and phonological skills, and therefore have difficulty decoding. Unless teachers check foundational phonemic awareness and phoneme manipulation skills, these students continue to struggle and believe that reading is too hard. It is ethically and professionally problematic when students' learning is hindered because they have not had the explicit teaching they need.

Explicit teaching involves the use of structured lessons that include goal setting, worked examples, multiple exposures; and expert questioning, use of metacognitive strategies, guided practice, and task-related feedback and review (Hattie, 2017; Rosenshine, 1986). Additionally, the guidelines from research emphasise planning (along a learning progression); frequent review, practice and response opportunities, frequent assessment; scaffolding; fast-paced sessions interspersed with other learning activities; and regular recaps of what has been taught (Mitchell, 2018). Explicit teaching can be whole class, small group, or individual depending on what is needed. The use of flexible groupings allows teachers to target students who need explicit teaching, and ensures that students only participate in lessons that will enhance their learning.

Scaffolding is assistance or support which is phased out as it is no longer needed. It is the "temporary adaptive support" that is provided until students are capable of achievement without assistance (Shvarts & Bakker, 2019). The two keys to scaffolding are that it responds to learners' needs and is reduced as learners accept increased responsibility for their own learning. Scaffolding can be provided by teachers in different ways. It can be offered through dialogue which varies in directness and intensity as needed, or by the flexible use of teaching strategies and tools that are available (Bakker, Smit, & Wegerif, 2015). This strategy is highlighted by Tomlinson (2017a) as an effective way of supporting reading and writing, by using graphic organisers, mnemonics, and prompts.

Activity

There are many scaffolds available for teachers to use to support their students' learning. Search the internet or Google Scholar for *scaffolds for learning* associated with a discipline area (e.g., reading, mathematics, science, social skills) and see what you can find. How can you incorporate these ideas into your teaching?

Cooperative group teaching

Cooperative group teaching is a vital approach for responsive teaching as it supports the use of flexible groupings and learning relationships. Optimising the use of classroom talk by organising cooperative or collaborative group activities provides opportunities for students to learn and practise the interactive capabilities that are needed throughout life. There are three main types of cooperative group learning – cooperative base groups, informal groups, and formal learning groups – that teachers can incorporate into their practice (Johnson & Johnson, 2008).

Cooperative base groups have a stable membership. Students meet regularly over a period of a term or school year and support each other's learning and participation (Johnson & Johnson, 2008). Many schools have systems of home groups which align with this model. These groups often focus on issues of social and emotional learning, and support students when there are critical incidents that affect the school.

Informal cooperative learning is carried out within ad hoc groups formed for a short time as part of whole-class lessons. These groups are often formed to engage in discussion around aspects of a presentation. Group members may be asked to summarise content, give a reaction to the information presented, predict what is to be presented next (hypothesise), solve a problem, relate information to past learning, and integrate it into conceptual frameworks, or resolve conceptual conflicts created by the content.

Formal cooperative learning is supported when students work together in carefully organised groups on substantial activities with joint goals. Successful groups need to have built-in interdependence, rather than functioning as a group of individuals with their own interests (Johnson & Johnson, 2008). Effective collaborative learning in formal groups is supported by promoting interactions that:

- Strive for mutual benefit
- Efficiently and effectively provide each other with assistance and resources
- Offer feedback about performance, assigned tasks, and responsibilities
- Challenge conclusions and reasoning
- Accept perspectives of others
- Combine effort to achieve mutual goals
- Are trustworthy
- Provide lower levels of stress and anxiety for participants (Johnson & Johnson, 2008).

When these groups function well and everyone is engaged, contributing, learning, and producing artefacts together, they are ideal learning opportunities (Chi & Wylie, 2014). Teachers make many decisions when organising cooperative group learning activities. They require considerable time for planning and materials preparation, but once teachers adopt a cooperative or collaborative group learning mindset, they can adapt many learning activities into standard structures.

Think-Pair-Share is one standard structure that is commonly used in tertiary education. The components of *Think-Pair-Share* are:

> *A provocation is presented, and students are asked to think about it and capture their thoughts for themselves.*
>
> *(Think)*

> *Students are then asked to share their thoughts with one other person. This can be structured in different ways, from being open to student interpretation, to being scripted for particular levels of response.*
>
> *(Pair)*

> *Students share their refined or combined thoughts with the larger group. Sharing can be organised in many different ways, including providing a written response to a concept; adding comments to a graphic organiser; selecting from a range of responses that are then tallied; or selectively contributing to a whole-group discussion.*
>
> *(Share)*

Jigsaw is a another highly effective strategy which prepares students to contribute meaningfully to a group. This is done in two phases. First, resource or expert groups are established within which students engage with specific content. Those groups are then reallocated into jigsaw groups (one student from each resource group) where each student shares their resources and contributes to a larger task.

An example of a double jigsaw, which has two phases of resource groups, is shown in Figure 9.4. This jigsaw was used with postgraduate teachers in a subject about literacy learning difficulties. There were 24 students in the class, who were initially divided into 12 pairs. Each pair was allocated a unique set of resources from academic research papers and government reports on literacy learning intervention, covering four subtopics (literacy learning, variability in literacy learning, assessment of literacy, and intervention – represented by different colours). The student pairs were asked to spend 20 minutes together making sense of the resources, so that they could share them with a larger sub-topic group in the first layer of the jigsaw.

The subtopic groups were made up of three pairs of students (six students) who all engaged with resources on the same topic. These students were asked to combine their knowledge to produce a one-page artefact on their topic (e.g., assessment of literacy learning). As each person took their version of the artefact page to the next group, they all needed to understand the contributions to it. Once in the final jigsaw groups, made up of one person from each sub-topic

138 Using the responsive teaching framework

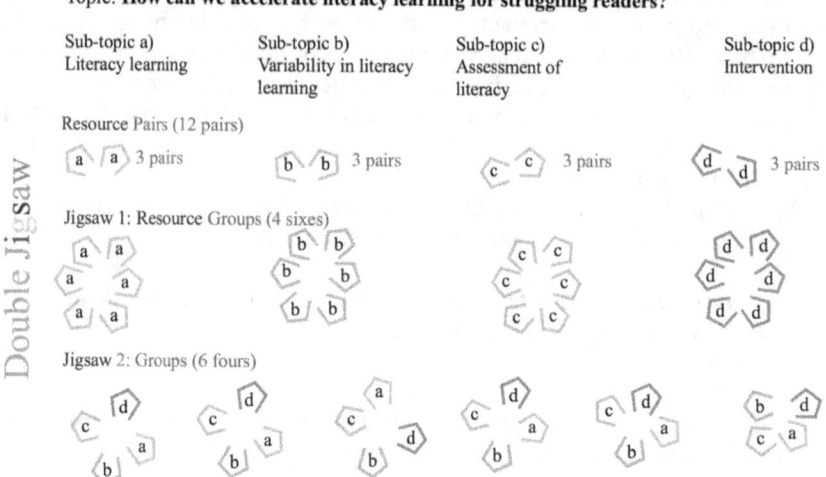

Figure 9.4 Example of a double jigsaw structure.

group (four students), the students shared all the information and created a poster that responded to the question: How can we accelerate literacy learning for struggling readers?

Many decisions are made when setting up a jigsaw activity. The number of students dictates how it can be done, as it works best with a number that can be divided flexibly, but it is also possible to provide additional roles or use rotating groups (as in speed dating) if required. Timing can be variable. In this case, the activity took place during a two-hour session with a group of dedicated, motivated adult learners. It will depend on how much time students need to engage with the information before they are responsible for sharing it. The amount of information can be varied, as can the level of literacy required, and the mode of delivery within different packages of information so that everyone is able to engage with their material. Higher-order thinking within cooperative groups can also be instigated by using explicit teaching and scaffolds or beginning scripts, so that students are equipped to contribute in a number of ways, such as through explanations, asking thought-provoking questions, elaborating, and engaging in reasoned argument, and sharing their cognitive and metacognitive insights (King, 2008).

Activity

Search the internet or your professional resources for models of jigsaw group activities. How can you use these models to plan interactive opportunities to learn for your students?

Developed within the context of teaching comprehension to struggling secondary students (Brown & Palincsar, 1987), reciprocal teaching is a process of collaborative learning with a significant evidence base. It is a cognitive and metacognitive approach where a teacher models and then students take turns to lead dialogue about comprehension passages. All members of the group have roles that are rotated after each passage. The students use a scaffold of four comprehension strategies – summarising, questioning, clarifying, and predicting (Ashman & Conway, 2018) – to shape their dialogue.

Problems with social interactions can occur in cooperative group learning activities and can be reduced by allocating roles and setting rules about how often and long students can speak, establishing participation rules, teaching conflict resolution skills, and providing mediation as needed (Mitchell & Sutherland, 2020). Creative teachers have many strategies for managing imbalances in participation, including providing a set number of talking tokens (which all have to be used up), or using a talking stick or ball of wool which the students pass on as they take turns speaking. This last strategy can be messy but provides a material representation of the interactions in a group activity which can be revealing and fun for students and teachers.

Peer-assisted learning is where students of the same or different ages tutor or teach other students, either with fixed roles or in reciprocal relationships (Alegre et al., 2020). Peer-assisted learning is an evidence-based strategy with the potential to accelerate learning (Alzahrani & Leko, 2018; Corwin Visible Learning Plus, 2021). Possibilities for the structure and process of peer-assisted learning are many and varied, and depend on the purpose of the activity (Can & Ginsburg-Block, 2013). Peer tutoring can be integrated into whole-class lessons by flexibly assigning pairs of students to work together to complete exercises or by forming more formal dyads (Mitchell & Sutherland, 2020). In all situations, it is important to teach the behaviours that are to be used by tutors, including presenting instructional cues, asking questions, providing positive feedback, correcting errors, and keeping records of the sessions (Mitchell & Sutherland, 2020). There is evidence that peer-assisted learning is valuable for the tutor when the tutoring is structured, same-age, and non-reciprocal (Leung, 2019). There can be resistance, however, as there is concern that more competent students are being used or kept busy as peer tutors and not provided with opportunities for extending their own learning.

Collaborative learning and peer assisted learning approaches sit comfortably within responsive teaching. These approaches can be used with close monitoring to ensure they are making a difference for all students.

Activity

Search the internet for *reciprocal teaching* and see what useful resources you can find. Take note of the source and whether the model has been adapted from Brown and Palincsar's (1987) research. Does the resource remain true to the original research? What are the reasons given for modifications to the original approach? Are they justified?

Learning opportunities

Within these teaching approaches (differentiated, culturally responsive, collaborative, explicit, and cooperative group teaching) responsive teachers design enjoyable, interesting, interactive learning opportunities within which they provide learners with the language (iU) and key concepts (T) to use in learning interactions (R) and opportunities for self-managed, active learning (M&A). Each teacher will develop their own preferred learning activities. Over time, they will build a bank of tasks, instructions, and materials that can be adapted for different curriculum content. The challenge is to match learning opportunities to the purpose of teaching and students' readiness, interests, *Sustainable Learning Profiles*, and intended learning outcomes. This involves clearly defining the tasks and associated instructions and materials, determining the intensity and arrangement of the tasks, deciding who is to mediate or support the learning activity of the students, and then setting up student options, groupings, the place and space, adjustments, and resources (Berman & Graham, 2018). Learning opportunities can be provided to the whole class, a small group, or individuals, depending on the purpose of each activity.

It is essential that there is alignment between the intended learning outcomes or goals of the teaching, the learning activities used in teaching, and the assessment which provides evidence of learning. Biggs and Tang (2011) call this 'constructive alignment', an approach which uses alternative verbs to delineate the quality of student expressions of learning. As illustrated in Table 9.2 learning activities should be aligned to the verbs and content of the intended learning outcomes (ILOs).

In this example, the multi-structural ILO is about defining terms and students' learning is supported by activities related to practising definitions, and producing one or more of the items listed (e.g., definition cards). Within the highest-level of SOLO (extended abstract), the ILO is about reflection and the task provides access to information so that students can develop products that demonstrate how they can reflect on the importance of light in medicine or communication.

Verbs for intended learning outcomes that are organised according to surface and deep learning in the SOLO taxonomy (see earlier Table 8.4) can be used to generate further activities and products of learning as shown in Table 9.3.

This example illustrates how it is possible to develop tasks which include the full range of thinking, from recalling facts to extending knowledge into new ideas or contexts. These tasks can be related to problem-solving within real world issues. From a responsive teaching perspective such tasks are invaluable since they "address a range of outcomes, authentically represent the ways in which knowledge and skills will be used in the future and elicit a range of student responses" (Aubusson et al., 2014, p. 220). The collaboration, complexity of meaning-making, real-world alignment, and social value of such learning experiences (Aubusson et al., 2014) allow for students to practise successful intelligence (Sternberg, 2002). Sternberg (2002) defines this as analytical thinking about remembered information that is applied practically, creatively, and with wisdom. The verbs which describe the actions of successfully intelligent learners (Table 9.4) can scaffold teachers to design further learning activities that include multiple aspects of content and levels of thinking. While memory is not included as a dimension in more recent versions of Sternberg's model, aspects of wisdom have become more prominent. Both are included in this table.

Table 9.2 Learning activities and products aligned with learning intentions for Year 9/10 Physics (Energy)

Generalised learning intention
Recognise that light and sound are types of energy that are detected by eyes and ears

SOLO levelled ILOs	Intended learning outcomes	Learning activities	Products
Multi-structural level intended learning outcome	Defines the terms *light* and *energy* and identifies some properties of light.	Access information (provided, guided, or searched for) in presentation, text, online resource; practise defining or listing properties for others, on cards, in infographic or glossary. And then produce…	Definition cards, matching questions in quiz software, a concept map, an infographic or diagram.
Relational intended learning outcome	Knows that light can be transformed into other forms of energy.	Access information about types of energy, observe or carry out experiments that demonstrate changes in energy, observe natural phenomena which involve changes in energy. And then produce…	Flow charts, an animation, cartoons; a magazine article, a children's book, a song or poem, or a report.
Extended abstract intended learning outcome	Reflects on the importance of light in medicine and communication	Access information (provided, guided, or searched for) in presentation, text, or online resource about the use of light in medicine and communication; excursion to local medical scanning laboratory; experience the use of light in communication (from historical perspective). And then produce…	An oral presentation on phototherapy or other use of light in medicine, a video documentary or podcast for children, a written explanation of how a light scan reveals information about the body, a magazine article, a children's book, a piece of music, an artwork or a report.

Learning intentions from Martin, 2011, p. 22.

Table 9.3 Learning activities and products aligned with surface and deep learning

Quantity of learning (surface)	Quality of learning (deep or higher thinking)	
Knowing one or more aspects (Unistructural and multistructural)	Knowing how the multiple aspects relate to each other (Relational)	Knowing how these aspects can be extended into different ideas or contexts (Extended abstract)
Description, list, tree diagram, table or matrix, glossary, definition cards, labelled diagram, online quiz (matching, ordering, defining), recitation, mnemonic, procedural report, set of instructions, flow chart, illustrations, highlighted text…	An explanation, a plan, a set of predictions, a conclusion, (therefore), a review, an argument or thesis, infographic comparison, debate, built model, justification for a design, rewritten speech, examination of presentation, translation, problem solution…	A proposal, set of principles, generalisation, set of reflective questions, composition (written or musical), screenplay or novella, science fiction animation, written proof, an original case…

Table 9.4 Successful intelligence

Memory	Analytical thinking	Practical thinking	Creative thinking
Recall	Analyse	Apply	Create
Recognise	Critique	Use	Invent
Match	Judge	Put into practice	Discover
Verify	Compare/contrast	Implement	Imagine if…
Repeat	Evaluate	Employ	Suppose that…
	Assess	Render practical	Predict

Wisdom

The use of intelligence, creativity, and knowledge toward a common good by balancing intrapersonal, interpersonal and extrapersonal interests over the long and short terms through the infusion of values by adapting to, shaping, and selecting environments.

Sternberg, 2002 and Sternberg & Grigorenko, 2007.

Much higher-order learning, or creative, practical, or wise thinking, needs to be taught within inquiry-based learning activities. However, the inquiry processes need to be well guided (Jerrim, Oliver, & Sims, 2020) by putting constraints around the scope of the inquiry, and providing feedback, prompts, scaffolds, or explanations as needed during the inquiry process (Lazonder & Harmsen, 2016). Inquiry learning can be carried out in multiple modes, including drama (Farrand & Deeg, 2020). As with any learning opportunity, it is the guidance and use of teaching strategies by the teacher or others that make this type of learning opportunity a successful experience. Additionally, it is important to note that there is a need for explicit teaching of aspects of the inquiry process and to check students' foundational knowledge in order to set up meaningful, inquiry-based learning activities.

Activity

Alan Reid (2021) has written that:

> For some time now the education debate in Australia has been marred by the presence of a simple binary: explicit teaching or direct instruction versus inquiry-based teaching. Simply put, explicit teaching is a structured sequence of learning led by the teacher, who demonstrates and explains a new concept or technique to students who then practise it. It is sometimes described as a process that moves from 'I do' through to 'we do' and 'you do'. Inquiry-based teaching is used as a catch-all term for models of teaching that are student-centred and involve the students, guided by the teacher, creating essential questions, exploring, and investigating these, and sharing ideas to arrive at new understandings.

What are the pros and cons of these approaches? What is missing from this debate?

In terms of the fundamental of student engagement, ICAP is a taxonomy that assists teachers to be conscious of this feature of instruction in learning activities. The ICAP taxonomy distinguishes between tasks which require students to be interactive, constructive, active, or passive (ICAP; Chi & Wylie, 2014). Responsive teaching acknowledges that all these levels of activity are important at different times, and that students will choose their level based on aspects of ATRiUM capabilities (such as motivation, confidence and self-efficacy, and connectedness). However, since responsive teaching advocates strongly for active learning, learning sessions can be arranged to provide relevant opportunities for active, constructive and interactive engagement.

Deeper learning processes result from an emphasis on the interactive and constructive modes. There needs to be as much active learning as possible, as every teaching moment in a learning period needs to be optimised, a sharp contradiction to the traditional engaged classroom where students work on their own (Chi et al., 2018). Instead, every student can be engaged in active learning using dyads and small groups, skills of interaction (including active listening), and tasks that require the participation of all. Such tasks are described using verbs that elicit generative collaboration such as "debate" or "challenge or confirm each other's ideas" (Chi et al., 2018, p. 1824). The ICAP taxonomy (Chi & Wylie, 2014) has been used to analyse the interactions of students within groups and has shown that friendships can ameliorate shyness (Chen et al., 2021), which means teachers need to carefully create groups for interactive learning taking into account student connections and their capabilities for relating to others (R).

Educational settings have been moving away from lectures as a group activity and instead have been providing asynchronous access to information, followed by convening in person to engage in interactive learning activities based on the content. Flipped or inverted classrooms (Akçayır, & Akçayır, 2018) have thus set expectations that individual work is focused on receiving information (passively or actively), while group time is used for constructive and interactive learning activities. The Covid-19 pandemic accelerated this process. This change towards online learning means that students need capabilities for accessing information (including facility with ICT) and filtering and organising it, so that they are prepared for group activities. There are many activities teachers can use to check students' learning. Quizzes, sets of questions, summaries, extended writing tasks, crosswords, concept maps or other graphic organisers, and creative works can all be used as ways to frame and filter information.

Taking the importance of engagement into account, teachers can use the principles and guidelines of UDL to plan a range of opportunities for active, constructive, and interactive learning for all students. The UDL guidelines are an organising tool that can support educators to flexibly design learning opportunities and select the materials and teaching strategies that suit the needs of learners in any class or grouping (Figure 9.5).

Purposeful and motivated learning

Access to learning	Building learning	Internalising learning
Recruiting Interest • Optimise individual choice and autonomy • Optimise relevance, value and authenticity • Minimise threats and distractions	**Sustaining Effort and Persistence** • Heighten salience of goals and objectives • Vary demands and resources to optimise challenge • Foster collaboration and community • Increase mastery-oriented feedback	**Self-regulation** • Promote expectations and beliefs that optimise motivation • Facilitate personal coping skills and strategies

Resourceful and knowledgeable learning

Access to learning	Building learning	Internalising learning
Perception • Offer ways of customizing the display of information • Offer alternatives for auditory information • Offer alternatives for visual information	**Language & Symbols** • Clarify vocabulary and symbols • Clarify syntax and structure • Support decoding of text, mathematical notation and symbols • Promote understanding across languages • Illustrate through multiple media	**Comprehension** • Activate or supply background knowledge • Highlight patterns, critical features, big ideas and relationships • Guide information processing and visualization • Maximise transfer and generalisation

Strategic and goal-directed learning

Access to learning	Building learning	Internalising learning
Physical Action • Vary the methods for response and navigation • Optimise access to tools and assistive technologies	**Expression & Communication** • Use multiple media for communication • Use multiple tools for construction and composition • Build fluencies with graduated levels of support for practice and performance	**Executive Functions** • Guide appropriate goal-setting • Support planning and strategy development • Facilitate managing information and resources • Enhance capacity for monitoring progress

Figure 9.5 UDL guidelines for designing learning opportunities.
Adapted from CAST, 2018b.

Choosing from a range of activities within the UDL approach increases students' sense of agency and motivation for learning (Brennan, King, & Travers, 2021). It is important that responsive teachers provide as much choice as is appropriate to ensure students engage in activities within their zone of readiness and are increasingly challenging. There will be times when teachers need to limit choices with a view to extending the interests of students and the ways they engage with curriculum. There will also be situations when students are not confident in making choices or may need assistance in decision-making (Brennan, 2019).

Activity

Universal Design for Learning (UDL) and differentiation belong together in inclusive learning environments.

How are these approaches different from one another? How are they the same? What makes them so complementary in contemporary learning environments?

Teaching for all our students

RTF 5 asks how we can teach for all our learners. This consideration is very complex. Decisions about how to teach are informed by research evidence which points to a range of teaching approaches that complement each other and are used at different times depending on the needs of students and their intended learning outcomes. There is also considerable evidence about the learning strategies that effective learners use that can inform our teaching of those capabilities. Additionally, teachers must keep in mind that many students bring with them barriers associated with previous learning experiences, disabilities, or learning difficulties. Teachers can build on students' strengths and provide the conditions for their capabilities to develop and for them to experience success.

Even though it is important to draw on research about effective teaching approaches and strategies, it is not enough. These strategies have to work for students in a wide variety of educational settings. It is vital that evidence of learning is taken into account when instructional decisions are made. In the last three steps of the *Responsive Teaching Framework*, we explicitly consider how to gather evidence of what students have learned:

RTF 6. How do I gather evidence of student learning?
RTF 7. How do I use feedback to support learning?
RTF 8. How did my teaching support my students' learning?

These three steps complete the *Responsive Teaching Framework* and lead to making subsequent decisions about how best to teach.

10 RTF 6: How do I gather evidence of student learning?

RTF 6. How do I gather evidence of student learning?

How will I know how each learner and the learning group respond to teaching in relation to: (i) the intended learning outcomes; (ii) unintended learning outcomes; and (iii) factors that support and hinder learning? How will sustainability be evidenced (maintenance and transfer)?

Introduction

Responsive teachers use screening and monitoring of student learning, both in terms of curriculum learning and development of ATRiUM capabilities, to know how students are progressing. Assessment serves different purposes and is conducted in different ways. It is integral to every step of the *Responsive Teaching Framework*. In RTF 6, the purpose of assessment is to know what the students are learning as they do it, and what they have learned at the end of a teaching period.

The WHY and WHAT of assessment in RTF 6

To carefully consider what it is that responsive teachers do in assessment within RTF 6, we return to the framework introduced in Part I, which helps our thinking about the WHY, WHAT, and HOW of assessment. The WHY and WHAT of assessment in RTF 6 are shown in Figure 10.1.

WHY? Purposes of assessment RTF 6	WHAT? Content of assessment RTF 6
• Assessment in RTF 6 is done to determine the extent and nature of student learning • Students and teachers need this information to provide a baseline for future teaching and learning • Schools and education systems need this information for evidence of effectiveness	• Content of assessment is defined by ILOs and associated development of ATRiUM capabilities

Figure 10.1 The WHY and WHAT of assessment in RTF 6.

DOI: 10.4324/9781003299813-12

The purpose (WHY) of assessment within RTF 6 is to show the extent and nature of learning of the taught material. Most education systems and schools advocate for assessment as a way of improving learning, which is fundamental in responsive teaching. Within the bounds of RTF 6, the primary purpose is summative; it is *assessment OF learning*. The teacher's task is to make judgements about student achievement based on intended learning outcomes or goals, curriculum capabilities, or developmental progressions. Accepting that we need to provide opportunities for our students to demonstrate what they have learnt, we also need to consider what this information is to be used for, and by whom – students and their families, teachers, schools, and/or education systems. As with all responsive teaching considerations, multiple people have an interest in the evidence gathered about student learning. These interests do not necessarily align and may create tensions that influence how assessments are conducted and reported.

At the most fundamental level, assessment is for the benefit of the students and supports their teaching-learning relationships and future learning. It is the students' chance to show themselves and their teachers what they have learnt, and it produces a record of that learning. Assessment allows students to track their learning and to be able to say where they came from and what they know and can do now. It is also the basis of reports or certification which are concrete representations of the learning of specific content at a particular time in reference to a particular teaching period.

Teachers also need to see what their students have learned, at the individual student level and across the learning group. Based on the evidence gathered, they can then make firm statements about what students can do or know, and how well learning has happened. Teachers are also interested in any unintended learning outcomes, evidence of what has contributed to learning, or hindered learning at this time. From this evidence, teachers generate reports for each student and for the learning group. The reports go to their students and families. Families are interested in what their children have learned and depend on reporting to inform them about their children's progress.

Schools are interested in the results of summative assessments so that they can account for not only students' learning, but also the teaching that has been provided. Schools need this type of evidence so they can demonstrate the impact of teaching in the school. Education systems also seek this assessment information and use it for a number of purposes that are evaluative and bureaucratic. Although this assessment should be primarily about determining learning and, thereby, supporting it, it does also meet other needs related to accountability and evaluation within the ecology of teaching and learning.

The content (WHAT) of the assessment is what teachers intend students to learn. These intentions are detailed through intended learning outcomes which are explicitly and formally defined as the basis of planning, and around which learning activities are designed. Responsive teaching also focuses on the processes of learning, and the ATRiUM capabilities that are drawn on when demonstrating learning. The ATRiUM capabilities provide a way for teachers to see their students' learning through a whole-of-student lens and to notice how capabilities are used to support learning or how they may hinder learning and students' demonstration of understanding.

Such assessment is summative *and* formative, revealing achievement after a period of teaching and informing subsequent teaching and learning. Because periods of learning vary, assessment of learning can happen at the end of a year, semester, term, or topic, as traditionally done. However, for responsive teachers to use information formatively, assessment needs to be carried out regularly (Mitchell & Sutherland, 2020). Teachers need to assess and monitor as appropriate so that they and their students can monitor learning as it is happening. It is interesting to note, that monitoring of progress is considered an alternative assessment in the Global Research Database (Corwin Visible Learning Plus, 2021) because it is different to the traditional end-of-topic tests or examinations. However, responsive teaching considers that regular monitoring of learning is essential and should be built into all teaching and learning opportunities. Assessment in RTF 6 aims to gather evidence of students having achieved intended learning outcomes. It can also take note of unintended learning, as well as any factors that support and hinder learning.

Intended learning outcomes

Intended learning outcomes, set within the curriculum focus for teaching, are the starting points for assessment in RTF 6. It is essential that there is alignment between the intended learning outcomes or goals of the teaching, the learning activities used in teaching, and assessment which provides evidence of learning (Biggs & Tang, 2011). Assessments are developed in relation to the intended learning, not the acquisition of other skills or knowledge. For example, a science assessment that asks a student with reading difficulties to read a large block of text and then provide responses is testing both skills in reading and the ability to understand scientific concepts. It is important to ensure that what is being assessed is based on the goals set for learning.

Assessment of intended learning can often be carried out by re-administering the same assessment task used at the beginning of a unit. If there is a learning progression on which the intended learning can be mapped, it is possible to share this with students so they can see where they were at the beginning of the unit and where they are at the end.

Outcomes assessment is evidence of what students know and can do after teaching and is usually in comparison to some similar assessment given beforehand. A spelling test of a set of words before teaching and then after teaching is the simplest form of baseline-outcomes assessment and allows for direct comparison of correct spelling before and after teaching.

There can be problems with asking students to do tasks or answer questions about things that have not yet been taught, so teachers may need to adapt the initial assessment to avoid generating a sense of failure or inadequacy. If the intention of teaching (DART 1) has been well negotiated and there is trust in the relationships, it may be possible to provide students with a task that they are not yet able to do, while clearly indicating that they will be able to do it by the end of the unit. It can be helpful to have other strategies to help gauge what the students already know and can do, such as whole class discussion about a topic captured on a whiteboard or mind mapping software. Another way to gauge knowledge is to ask the students to share what they know about a particular topic in a written or graphic format. Giving students stick-it notes and asking them to list all the things they know about a topic creates a set of movable pieces of information that can be organised on a wall to show what is already known – and what can be added to as the topic progresses. This strategy can be used with wiki software (e.g., Padlet). These strategies allow teachers to find out what is already known and use this information to decide how to teach the topic.

Assessment of knowledge can be done in many ways, such as by asking direct questions or using multiple choice or matching questions. It can also be included within higher order tasks; however, this raises a complication for teachers. For example, when assessing both knowledge and skills in a written essay, it is necessary to make a distinction between these two different learning outcomes. Responsive teachers provide opportunities for students to both write essays when needing to recall all the content, and when they have ready access to content. For example, open book exams are designed to reduce this concern and make assessment tasks more authentic.

Sustainability of learning, or the maintenance and transfer of intended learning outcomes, also needs to be the considered in planning and administering assessments. Maintenance is when the knowledge and skills are known sometime after they have been taught. These can be assessed using the same assessment tasks that determined the achievement but administered after a subsequent period. *Sustainable Learning* is about cumulative learning which is maintaining what has been learnt and building on it. Transfer of learning is established when students can use knowledge and skills in contexts different to those in which the learning happened. Assessing transfer requires assessment tasks or contexts that are diverse. It is helpful to be able to establish that students can use their learning in different contexts, which is evidence of the kind of adaptability and flexibility needed in our complex world.

Unintended learning outcomes

Responsive teachers deliberately look for indicators of learning and development outside the intended learning outcomes. There are often untargeted learning outcomes that we need to notice and take account of – these additional outcomes are either positive and welcome, or negative and unwelcome.

Positive unintended outcomes are aspects of the curriculum that were not necessarily the focus of the learning activity but are observed to have developed. A deepening of interest or evidence of connections being made between intended learning and other curriculum domains, or previously taught material is notable. They may be the result of opportunities to apply or practise previously taught knowledge or skills. On the other hand, students may take a direction that is unintended, but still a valuable focus of learning.

Relationships between students while they are engaged in learning activities can be the basis of learning in terms of ATRiUM capabilities. Responsive teachers try to group students in a diversity of ways so that they can generate learning relationships that allow students to contribute as *more competent others* whenever they are able, and to learn from their peers when appropriate. Some groupings of students will create positive relationships which are important to notice and to build on.

A teaching opportunity occurs when students ask curious and enquiring questions that take a topic in a different or unexpected direction, or further than anticipated. Responsive teachers make the most of these teaching moments. When a learning activity is not well received or fails to engage students' behavioural reactions may result. Perhaps the learning opportunity did not activate learning and needs to be changed, or it might be that aspects of ATRiUM capabilities hinder learning, for example, a developing frustration or reluctance to engage (A & M). Undesirable outcomes or responses to learning activities can also be curriculum based (as in misconceptions, inadequate knowledge, or skills for the task).

Factors supporting and hindering learning

Responsive teachers need to know what has supported learning or hindered it so they can foster positive experiences and reduce barriers in the future. *Sustainable Learning*, particularly *learning that lasts*, focuses on the development of processes that are both the vehicles for learning and which build capabilities. Teachers are advised to focus on processes rather than on finite, fixed bodies of knowledge and skills, because we live in a dynamic, changing world that requires learners to be adaptive, flexible, and persistent. Within each ATRiUM capability there are many possible processes or skill sets. Figure 10.2 includes the factors which are highlighted in the following discussion.

THINKING
- Attention
- Perception
- Memory
- Cognitive processing
- Executive functioning
- Expression
- Information-gathering
- Building understanding
- Successful intelligence
- SOLO levels
- Strategic & Reflective thinking

RELATING TO OTHERS
- Cultural practices
- Social communication
- Social skills
- Group skills
- Friendship skills
- Conflict resolution
- Seeking & receiving help

USING LANGUAGE, SYMBOL SYSTEMS & ICT
- Receptive & expressive language
- Literacy
- Numeracy
- ICT skills
- Use of assistive technology
- Auslan
- Multiple modes

ACTIVE LEARNING
- Engagement
- Motivation
- Interest
- Enjoyment & happiness
- Prior knowledge
- Curiosity

MANAGING SELF
- Self-awareness
- Self-efficacy
- Self-evaluation
- Self-regulation
- Effort management
- Planning
- Persistence & perseverance
- Confidence
- Metacognition
- Emotion and mood regulation

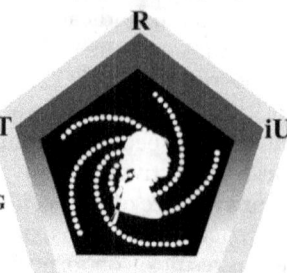

Figure 10.2 ATRiUM capabilities elaborated.
Adapted from Berman & Graham, 2018, p. 127.

There are no absolute boundaries between ATRiUM capabilities since some factors are relevant to more than one capability. Additionally, the lists are not exhaustive since there will be other ways of defining and describing aspects of each capability, and a body of scientific research and associated models explaining how it works. This list can be altered to suit contexts and the meaning that teachers, students, and families make of student capabilities.

Active learning (A)

Active learning involves engagement, motivation, and interest in learning, enjoyment, and happiness. It depends on curiosity, connections with prior learning, and perceptions of the intentions of learning. Engagement has been defined in many ways and can refer to behavioural, emotional, and cognitive aspects of functioning. Because some of these are overt and some are covert (Quin, 2017), teachers will need to notice behaviours and make inferences about the internal functioning of students. The Global Research Database has defined the term 'concentration-persistence-engagement' as a student's ability to concentrate on a task and to persist despite challenges. One of the meta-analyses cited on this database was focused on the resilience of at-risk students (Corwin Visible Learning Plus, 2021). This emphasises how engagement is intertwined with other concepts that are also aspects of managing self (M). Another way to think about engagement is in reference to the interactive-constructive-active-passive (ICAP) dimensions of learning activities (Chi & Wylie, 2014) which stress the need for active learning, and include notions of students being constructive (A & M) and interactive (R) in groups.

Motivation to engage in tasks and with learning processes is influenced by students' self-expectations, social context, and self-regulation; their goals (performance, mastery, and social); the learning task (locus of control and value); and their perceptions of costs (effort, opportunity, and emotions) versus benefits (agency, autonomy, pride, compliance, and satisfaction; Hattie, Hodis, & Kang, 2020). This conceptualisation, drawn from multiple theories, illustrates the complex and multidimensional nature of motivation. Interest in learning is related to motivation, and has been emphasised within RTF 4, where it is considered a foundation for active learning, and a characteristic teachers need to understand about their students. In fact, enjoyment and happiness are positively related to active learning, while boredom, frustration, procrastination, and a surface approach to learning have a negative effect on mood (Corwin Visible Learning Plus, 2021).

Prior knowledge and skills support active learning because students can build on what they already know, understand, and can do, and can draw on their knowledge of context to position their new learning. Recent research in neuroscience has revealed that there is a link between curiosity and prior knowledge, with optimum proximity to new information activating curiosity and supporting learning (Wade & Kidd, 2019).

As already emphasised, a key component of active learning is knowing the intention of learning. For example, setting clear, appropriately challenging goals with defined success criteria supports commitment to learning and more successful achievement (Corwin Visible Learning Plus, 2021). DART 1 emphasises the need to establish the general intent of teaching and RTF 4 provides structures for developing and sharing intended learning outcomes in ways that support active learning.

Thinking (T)

The thinking capability can be understood from many different perspectives depending on what makes sense for teachers. We have selected two models for this discussion: information processing theory; and an integrated model which includes levels of thinking. These models can be combined with other models such as SOLO (Biggs & Collis, 1986) and Successful Intelligence (Sternberg, 2002).

Information Processing theory (Figure 10.3) assists teachers to focus on ways that thinking skills support and hinder their students' access to the curriculum and their demonstration of thinking.

The information processing model helps teachers to focus on potential barriers for students as they take in information, process it, and respond verbally or nonverbally. There may be difficulties with any of these aspects of thinking – and it is helpful to identify problems as soon as possible so that strategies can be put in place to build the capability or to work around it. As an example, attention can be a barrier to taking in information for some students. Selective attention (knowing what to pay attention to) is the filtering of complex and competing stimuli that are present in educational settings. Sustained attention is needed to support persistence and completion of activities. These processes are both needed for information to be encoded into working memory (Arnicane & Souza, 2022). Learners need to pay enough attention to the information, for long enough, to be able to make meaning of it. For students with ADHD, for example, attentional difficulties often interfere with the filtering of information. This affects the quality of subsequent processing

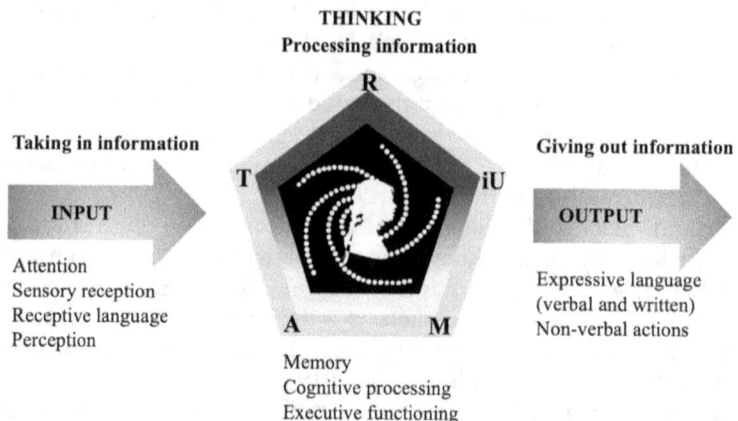

Figure 10.3 Information processing model.
Adapted from Berman & Graham, 2018, p. 49.

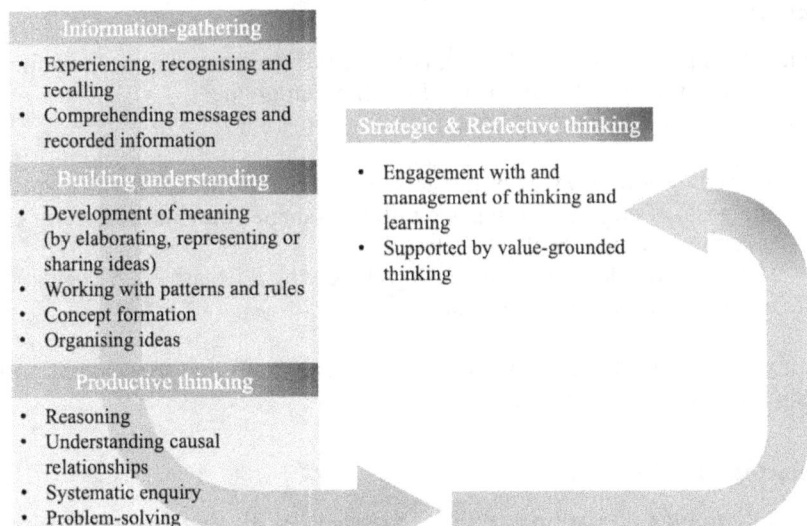

Figure 10.4 An integrated model for understanding thinking.
Adapted from Moseley et al., 2005, p. 314.

and may compromise the output. Each aspect of this model can be the source of potential barriers in thinking.

An alternative model focuses on other important aspects of thinking. Derived from analysis of more than half a century of theory generated to explain thinking (Moseley et al., 2005), the model in Figure 10.4 distinguishes between three phases of lower order cognitive skills (information gathering, building understanding, and productive thinking), and two higher order thinking skills that involve strategy and reflection.

These two levels interact, with metacognitive skills used iteratively alongside basic thinking skills. Strategic and reflective thinking happens when students are conscious of how they think and can identify the thinking processes that work best for them, and in what situations. This can be referred to as 'metacognitive thinking'. It occurs when students have a repertoire of learning strategies from which to select; can identify how they thought about a task and evaluate that thinking; actively seek feedback to assist in understanding how they are learning; and actively take responsibility for their learning (Hattie, 2017). Metacognition is one dimension of self-regulated learning (M), and is enacted in conjunction with emotional, behavioural, and contextual self-regulation. It involves goal setting in the context of prior knowledge and metacognitive knowledge; being aware of thinking and deliberately monitoring it; selecting and adapting thinking strategies for learning; and making judgements and attributions about thinking and learning (Pintrich, 2000, 2004). The reflective questions within this model are designed for students, but also prompt teachers to consider how students' thinking skills are supporting or hindering their learning.

Activity

In her 2020 paper, Elizabeth Norman discusses three ways that metacognition might derail learning. What do you think these might be?

The three ways are:

1. Metacognition may sometimes actively interfere with task performance.
2. The costs of engaging in metacognitive strategies may under certain circumstances outweigh its benefits.
3. Metacognitive judgments or feelings involving a negative self-evaluation may detract from psychological well-being.

Can you give examples from your experience of ways that metacognition is helpful and not always helpful?

Relating to others (R)

Within complex educational settings, the social skills that support learning include conversation skills, coping with conflict, friendship skills, and group skills. All of these depend on sensitivity to social interactions and cues, role taking and responding to others, social insight, moral judgement, social communication, and social problem-solving (Mitchell & Sutherland, 2020). There are many models that explain the complexity of social interaction capabilities (R), but for the purposes of this chapter we return to the one used for Thinking (T) (Figure 10.5) and apply a social perspective to it as some researchers have done (e.g., Crick & Dodge, 1994).

Looking at capabilities for social interactions in reference to the information processing model allows teachers to consider how their students receive and make sense of social information, and how they respond to it (Crick & Dodge, 1994). This simplification helps everyone focus on where difficulties might be experienced and how they might lead to barriers in engaging with others. For example, attention to appropriate social cues may need to be explicitly taught to some students. Similarly, generating socially appropriate

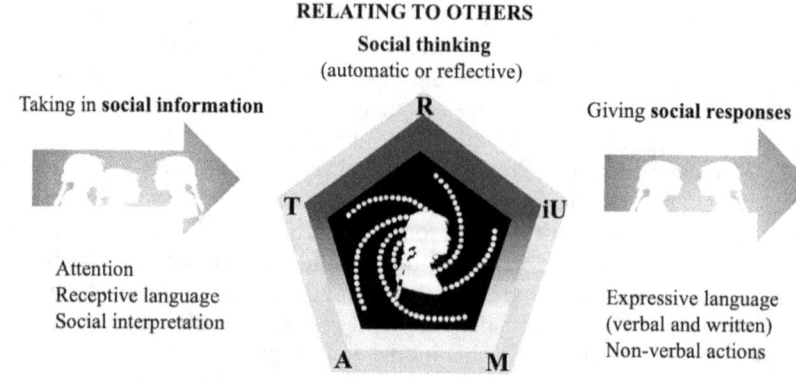

Figure 10.5 Social information processing.

responses (verbal and non-verbal) to group challenges may have to be taught. Extension of this model has included consideration of neurological development and social contexts (e.g., family function and environment, socioeconomic resources, and culture) which all influence the development of social capabilities (Beauchamp & Anderson, 2010). Approaches to teaching capabilities for relating to others (R) are more than social skills training. They seek to teach for social competence which recognises the complex dynamic systems involved in acting in socially capable ways (Winner & Crooke, 2016). Social problem solving and critical thinking are needed for this capability, not merely producing correct behaviours on cue.

Interventions to support social capabilities vary according to the focus of the teaching. Learning new skills might best happen in individual sessions; performance in response to a social cue can be assessed and taught in social settings; and building fluency of performance can be supported by introducing structures for students to monitor their own performance (Winner & Crooke, 2016). Another aspect of developing social capabilities is whether students rely on automatic responses or reflection or problem solving to support more considered behaviours (Verhoef, van Dijk, & Castro, 2022). Both are important, but many difficulties with social situations happen when reactions are not considered.

Within layers of responsive teaching, monitoring, and assessing behaviour is imperative, so that teaching of behavioural/social skills can be provided more intensively as needed. Help seeking and receiving assistance are core skills that need to be expected and responded to in teaching and learning. Teachers make themselves available to students who seek help (DART 2). These students' sense of belonging and self-efficacy supports their help-seeking (Won, Hensley, & Wolters, 2021). When help is sought, responsive teachers provide an optimum amount of assistance so that students can resume responsibility for their learning, with just enough help to manage it. Teachers need to notice when students have not sought help when needed. They also need to be cognisant of when students have sought help from peers or family (Martín-Arbós, Castarlenas, & Dueñas, 2021) and see if further strategies needed for students to work more closely with their teachers. There will be times when students seek help more than necessary, indicating a low level of self-efficacy (M) and tendency to depend on others.

Using language, symbol systems, and information communication technology (iU)

Language, symbol systems, and ICT are the vehicles through which we share and develop knowledge. It is vital that teachers identify how these systems support and hinder learning. Language is the medium of teaching, and many children come to school with more than one language. For example, 37% of children in NSW government schools have more than one language, and this population comprises 243 different language backgrounds (NSW Department of Education, 2020). In the Northern Territory more than 100 languages and dialects are spoken (Northern Territory Government of Australia, 2022). This means that many students bring languages other than the instructional language with them to school and are learning in a language outside their culture. In the Northern Territory bilingual education is being established in consultation with communities. Programs aim to teach 30–50% of curriculum in an Aboriginal language so that the students can "use the language they bring to school to learn curriculum content while they are learning English" (Northern Territory Government, Department of Education, 2022). Bilingual education exists in many different contexts, and there is complexity to acknowledge in the research evidence (Bialystok, 2018). The *Responsive Teaching for Sustainable Learning* approach acknowledges the crucial role that language plays in students' cultural identity and belonging and that linguistic and cultural resources are important for student learning (Gleeson, 2022). Dialect use, on the other hand, is an influential factor which may hinder learning (Corwin Visible Learning Plus, 2021).

Some students will come to school with disabling conditions related to language use that require support from speech pathologists. For students with language disabilities using assistive and augmentative technology can support their communication in educational settings: For some students this is essential for them to engage socially and educationally. Technological devices and software are evolving constantly and becoming more widely used. For example, voice to text, or dictation software was once exclusive and required advocacy and funding to access. Now applications are built into personal computers and mobile devices, and are used by many people for many varied reasons and in various ways. These include mobile technology, apps, wearable devices, virtual and augmented reality, and artificial intelligence (Mitchell & Sutherland, 2020). The skills needed to interact with students who use these supports can cause barriers for learning and need to be considered when teachers are making sense of students' use of language in learning.

Written language is central to formal learning, and student capability with it can support or hinder learning. All teachers need to be aware of how this happens. More than 20 years ago, Scarborough (2001) developed a metaphorical reading rope which delineated word recognition and comprehension as the two main components of reading; word decoding involved phonological awareness, decoding and sight vocabulary, and comprehension relied on background knowledge, vocabulary, language structure, verbal reasoning, and literacy knowledge. These separate skills become increasingly strategic and automatic as readers develop competence, and teaching needs to focus on all of them. This representation of the multidimensional capability of learning to read captured the imagination of teachers and parents and is widely used. More recently, Sedita (2019) used the same metaphor to explicitly articulate the skills that are needed for writing. *Responsive Teaching for Sustainable Learning* uses this metaphor in reference to the Australian National Literacy Progression which specifies five domains of skills development: speaking and listening; decoding and word recognition; fluency; comprehension; and writing (ACARA, 2020b; Figure 10.6).

Difficulties in learning within this capability present themselves in any one or more of these strands of development n Figure 10.6. The responsibility of teachers is to explicitly teach and monitor student progress within all strands of literacy and to provide opportunities for students to become increasingly

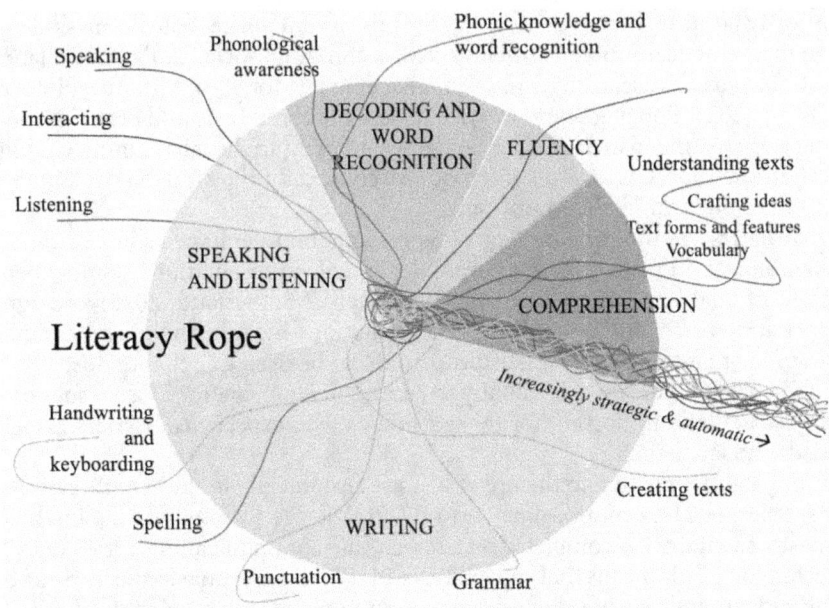

Figure 10.6 The literacy rope.
After Scarborough, 2001 and Sedita 2019.

strategic and automatic in their use of spoken and written language. It is evident from research that literacy is developed by systematically teaching reading, ensuring that there is adequate explicit instruction of decoding and word recognition and of comprehension (Mitchell & Sutherland, 2020).

Symbol systems are inherent in many disciplines and need to be taught explicitly as they are needed. Mathematical learning has a system of numerals that represent quantity, which students need to be able to encode and decode with fluency so that they can manipulate and apply functions to numbers. There are parallels between the way the numeric system works and how the alphabetic system encodes sounds, words, and stories. Mathematical orthography involves numerals that encode quantities and other symbols that represent operations on those quantities, the understanding of these symbols is essential knowledge that is built on in later years of mathematical learning (Douglas et al., 2020). However, mathematical learning also requires language, and a significant amount of that language has different meanings when used in Mathematics. Ensuring young children learn mathematical language that refers to quantities and spatial relations is important for early mathematical learning, since many basic concepts in language are foundational for mathematical ideas (Purpura, Napoli, & King, 2019). Mathematical symbols and concepts are combined with language in much of the mathematics curriculum, providing a multi-layered set of codes for thinking, representing, and problem-solving.

Using languages of computing, or coding, was initially a focus in schools in the 1980s. This area has experienced a recent resurgence as an educational priority because there is evidence of the positive influence that coding skill has on mathematical problem-solving, critical thinking, social skills and collaboration, and active learning and self-management (Monteiro, Miranda-Pinto, & Osório, 2021; Popat & Starkey, 2019). Coding is about logic and problem solving and creating instructions for activities inherent in the curriculum. Coding is not a new idea, but it is a contemporary context for the kind of thinking that needs to be included in education.

Teachers use multiple models of representation to enhance student understanding of information. For example, visual representations complement conventional linguistic information (Mitchell & Sutherland, 2020) and support and enrich thinking. Visual representations include pictures, diagrams, graphic organisers, and social stories, and can be used to help organise classrooms and to increase accessibility to conceptual information. Visual supports are particularly important for those students who experience barriers associated with language.

Capabilities relating to the use of ICT are also integral to the activities of students in the 21st century, since most information is accessed via the internet, most written work is completed on a screen, and communication carried out via technology. This means that capabilities with ICT are essential to the learning of all students and also life after school. Recognition of this has led to the development of models of what students need to know and do with ICT. An example is the Australian Curriculum ICT capability (Version 8.4) which includes investigating, creating, communicating, managing, and operating ICT, and applying social and ethical protocols and practices while doing so (ACARA, 2022c).

Capabilities with ICT (digital literacy) are influenced by many factors including access to technology. Even before the Covid-19 pandemic, it was evident that socioeconomic resources and ICT access contribute to young students' capabilities, attitudes, and experiences (Sweeney & Geer, 2010). The pandemic increased the demands on the capabilities of students and teachers as they engaged in online teaching and learning. Noticing how capabilities in ICT are supporting or hindering learning is important for teachers, as such technologies are integral to teaching and learning. Additionally, exposure to the world through technology creates vulnerability for students and internet safety must be a priority for all teachers and their students.

Activity

Consider how capable you are with ICT in reference to the Australian Curriculum capability (ACARA, 2022c). Are there aspects of this capability that you could further develop? ICT capabilities are associated with student self-control, stress associated with technology, and engagement in learning (Peng & Yu, 2022). Reflect on whether this is an issue for any of your students and consider what you might be able to do to address this.

The two examples, literacy and digital literacy, provided in this section illustrate the depth of the capabilities involved in using language, symbol systems, and ICT, but do not cover the broad range of capabilities related to symbol systems. There are other symbol systems in many other domains of life and education that can be considered.

RTF 6: How do I gather evidence of student learning?   159

Managing self (M)

Managing self (M) is also about regulating social, emotional, and behavioural aspects of functioning. Educational settings contain complex dynamics with many stressors, and it has become common for schools to incorporate social and emotional learning into schoolwide positive support structures. Social and emotional learning includes a focus on self-awareness, self-management, social awareness, relationship skills, and responsible decision-making (CASEL, 2022; Ross & Tolan, 2018). Managing self (M) is highlighted in this context to be about: managing stress and emotions; using self-discipline and self-motivation for setting goals, planning, and organising; taking initiative and demonstrating personal and collective agency; and making constructive choices about behaviour and interactions which are all supported by self-awareness, social sensitivity, and relationship skills including help-seeking (CASEL, 2022). Managing self entails fulfilling the role of a learner in educational settings over many years. During their schooling, students go through profound developmental changes and build important capabilities as they interact within their learning environments. The aim is for students to take responsibility for their learning in conjunction with their families, teachers, and other students and to regulate that learning. Models of self-regulated learning illustrate that there is a complex web of factors at play in how, and whether, students engage with and monitor their learning. For example, Pintrich's model assumes that learners are active and constructive and have potential for control and choice in their learning (Schunk, 2005). It draws together active learning (A) and managing self (M).

Pintrich's model of self-regulation has four phases (forethought, planning and activation; monitoring; control; and reaction and reflection) which are influenced by personal aspirations and the context of learning (Pintrich, 2004). Student personal agency is an aspect of self-regulation (Moseley et al., 2005), as are self-determination and self-efficacy (Mitchell & Sutherland, 2020). These components of self-regulation all play a part in how well a student can plan, monitor, control, and reflect on their learning processes. Teachers can contribute to students' sense of agency and belief in themselves as learners (DART 1). They also do this by ensuring that learning tasks are within the students' zones of readiness so that students experience success.

Self-regulation includes strategies such as elaboration and organisation of information, strategy monitoring, concept mapping, metacognitive strategies, and elaborativeinterrogation (Hattie & Donoghue, 2016). Effective learners become fluent and automatic by selecting and using strategies for learning. Many do this implicitly, while other students need explicit teaching and opportunities to practice these learning skills.

Since learning is a social activity, it is also necessary to consider co-regulation and socially shared regulation of learning (Hadwin, Järvelä, & Miller, 2017). Co-regulation happens as part of the teaching-learning relationship, specifically within DARTS 3 and 4, where teachers negotiate goals for learning and processes for monitoring, and tune into the current and potential competence of students. Socially-shared regulation is a function of the cohesiveness of groups in cooperative learning and describes how regulation dynamically shifts between individuals and the group (Järvelä & Hadwin. 2013). While "good teaching is inextricably linked to good regulation of learning", cooperative learning also supports the development of both socially shared regulation and co-regulation (Quackenbush & Bol, 2020, p. 7).

Anxiety can hinder learning. It can be related to specific aspects of the educational setting or more generalised. Some students come to school with clinical levels of anxiety which interfere with all aspects of engagement (A), relationships (R), and managing learning (M). Some research shows evidence-based instructional practices (e.g., cold-calling and asking for volunteers to answer questions) instigate social anxiety for some students, while non-graded individual tasks and lectures are the least anxiety provoking (Hood et al., 2021). Answering questions is an exposing situation for many students and is contaminated by fears of getting things wrong, therefore students who may experience social anxiety find these anxiety-provoking situations (Hood et al., 2021). Accomplished inclusive teachers make sure that students who are asked to answer questions in front of the group will be able to do so successfully. This is ensured by checking or rehearsing incidentally and privately beforehand. Such respectful and supportive use of questioning to share success is important. Questioning should never be used to expose failure. Positive changes in anxiety ratings for students are most likely to occur when the climate and culture of the educational setting is positive (Hood et al., 2021).

Assessment of the capabilities of self-managing and active learners who use thinking and language and other symbol systems to engage in teaching and learning relationships is a significant part of the general assessment of learning in classrooms. The discussion in these sections has illustrated how complex and interwoven – and important – capabilities are for all learners. Assessment in each capability can be done at a superficial and incidental level or more substantively by specialist assessment professionals if deeper investigation and understanding is needed.

Criterion and/or norm-referenced assessment

As is clear in this chapter, criterion-reference assessment, which uses curriculum and ATRiUM capabilities as the basis for criteria, is what is needed for assessment that supports *Sustainable Learning*. Responsive teachers set teaching intentions which become the criteria for assessments. Teachers can then determine how well and in what ways their students have achieved the intended learning. Norm-referenced assessment is also prevalent in our education systems and needs to be understood so that teachers can make valid and meaningful interpretations of related assessment findings and use data from them in constructive and supportive ways.

Norm-referenced assessment is anchored in psychometric test development procedures, where a test is developed and administered to a large group of people so that what is 'typical' at different ages can be determined. This is an important approach in many contexts, particularly child development. It means that health and educational professionals can compare the development and learning of students against others of the same age and use that information to help in deciding whether students are gifted, have age-appropriate development and learning, or experience delays or disorders. This is important for providing evidence that can be used to access programs and funding that are usually only available to those with significant differences in development and learning. However, there are problems if the information gained from such tests is misused to lower expectations for students. Such norm-referenced assessment results are usually snapshots of development and learning and may not reflect future possibilities. High expectations support teaching and learning and are an essential emphasis within teaching-learning relationships (see DARTs).

The ideas from norm-referenced approaches are also used informally in teaching when teachers provide total scores and grades and thereby give students ways to rank themselves against their classmates. This can lead to a situation where gifted students deliberately manage how well they do so that they do not stand out in the group. Students may be hindered in their learning and in their demonstration of learning. The practice of summing up performance in an assessment by an accumulation of scores or by a grade is a simplistic practice. It reduces the complexity of learning to one figure or letter and removes all details of what was learnt and what students can now do.

Teachers need to be very aware of how scores or grades can hinder their students' active learning and self-management. Teachers may still need to use grades and scores but can do so in sophisticated ways that do not block students' learning. Approaches to this challenge are covered in the next chapter on feedback for learners.

The HOW of assessment of learning

Responsive teachers consider both the curriculum content and ATRiUM capabilities as they design assessment activities and interpret assessment information. However, it is not easy to capture student responses in real time in such a way that it becomes credible evidence of learning. Instead, teachers devise more formal assessment events where students demonstrate learning in ways that are easier for teachers to interpret and compare. Conventionally, much of this type of assessment is done by organising groups of students in the same place at the same time and giving them written questions or stimulus materials. Students' responses in writing are then collected as evidence of learning. Having results on paper or within computer programs allows teachers to revisit, analyse, compare, and make judgements about what has been learned. It also supports quantification of outcomes and ranking of results. These traditions in assessment of learning might be convenient and efficient but are not necessarily helpful for learners or genuine in their acknowledgement of the fundamental purpose of assessment, which is to support learning.

Teachers are responsive to each learner by understanding what they bring to their learning (RTF 3), what they need to learn now (RTF 4), and how they can best be taught (RTF 5), using group written tests discounts their intent. By using the same conditions and formal ways of accessing evidence of learning,

> **HOW? Approach to assessment RTF 6**
>
> - What is the best way to assess the content and provide the information for the purpose?
> - What is the full range of the content?
> - Does the assessment approach include any other content (such as reading skills) that should be taken into account?

Figure 10.7 The HOW of assessment.

teachers may create barriers for many students, particularly those who experience anxiety about testing and those for whom written language is difficult.

Responsive teachers design assessment to ensure that students demonstrate what they have learned (see Figure 10.7). Because there are many different ways to assess learning, the strategies used depend on a clear understanding of the purpose and content of the assessment. It is important to differentiate by providing multiple options for students to demonstrate their learning. Teachers need to decide on the best ways for their students to do this, so that the information gathered is fit for purpose and reflects the intended learning.

Assessment needs to be aligned with intended learning outcomes and provide an opportunity for students to demonstrate the learning that is explicit in the ILOs. The recommended way to develop an assessment that reflects UDL principles is to use formative assessment which embeds student choice and evaluates student learning against clearly articulated success criteria. For example, when students are required to provide an oral presentation but are non-verbal, they can use technology that reads their presentations for them, rather than being excluded from the task. Similarly, students with anxiety disorders can record their tasks privately for the teacher and/or class to listen to. While education system requirements around assessment in the final years of schooling are not adaptable, internal school assessment has flexibility which should be used to support learning.

It is vital that teachers are clear about what it is that they are assessing. as it is very easy for intended learning outcomes to be contaminated by the need for other skills or knowledge that may hinder some students' abilities to demonstrate learning. A classic example of this is the provision of a written examination which prevents some students from showing what they have learned because of their delayed or disordered written language skills. The intended learning is therefore not validly assessed. Content validity is vital to ensure that students can show what they have learnt. A common situation within which content validity is contaminated is when assessment of mathematical problem-solving involves literacy levels that are barriers for some students. These students are not given sufficient chance to demonstrate their mathematical skills because of literacy barriers and both learning achievement and teaching effectiveness are not validly assessed.

Assessment tasks can be informal and integrated into everyday interactions. In fact, every interaction with students is assessment and, if captured, can provide comprehensive evidence of learning. Often this is the assessment that teachers use to make sense of how a student is going (monitoring), and sometimes it is when problems are identified and explored. However, gathering evidence from such incidental and complex interactions is not easy to manage and not always helpful, so teachers usually make a distinction between learning and assessment. This means that some form of product is requested from students, from which learning can be inferred by the quality of that product. This is typical for assessment of what has been learned at the end of a topic.

Assessment products are generated when students are asked to enact the actions defined in their ILOs (see Table 9.3 for a list of products aligned with ILOs and learning activities). The possibilities depend on the intended learning, the interests of the students, and the teacher's effort required to clarify and manage criteria for success across a range of possibilities. There are many products that can be produced, and these include short answers to sets of questions, extended written responses to questions, topics, or situations, worked problems, reports of experiments, graphic organisers or infographics, scripts for plays or screenplays, musical compositions, paintings, animations, conceptual frameworks, board games; just about anything can be the basis of an assessment activity.

If the intent is that students will be able to automatically recall facts with speed, then this can be built into the assessment task, but it is important that students have had time to rehearse and practise the task so that they are set up to succeed. For this type of learning, specific, measurable targets (as in SMART goals; RTF 4) are appropriate, with the provision of spaced practice throughout the learning period and recording of performance (monitoring) to see how learning is progressing. Student involvement in recording of performance allows student control of the process and the development of consciousness of how learning is progressing.

On the other hand, if the learning is about ordering a set of information, then it may be that a strategy (e.g., mnemonic) has been taught and practised, and students demonstrate their sequenced knowledge in pairs (with the possibility of feedback), then prepare to demonstrate to the class or the teacher or present it in a formal written task. Often this sequenced knowledge is needed for use in higher order tasks (e.g., problem solving) and so there are two steps in demonstrating learning. The recall and organising of the information, and then having it available for use in application, explanation, or argument. Students who have difficulty recalling sequenced knowledge are not able to demonstrate the higher order thinking. Responsive teachers thus need to be clear about whether they want both aspects or set two separate tasks that assess recall and application of available information.

Formal events can be the basis of assessment of learning, particularly for summative assessment (as in RTF 6) and can take the form of traditional examinations, assignments, observed group activities, exhibitions, presentations, or performances. Examinations are used for schoolwide and system-wide assessment, and produce quantified results and subsequent ranking of students. Procedures exist for the writing of questions, generation of possible responses, and procedures for multiple markers, so that results are as objective as possible in matching outcomes to set criteria.

Assignments often serve the purpose of being an assessment task as well as a learning task, since they can require students to research information, and then produce an extended piece of procedural, persuasive, or creative writing, a poster or infographic, a video report, a storyboard, or other substantial piece of work. This is typical for senior school and for tertiary study. Success criteria are provided (often as a rubric defining different levels of quality across dimensions of the task) and sometimes students are also asked to self-assess as part of their submission.

Observed group activities are also appropriate for assessment. However, determining the criteria, and setting up the activities so that it is possible to gather evidence of individual learning outcomes is complex. Groups are inherently dynamic with students contributing more in response to their motivation, or to compensate for what they perceive as lesser contributions by others. Teasing these complications apart so that evidence of individual student learning can be derived is not easy. For this reason, perhaps, groups are not used often in assessment, even though they may have been the context for the learning. Resolving the contradictions between teaching for cooperative learning and group work, and then assessing individually is a challenge for responsive teachers. Again, it is important to be clear about what the purposes are, so that assessment opportunities align to meet those needs.

Exhibitions of work of any sort provide opportunities for students to demonstrate their learning along with others and to celebrate the accumulated learning of the group. Many domains of learning require exhibitions, performances, or presentations, and these can be set up and assessed in different ways. Such exhibitions lead to the comparison of work, which teachers need to carefully manage. Performances or presentations, in many different media, can be important demonstrations of learning. While some students will be able to script, rehearse, and present a speech without notes, others will need assistance in structuring the talk, and remembering it, and confidence boosting, so they too experience success.

Finally, in this section, we consider special provisions in assessment, which are designed to ensure that students with disabilities are not disadvantaged in demonstrating their learning. In line with the Disability Discrimination Act (1992) schools put in place adjustments that are allowed to support students in state-wide assessments, some of which can be provided by schools, and others approved by examining authorities (e.g., NESA, 2021b). Most of the provisions are concerned with access to the content of examinations and support for producing written responses. Supports include the use of assistive communication technology, readers, and writers, as well as extended time. It is important that these provisions "reflect the kind of support and assistance provided in the classroom in order for students to demonstrate what they know and can do without being limited or impeded by their disability" (National Assessment Program, 2022). There is considerable inequity around these provisions as it has been shown that they are disproportionally accessed by independent schools and families who have the resources to access medical and allied-health casework assessments for the purpose of gathering evidence to apply for special consideration (Baker & Gladstone, 2021).

Assessment-ready and -capable learners

What responsibility do teachers have to make sure that students are assessment ready? This discussion raises questions for teachers along a continuum of ideas from explicit and direct teaching to the test to providing no preparation for assessment. Both ends of this spectrum are inappropriate, but there is a responsibility to ensure students are familiar with assessment procedures and that they are assessment capable; in other words, that they can demonstrate their learning on assessment tasks when needed (Hattie, Fisher, & Frey, 2018).

Education systems provide practice tests for students and there are many commercially available preparation texts for large-scale assessment. Assessment readiness is about building familiarity with the format and processes of assessment. This is necessary, of course, since teachers do not want a lack of familiarity with a platform or process to become a barrier for students trying to demonstrate their learning. A deeper approach to this issue, however, is about building the capabilities for demonstrating learning into instruction and consideration of students' depth of engagement in learning.

Likewise, assessment capability is when students are conscious of what they are learning, how well it is happening, what they can do to drive and support their learning (feedback, tools and resources, monitoring strategies), and their ability to teach others what they are learning (Frey, Fisher, & Hattie, 2018). This description aligns directly with the active learning (A) and managing self (M) capabilities in ATRiUM.

Assessment OF learning becomes assessment FOR learning and assessment AS learning

In RTF 6 responsive teachers consider what students have learned in reference to both intended and unintended learning outcomes and what factors influence that learning, in order to determine the extent and nature of student learning. Responsive teaching aims to bring students from where they are were before teaching, to where we want them to be, that is, to close the gap between knowledge and skills in relation to learning goals. All assessment morphs from assessment OF learning into assessment FOR learning. In assessment FOR learning the focus is on where the learner is now, where the learning is going, and how to get there (Hattie & Timperley, 2007; Wiliam, 2013). In Wiliam's (2013) framework, the five strategies of formative assessment (assessment FOR learning) are:

1. Clarifying, sharing, and understanding learning intentions
2. Engineering effective discussion, activities and tasks that elicit evidence of learning
3. Activating students as learning resources for one another
4. Activating students as owners of their own learning
5. Providing feedback that moves learning forward (Wiliam, 2013, p. 16)

This set of strategies aligns strongly with responsive teaching and delineates what assessment needs to be in order to support learning. Assessment is clearly integrated into teaching and learning and is used in all educational settings. Self-reliant learning is what responsive teachers aim for, so that all students progress to being sustainable learners who actively self-manage their engagement and learning in school, higher education, and throughout their lives. A conceptual framework and a set of conditions under which assessment supports student learning have been developed in the UK by Gibbs and colleagues (Gibbs & Simpson, 2004; Gibbs, 2006). Four conditions, which refer to student effort, assist considerations of how to assess.

> Condition 1: Assessed tasks capture sufficient study time and effort
> Condition 2: These tasks distribute student effort evenly across topics and weeks
> Condition 3: These tasks engage students in productive learning activity
> Condition 4: Assessment communicates clear and high expectations to students (Gibbs & Simpson, 2004; Gibbs, 2006).

In the context of higher education, student effort and time spent on learning is supported by multiple assignments spread throughout the course and topics (Gibbs, 2006). Translating this point into school education suggests that multiple, regular opportunities for students to demonstrate what they are learning are needed. These opportunities do not all need to demonstrate that learning to teachers with the same intensity, instead they can involve either peer feedback or structures within which to self-assess. Again, we draw on Vygotsky to advocate for constant opportunities for students to demonstrate learning and to receive expert teacher feedback, which models the language and emphases that are most powerful in supporting learning. In this way, students begin to use self-talk and conversations with peers to strengthen their own skills in judging learning and directing future learning goals. This means that all learning opportunities can be also assessment opportunities – *assessment OF learning* becoming *assessment AS learning*.

The second dimension of Gibbs' (2006) conditions for assessment-supporting learning focuses on assessment tasks that are designed as productive learning activities with clear and high expectations. It is well known that short answer or multiple-choice questions do not necessarily provide valid evidence of deep, conceptual learning. The use of "larger, more complex and open-ended assessment" that requires demonstration of understanding is more likely to generate deep learning (Gibbs, 2006).

In conclusion, responsive teachers use assessment referenced to the curriculum and ATRiUM capabilities to gather evidence of learning. Assessment activities should provide opportunities for students to engage in the actions that are the focus of the intended learning outcomes and demonstrate their learning. Student choice about how to demonstrate learning is integral to a differentiated approach. When students engage in formal assessment, they need to be assessment-capable for that assessment and not hindered by aspects of the assessment that are not the focus of the assessment.

As this chapter has shown, summative assessment (assessment OF learning) can turn into formative assessment (assessment FOR learning). The next chapter provides a discussion of the feedback that needs to happen for any assessment OF learning to become assessment FOR learning, and how responsive teachers can provide feedback in effective ways.

11 RTF 7: How do I use feedback to support learning?

RTF 7. How do I use feedback to support learning?

What quality, quantity, and timing of feedback is needed? How do I teach students to give themselves feedback? How do I get students to respond to feedback?

Introduction

This seventh step of the RTF focuses on how responsive teachers can strategically use feedback to powerfully support learning (Fuchs & Fuchs, 1986; Hattie, 2009). Feedback is "part of the joint search for success" (Mitchell, 2017, p. 77) between teachers and students. It is complex and yields differential effects dependent on the context (Wisniewski, Zierer, & Hattie, 2020). Assessment within responsive teaching aims to determine the extent and nature of student learning. Feedback is the sharing of evidence of learning which has been provided through assessment and has the potential to accelerate learning (Corwin Visible Learning Plus, 2021). Both research and evidence from professional practice provide guidance about how to facilitate feedback for learners. In this chapter, we consider the conditions that support student learning through a focus on the quality of feedback, the quantity and timing of feedback, and the actions taken by students in response to feedback (Gibbs, 2006; Gibbs & Simpson, 2004).

Research attempts to estimate a mean effect size for feedback in learning (Corwin Visible Learning Plus, 2021; Hattie, 2018; Hattie & Timperley, 2007; Wizniewski et al., 2020), but this is difficult because of the many variables influencing its use. Feedback meets different purposes (WHY), has different foci (WHAT), and encompasses a variety of approaches (HOW). Meta-analyses attempt to take this variability into account and make sense of evidence about the effect of feedback on learning. From the perspective of *Responsive Teaching for Sustainable Learning* feedback makes a vital contribution to learning as an essential action that follows assessment; it informs future teaching and learning and is an explicit and embedded aspect of dialogic teaching and the deliberate actions of responsive teachers (DARTs).

Feedback needs to be built in when designing assessment activities (Wiliam, 2013), because assessment is meaningless for learning unless it incorporates feedback that moves learning forward. Thus, feedback is deliberate and explicit in assessment activities and is inherent in all learning activities and interactions in classrooms. Feedback can come from teachers, others in learning groups, and through student self-talk. It can be provided personally or through written, video, or audio recorded means. It may be reduced (i.e., scores, grades, rewards, or punishment) or elaborated.

While students depend on feedback from external sources, they tend to remain passive learners. *Responsive Teaching for Sustainable Learning*, therefore, aims not only for effective use of feedback provided by others, but for active generation of feedback by students. Students thus take a "substantial role" in the feedback process, as is inherent in the dialogic model of teaching and learning (Van der Kleij, Adie, & Cumming, 2019). An underlying aim is to build students' capabilities in self-judgement so that self-talk and reflections on learning (self-feedback) support learning throughout their lives. Students constantly make judgements about their own learning which can be instrumental in supporting learning. Such self-generated feedback aims to "inform adjustments to processes and products that deepen learning and enhance performance" (Andrade, 2019, p. 2). Sustainable learners need to be able to frame their own feedback constructively with a view to growth and learning, and they need to be explicitly taught how to do this. The quality, quantity, and timing of feedback associated with assessment tasks will now be considered, followed by processes for feedback integrated into dialogic teaching, and how supporting students' 'self-feedback' underpins active learning (A) and managing self (M).

Quality of feedback

Responsive teaching aligns explicit intended learning outcomes (RTF 4) with learning activities (RTF 5) and assessment tasks (RTF 6), and thus provides meaningful evidence of learning upon which feedback is based (RTF 7). Responsive teachers design quality feedback that focuses on learning. Their feedback is explicit, linked to task assessment criteria and strategy use, and provided in manageable units so it is understandable and useable by learners (Gibbs, 2006; Mitchell, 2018).

Not all feedback is equal. Some has more positive influence on learning than others. It is important to distinguish between simple reinforcement (positive and negative), corrective feedback, and high information feedback, which is correction plus reference to self-regulation, attention, emotion, and motivation (Wisniewski, Zierer, & Hattie, 2020). Much of the research literature about feedback for learning concerns the correction of errors. However, it is important for teachers to notice correct responses and evidence of learning. Learners benefit from affirmative feedback which acknowledges what they now know and can do. Feedback that is derived from the alignment of ILOs, learning opportunities, and assessment tasks (Figure 11.1) acknowledges what students have learned in reference to what was intended, and is future oriented.

When intended learning outcomes are well constructed, they are the basis of feedback about the task, and about processes or procedures used within learning activities. Reinforcement and provision of cues necessary to advance

170 Using the responsive teaching framework

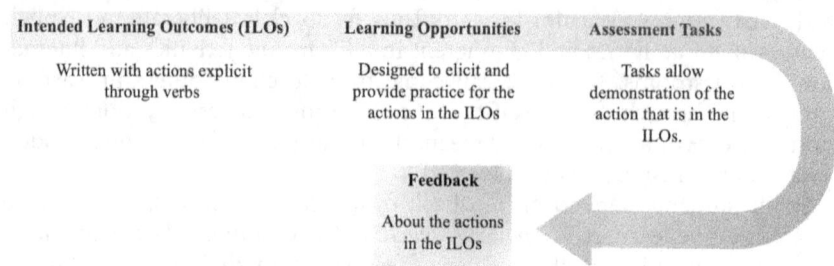

Figure 11.1 Feedback within constructive alignment.
Derived from Biggs & Tang, 2011.

to the next steps in learning have potential to accelerate learning (Corwin Visible Learning Plus, 2021). Specifically, the quality of feedback can be increased by making sure it is informative about tasks and the processes used within tasks (Hattie & Timperley, 2007; Wizniewski et al., 2020). Quality feedback also requires a match between the specific information provided and that which is needed at any time by students. Some students will need generalised feedback, while others will require feedback to be more direct or detailed. At times students may only need questioning about an aspect of a task to prompt them to check their work, while others need more explicit direction about what needs to be changed and how to do it.

Structured rubrics that define different levels of depth within learning outcomes have built-in feedback and take considerable time to construct. Unless the rubrics are built on a sound theoretical basis which has been validated, they are merely a set of descriptors that may or may not match the reality of learning and development and can be confusing for students and assessors. It is important for teachers to understand how detailed rubrics are received and used, and how they support or hinder engagement with assessment activities and subsequent feedback. Rubrics can reduce self-efficacy before an assessment task is even started, creating a barrier for learning. Responsive teachers need to be able to use rubrics flexibly so that they provide meaningful feedback. For example, rubrics could be limited to three levels that represent a recent achievement level, the current unassisted, and the assisted levels of learning, so that the success criteria are understandable and achievable because they are linked to students' zones of readiness.

Activity

Search for rubrics or marking criteria on the internet and see what professional resources are available for teachers. Consider these in light of the discussion in this chapter. Make judgements about how the rubrics would support your provision of feedback to students about their learning. Develop your own format for this kind of feedback and trial it with your students.

In conclusion, quality feedback is affirmative of students' achievements and provides direction for future learning. It is a natural extension of the alignment between intended learning outcomes, learning opportunities, and assessment tasks, and provided with reference to the task and processes of learning that were the focus of teaching. Quality feedback is also differential in response to readiness and *Sustainable Learning Profiles*, so that it supports the continued learning of each student. Because feedback is a powerful aspect of responsive teaching and it makes a considerable difference to student learning, we need to make decisions about how much to provide and when.

Quantity and timing of feedback

As well as ensuring quality feedback, it is important to consider both the amount and the timing of it. Often there are aspects of a product of learning which need strengthening, but if feedback details all of these, students may be discouraged and give up. Finding the right amount of feedback by selecting the most important aspects of a task at any time is challenging. Responsive teachers select the most important foci for detailed feedback relating to each student's readiness for learning. It is helpful for teachers to negotiate the focus of feedback by asking students what is most important to them in the activity, and what they would like the feedback to focus on at this time. When there is trusting teaching-learning relationship students are comfortable to reveal and discuss their learning (DART 2) and can ask teachers to notice aspects of it (DART 3) and support their self-regulation (DART 7) through specific or targeted feedback. Teachers can then make general comments about some aspects of the product, together with more detailed feedback on one aspect of it. For example, if a student is focused on developing skills of showing their work in a mathematical proof, then this can be the focus for feedback. This does not mean the teacher ignores the problem-solving, the calculations, or the solution, it just means that there will be more detailed feedback about the presentation of the thinking at this time.

A process for self-assessment and request for feedback as part of assignments or learning activities can support student agency in relation to feedback. This allows responsive teachers to deliver feedback that is most needed at the time, and in the quantity and detail that will be most effective in supporting learning. Self-assessment is feedback (Andrade, 2019) and is imperative for successful active learning (A). A scaffold for student self-feedback in reference to assessment in *Responsive Teaching for Sustainable Learning* (RTF 6) is shown in Figure 11.2. It is informed by Hattie and Timperley's model (2007) and Andrade's (2019) taxonomy.

Use of a process like this, which explicitly extends teaching-learning interactions and maintains relationship expectations related to the DARTS, allows students to actively engage with feedback as a strategy to support their learning, and to provide direction for feedback to teachers so that feedback is differentiated and useful for learning. The ideas in this scaffold can be adapted to suit the context of a variety of educational settings.

Feedback needs to be provided quickly and often enough to support learning (Gibbs, 2006). Item-based computer feedback has been shown to be most effective when immediate and accompanied by an explanation (Van der Kleij, Feskens, & Eggen, 2015), however, the issue of immediacy or delay in access to

Open-ended critique of the product and associated learning
What have you produced and what have you learnt while doing this?

Criterion-referenced evaluation of the assignment
How well have you met the success criteria?
How well have you achieved the intended learning outcomes?
What do you need to learn now?

TASK

Open-ended critique of processes and procedures used in completing the task
How did you do this?
How could you do this differently?

Criterion-referenced reflection
How did the use of ATRiUM capabilities support and hinder completion of the task, and the learning involved?
(A) How were you active in your learning?
(T) How did thinking support your activity?
(R) How did you relate to others?
(iU) How did you use language, symbol systems and ICT in this activity?
(M) How did you manage yourself?

CAPABILITIES

Request for feedback   *What would you like feedback about?*

Figure 11.2 A process for self-assessment and request for targeted feedback.
Derived from Andrade, 2019 and Hattie & Timperley, 2007.

feedback is complicated and can be further complicated by aspects of the context including the type of learning and phase of learning (Kulik & Kulik, 1988). Generally, feedback about formal assessment tasks needs to be as immediate as possible so that the experience of the task is still present enough for the feedback to be meaningful and connected to the effort expended. This is an admirable and important aim, but in the complex and busy interactions of teaching and learning, it is unlikely to be provided often enough and in enough depth for every student to benefit.

The most immediate form of feedback exists within interactions between teacher and student, and it is inevitable that every "teaching strategy, every interaction will be received by the learner as feedback" (Berman & Graham, 2018, p. 198). As teachers move around their classes interacting with students as they engage in learning activities, they strategically use different types of responses to check for learning, as well as to offer further teaching. Teachers offer informal feedback at different levels, based on their judgement of the support required at the time, and depending on their students' responses to instruction. Responsive teachers change how they interact with individuals and groups of students based on often unconscious interpretations of student learning needs at the time. They differentiate language, tone, facial expressions, gestures, pauses, explanations, modelling, deliberate linking with prior knowledge or activities, encouragement, and affirmation, often without conscious awareness of what they do and why. This is the most powerful form of feedback that can be given to support student learning. It is immediate, often pre-emptive and students have the opportunity to take advantage of it as they learn.

Making sense of feedback within interactions

The *Deliberate Actions of Responsive Teachers* (DARTs; Figure 9.2) emphasise the integral nature of feedback. This concerns the processes established for noticing growth and change through learning (DART 3) and how this information is shared within teaching-learning relationship (DARTS 2-6), and then made the focus of reflection on learning (DART 7). Teachers interact and differentiate intuitively in response to how they see each student's needs, for example, by slowing down, providing chunked explanations, giving elaborated information, or asking questions. Interpretation of these interactions allows further insight into the learning needs of students, and the type of feedback needed.

Sometimes teachers may act on incorrect assumptions and may unintentionally hinder student agency or self-efficacy. For example, it is common for teachers to fill silences, as it is a social skill that protects participants from awkwardness and the possibility of revealing that one person does not know how to respond. However, it has been shown that silences or pauses in teaching-learning interactions are important. A pause or wait-time of three seconds has been shown to set an expectation that a student is able to respond and allows time for elaboration if a student has given a brief immediate response (Wasik & Hindman, 2018). Wait times can increase the number, length, and accuracy of voluntary responses and can also influence student achievement (Mahmud, 2019). Teachers can deliberately build in these pauses by modelling waiting, thinking-out-loud, active listening, and careful use of time when it will be most useful and not disruptive (Wasik & Hindman, 2018). Wait time, after providing a cue, is also imperative when teachers need the attention of a group of students so they can provide verbal instructions (Richmond, 2007) or provide instructions for a whole group discussion or activity. Meanwhile, teachers provide feedback in everything they do and say, as every teacher response to their students is received as feedback on learning, either directly or indirectly.

The following table (Table 11.1) is an analysis of spontaneous teacher responses during dynamic assessment mediation (Graham, Berman, & Bellert, 2015). It is presented as an example of the types of strategies that teachers and learners rely on throughout daily classroom activities which function as feedback. Students draw conclusions about their learning from the type and intensity of teaching responses offered to them and to others during learning tasks.

Activity

Use Table 11.1 to analyse a video of your own teaching interactions or an observation of another teacher. See if you can identify the types of strategies you (the teacher) are using when interacting with students, and the

Table 11.1 Teaching interactions are feedback

Perceived learning needs or barrier to learning	Teacher-provided explicit feedback	Seeking student response
1. Required information is not understood	Provide or guide an explanation, description, or summary. *This is about…*	Seek an explanation, description, or summary: *What is this about?*
2. Task instructions are not understood	Repeat, paraphrase, or elaborate instructions. *The task is asking you to…*	Seek retell of the instructions: *What do you need to do?*
3. Previous information is not available	Tell or guide student recall of information: *Remember, we discussed…*	Seek recall of information: *Do you remember what we knew about these groups?*
4. Focus is not yet on important aspects of task	Direct or guide focus on a particular aspect of the task or question. *You need to look at… so that you can…*	Seek focus: *What part of this is important?*
5. Current approach or idea is not working	Provide or guide an alternative idea or approach to a task: *Let's try another way of thinking about this.*	Seek alternatives: *Is there another way you could do this?*
6. Connection to previous learning is not yet evident	Provide or guide to a link with previous aspects of the lesson or previous lesson: *You already know how to do this part.*	Seek a link: *Is this connected to what we did earlier?*
7. Needs manipulation of concrete material	Model or guide use of familiar or alternative materials or visual representation: *Watch me do this…*	Ask about use of materials: *Could you use… to help?*
8. Ready to be conscious of learning	Provide or guide a reflection on ideas or activities: *Let's think aloud now so you can see what you are doing.*	Seek reflection on ideas or activities: *How have you been doing this so far?*
9. Ready to evaluate	Provide or guide evaluation of an idea or attempt: *That idea makes good sense.*	Seek evaluation: *Did this work? Does that make sense?*
10. Ready to transfer	Provide or guide application to a similar task: *You can do the same thing with this problem.*	Seek application to a similar task or context: *Could you use that for this problem?*
11. Emotional support needed	Make explicit verbal comment about emotional status: *You are persisting with this even though it is hard – well done.*	Give non-verbal or verbal low-level gesture or acknowledgement of emotional effort: *Keep at it, it is working.*

Adapted from Berman (2001).

explicitness of each strategy. Can you see the justification for why particular feedback strategies have been selected? What was the range of these? Notice how students interpreted teacher interactions as feedback about their learning. How did the students use this feedback?

Peer feedback can also be used, but it needs to be carefully managed by teachers so that it achieves its aim of building learning conversations between students that strengthen the learning for all. Teachers, therefore, must make sure that providing peer feedback is not an activity used to criticise, but instead is a process of acknowledging strengths and making suggestions for improvement. The use of questions rather than statements assists in developing student mindsets for providing feedback that is helpful for others' learning and set up scripts for thinking about students' own work. Peer assessment can be integrated into learning activities in such a way that learners have the opportunity to look at examples of how other students have responded to the task. This provides a reference for students to make judgements about their own work, and how they could develop it further. Sharing examples of peer responses to assessments is particularly useful where there are creative components to tasks as students get to see a range of responses.

Self-feedback

Assessment is the basis of reflective conversations with students who are supported in actively driving and managing their own learning. We need to explicitly teach and give many opportunities for our students to practice the skills of reflective conversations which become the basis of internalising self-talk about learning and managing learning. In this way, we are acknowledging conversations about assessment as a powerful force in teaching and learning. As "ultimately the fastest and most frequent feedback available is that provided by students to themselves from moment to moment as they study or write assignments" (Gibbs, 2006, p. 33), we need to teach students to use self-feedback to support their perseverance and success in learning. Responsive teachers deliberately teach these strategies by modelling the language and providing opportunities to learn through reflective conversations with peers and teachers.

Wiliam recommends using a process that supports students to develop a critical eye for self-assessment and, therefore, the generation of self-feedback (Wiliam, 2016). His scaffold involves the following task: When students have finished a piece of work, ask them to identify something they found easy, something they found hard or challenging, and then something interesting. As well, Wiliam suggests asking students to nominate what they would do differently if they did this task again. The aim of this series of questions is to build thinking around how to improve learning and performance. In summary, William's questions are:

- How did you do this task?
- What was easy?
- What was hard?
- What was interesting about this task?
- If you could do this task again, what would you do differently?

Mediated learning (Skuy, 1997) is a natural context for the development of self-feedback. Within this context, teachers do not provide definitive statements about learning, but instead encourage and facilitate students' observations about their own learning. Responsive teachers need to be aware that self-feedback is complicated for students who experience self-doubt or mood disorders who can be highly critical of their work and capabilities. This is exacerbated by students comparing themselves to the highest achievers or against the highest level of quality in success criteria.

Scripts are provided as part of dynamic assessment and focus on the tasks and on ATRiUM capabilities. Teachers can use questions as a script for learners and probe their engagement in learning or assessment before, during, and after the task, and model the language of self-assessment (Table 11.2).

At the beginning of a learning activity, the questions are about clarifying the requirements of the activity, checking the information needed, and linking with previous experience. During the task, the questions are about the thinking and decision-making processes being used as well as seeking substantiation of those decisions (Lauchlan & Carrigan, 2013). The final questions ask students to reflect on what was done, whether it was valid, what was learnt, and what still needs to be understood.

Student role in feedback process

What students do with the feedback is critical. Responsive teachers engage respectfully with students' work, giving direction to what needs correction or further elaboration. This is a skill that depends on the trust in the relationship between students and teachers.

Students are all in their own unique place in learning at any particular time, which can colour the way they receive feedback and also what they do with it. For those students who are experiencing or who have a history of learning difficulties, and those who find the whole process of formal schooling discouraging, this process needs to be managed carefully. If feedback is seen to affirm students' beliefs that learning is too hard, they may react to frustration by

Table 11.2 Script for teaching self-assessment

When starting a task	During the task	When finishing a task
What do you have to do here? How is this the same as something you already know or can do? What do you know about this already? What do you expect to find out?	Tell me what you are doing. How is this the same as something you already know or can do? How do you know this is right? Is there another way you could do this?	Is your answer right? Do you need to change it? Do you need to add more? What have you learnt? Did you understand everything? Do you need to find out more? What did you like and dislike about the task? What did you find easy/difficult?

Derived from Lauchlan & Carrigan, 2013.

opting out or giving up. Finding the optimal feedback that encourages and moves students forward within their zones of readiness is not something that can be prescribed, although research has attempted to make more sense of the important components (the quality and quantity) that tend to be most effective.

Responsive Teaching for Sustainable Learning assumes a substantial role for students in the feedback process, one that is dialogic (Van der Kleij, Adie, & Cumming, 2019). If feedback is dialogic, then it will contribute to enhancing interactions and relationships. Dialogue containing feedback needs to enact high expectations by "pushing students that bit further, expecting that students can and will learn every day, while still caring for students individually and seeking to understand the underlying issues that might be getting in the way of learning" (Sarra et al., 2020). Key aspects of responsive teaching are echoed in Sarra et al.'s (2020) model for high-expectations relationships with Indigenous students, which includes knowing students, building trust, and having strengths-based conversations which acknowledge learning capabilities, achievement, and growth.

One of the features of explicit teaching is how students make use of feedback by receiving and attending to it and acting on it to improve their learning and work (Gibbs, 2006). This emphasis on what students do with feedback is also the target of research that previously focused on quality of feedback as the key issue (Hattie & Timperley, 2007). A distinction between feedback that supports students' sense of self and that which improves performance has been made (Kluger & De Nisi, 1996) suggesting that feedback has multiple effects on learners. It can support or hinder ATRiUM capabilities depending on how it is received.

Student use of feedback is supported by provision of time for them to reflect on their learning and to "engage with peers and their teachers on *how* to learn – not just what to learn" (Frey, Fisher, & Hattie, 2018, p. 48). This emphasis on social interactions with others as learning is happening points to the ATRiUM capability of relating to others (R). Reflective conversations can empower learners to be active in assessment of their learning, which in turn builds "a sense of accomplishment, comfort and confidence" (Weaver et al., 2020, p. 37).

In summary, provision of feedback to students is core business for responsive teachers, so it is important to understand how it acts as a powerful mechanism for learning. Feedback is a human interaction skill that depends on trusting relationships and can be strengthened through professional strategies. It does not need to be formalised, in fact, on-the-spot feedback with varied levels of directness or intensity can be effective for supporting students as they engage in learning activities. Importantly, feedback associated with assessment is not helpful for student learning unless there are constructive actions that are set up to follow it. Feedback is required to support quality learning that is future oriented, appropriate in quality and sufficient in quantity.

12 RTF 8: How did my teaching support my students' learning?

RTF 8. How did my teaching support my students' learning? What knowledge and skills do I need to further develop?

Introduction

The final step of the *Responsive Teaching Framework*, RTF 8, is about using evidence gathered throughout the teaching cycle to evaluate practice and to make subsequent decisions about teaching. When teaching approaches are evidence-based, and they produce successful learning experiences, it is important to carefully consider how well they contribute to student learning and whether they can be further strengthened. The two frameworks for evaluation drawn on in this chapter are realist or realistic evaluation (Tilley & Pawson, 2000) and implementation science (Blasé et al., 2012). Realist evaluations (Tilley & Pawson, 2000) seek to determine what works, for whom and why (Maxwell, 2018) by defining context, mechanisms, and outcomes, and then drawing relationships between them. These authors also recognise that there will never be an absolute answer since everything is variable and dynamic (Pawson & Tilley, 2001). Realist evaluation aligns with *Responsive Teaching for Sustainable Learning* with its focus on context and the actions of teachers and learners. Implementation science uses a triad of dimensions (i.e., competence, organisation, and leadership) against which to consider the mechanisms that underpin responsive teaching. Outcomes and conclusions about the effectiveness of teaching need to be put into context and understood in terms of processes to make sense of what worked to achieve learning.

Outcomes of teaching and learning

The starting point for reflection and evaluation is the difference between what students knew and could do initially (RTF 3 & 4) and what they know and can do now (RTF 6) after teaching. This step of the RTF answers the question: How well have the students learned?

At a whole class level, in reference to the curriculum, results allow teachers to determine who has achieved the intended learning, who has partially achieved these outcomes, who needs more teaching or practice, and who is struggling and in need of more explicit or targeted teaching. This information feeds directly into RTF 3 and RTF 4 of the next cycle of responsive teaching. Apart from being able to report this learning to students and their families, and to the educational system as required, this evidence can also be interpreted with a view to understanding how context and teaching practice contributed to learning.

The overall evaluative question is: How well have I taught all my students? As well as celebrating high achievement in the group, it is important to consider struggling learners and how well they have learned, and, therefore, been taught. Many students will learn despite teacher expertise, while some will depend absolutely on teachers making justified decisions about how to teach them. These are the students who are the real indicators of responsive teaching expertise. Consequently, even though responsive teachers identify and celebrate all students' achievement, they make judgements about their effectiveness in relation to those who struggle to learn.

In RTF 6, attainment of learning outcomes is determined through assessment. These comprise intended and unintended learning outcomes and factors that support and hinder learning. The difference between what the students previously knew and could do, and what they can now do and know, constitutes the basis for establishing achievement.

Context for teaching and learning

Contextual layers of influence feature in *Responsive Teaching for Sustainable Learning*. In RTF 1, we carefully considered multiple layers of influence, from international, national, local community, and within educational settings, as well as what teachers and learners bring to their relationships (RTF 2 & 3). These influences affect how teachers teach and how their students learn.

Additionally, some aspects of context are deliberately shaped, organised, and managed as part of professional practice, such as school culture, classroom climate, and ambience. It is important for teachers to notice how these aspects support and hinder teaching and learning. The reflective task in relation to RTF 1 is to make sense of how multiple layers of ecological influence affect teaching practice and student learning, and whether there is a need for them to be taken more into account in subsequent teaching. Context is well defined in *Responsive Teaching for Sustainable Learning* and is part of RTF steps 1, 2, and 3 which highlight the interactions between multiple layers of influence and what teachers and students bring to teaching and learning.

How well did I interpret and manage the influences on my teaching and the students' learning?

In the context of teachers who have students involved in state-wide assessment, responsive teachers ask themselves how this process influences their teaching and student learning. Is it possible that the specific needs of the testing, and any preparation has been included in decision-making? Chapter 5 contains more structure for this reflective process.

Processes of teaching and learning

Next, we are interested in the mechanisms or processes that lead to change in learning in context. This phase considers all the processes of teaching as outlined in the Responsive Teaching Framework including: awareness of the contextual factors (RTF 1, 2, & 3); understanding the learning needs of students and deciding how best to respond to them through developing teacher-student relationships, choosing teaching approaches, designing learning opportunities, and planning assessment and feedback (RTF 4, 5, 6, & 7); and the reflective practice that is inherent in all RTF steps, but explicitly defined in RTF 8, which asks: How did responsive teaching support student learning?

A systematic way to think about how the processes of responsive teaching practice make a difference comes from implementation science (Blasé et al., 2012) which focuses on competence, organisation, and leadership. Responsive teachers use the following reflective questions to better understand how these processes work.

- How was I competent in teaching these students at this time? What aspects of my competence supported learning? Which aspects of my competence need development? Were there things I did not know or could not do that were needed?
- How was I organised in teaching so that there was efficient and effective management of students, of learning tasks and materials, of assessment processes, and recording of assessment information?
- How was my leadership of colleagues and other personnel and of students effective in supporting competence and organisation?

Competence is expected at each step of the *Responsive Teaching Framework*. It comes from professional and cultural skills and knowledge (RTF 2); finding out about the students as learners (RTF 3), and understanding them in terms of their readiness, interest(s), and *Sustainable Learning Profiles* (RTF 4); setting up the conditions for positive learning environments and teacher-student relationships; and using a combination of differentiated, culturally responsive, collaborative, explicit, and cooperative group teaching approaches to teach curriculum intended-learning outcomes and ATRiUM capabilities (RTF 5); assessing learning (RTF 6); and providing supportive feedback (RTF 7). *Responsive Teaching for Sustainable Learning* also focuses on evaluation (RTF 8), specifically: How well were all four types of evidence gathered and used in teaching, and how well were changes of intensity in teaching, flexible groupings, and *Layers of Responsive Teaching* used?

 How well did my professional and cultural skills and knowledge support responsive teaching?

Responsive Teaching for Sustainable Learning stresses the importance of what teachers bring to their teaching (RTF 2). Who we are as teachers is fundamental within the *Responsive Teaching Framework* and distinct from decisions made about the learning environment, teaching approaches, and teaching for ATRiUM capabilities.

How well did I understand the students as learners?

Knowing students as learners is fundamental to responsive teaching and prevents responding to assumptions rather than to the real needs of learners. Understanding interest(s), readiness, and *Sustainable Learning Profiles* (RTF 3), defining intended learning outcomes (RTF 4), assessing learning (RTF 3 & 6), and considering feedback are all part of the process that needs to be reflected upon and evaluated.

How well did I construct Sustainable Learning Profiles and define intended learning outcomes?

Readiness for learning and the development of ATRiUM capabilities are considered when reflecting on RTF 4, as shown in the following examples. Example 1: Increased teacher immediacy and selective groupings for cooperative activities aimed to increase Anders' low level of engagement with his teacher and peers, and the associated fixed mindset revealed in his ecological map (Figure 8.6). Some recent observations have revealed that Anders is now interacting and seeking help from both his friends, and from two other students. He has also approached the teacher more than once a day to ask for clarification and to check he is on the right track with tasks. Anders' teacher makes sure he gets immediate responses and encouragement on every occasion this happens. Other adults have been also asked to ensure this happens. He has not yet approached others. The conclusion from this information is that the strategies have been effective and should continue, with increased involvement of more students.

Example 2: Bela's *Sustainable Learning Profile* (Table 8.1) identified her reluctance to write and indicated a need to investigate writing skills development and to incorporate scribes for written learning tasks. Assessment of Bela's literacy skills development revealed that Bela's oral language (receptive and expressive vocabulary) is more than age appropriate (she is 7). Bela's oral language capabilities have masked the difficulties in reading skills to date, but assessment has shown that these are not progressing as anticipated and will need systematic explicit and intensive teaching for a period. Bela is proving to be very self-aware and has responded well to conversations about her strengths and difficulties. Bela's family is supportive, and a joint school/home structured program of phonological and phonics skills has been established and is monitored by the class teacher. In the meantime, Bela has been taught how to use dictation software and to edit her writing on the screen. Support from the teacher, a teaching assistant and her peers is used flexibly to help Bela to practise relevant skills with immediate feedback where possible.

These examples show how careful understanding of students' learning needs and priorities for teaching can make a difference. Both students could easily have been overlooked or had their learning needs misinterpreted, and become used to being 'unsuccessful', year after year. It is not possible to overemphasise the effect of non-responsive educational settings. Anders' sense of control over his learning and his world would have become less and less, whereas Bela would possibly have become disruptive in her drive to belong socially as she struggled with specific aspects of learning. Reflection on these two individual students provide examples of how teachers knew their students and responded to their students' needs.

 *How well did I responsively differentiate and use a range of teaching approaches and learning opportunities to respond to my students' learning needs?*

Now we turn to the practices of responsive teaching that need to be reviewed and evaluated, with the view to determining how well practice supported teaching and learning, and what could be strengthened or changed in the future. Responsive teachers draw conclusions about what worked and what did not, in order to understand the context, processes, and outcomes for students. The relationships in the educational setting are the foundation on which teaching, and learning happen. In the two examples above, these relationships were considered.

Anders' ATRiUM capabilities (R) were targeted through the student-teacher and student-student relationships with immediacy (DART 2) emphasised, and by organising flexible groupings for success in those relationships. Bela's needs were related to using written language (iU) and required close assessment of her skills development, increased explicitness, and intensity of teaching and the use of resources within and outside the school. Bela's capabilities in oral language were being over-used as she avoided written language. Differentiation of assessment and subsequent teaching responded to Bela's specific learning needs. With close monitoring, it is anticipated that the need for intense and targeted instruction will diminish once Bela's skills decoding and encoding skills are firmly established.

Student voice in evaluation

It is important to incorporate student voices into teaching, and a perfect time to do this is when evaluating the effectiveness of instruction. Asking students what worked for their learning allows them to share their experiences, and supports self-awareness, thus reinforcing the development of ATRiUM capabilities (particularly A & M). In Figure 12.1, we draw on the questions that Lloyd et al. (2015) used with Australian Aboriginal students, blended with questions used in classroom-level consultation with students (Scarparolo & MacKinnon, 2022).

RTF 8: How did my teaching support my students' learning?   183

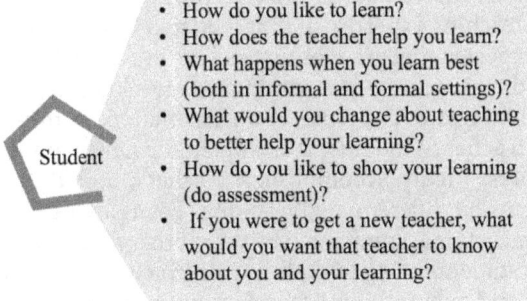

Figure 12.1 Questions for students evaluating their learning and teaching.
Derived from Lloyd et al., 2015 and Scarparolo & MacKinnon, 2022.

Student responses to these questions help teachers see teaching and learning from their students' perspectives. There are caveats around seeking student feedback on teaching, however. It is not helpful if students think they are being given the opportunity to criticise and judge their teachers. Students' contributions need to be focused on their own learning and how teaching best supports that learning. This conversation would be a continuation of the teacher-student relationship within which the aspects of teaching that supported learning are identified.

The last question in Figure 12.1 asks what students would like teachers to know about them, which leads to consideration of teachers' responsibility to get to know their students as learners. Knowing students as learners is a constant task, and at this time in the RTF cycle, responsive teachers revisit what they do know and alter that based on more recent evidence of learning and development.

The following sections contain a more fine-grained consideration of responsive teaching practices. Specifically, setting up conditions for positive learning environments and teacher-student relationships, and using a combination of differentiated, culturally responsive, collaborative, explicit, and cooperative group teaching approaches to teach curriculum intended-learning outcomes and ATRiUM capabilities (RTF 5), assessing learning (RTF 6), and providing supportive feedback (RTF 7). These are areas for focus in evaluation and include how well evidence was gathered and used in teaching, and how changes of intensity in teaching, flexible groupings, and *Layers of Responsive Teaching* were used (as needed) to support students.

Evaluating teaching approaches

Teaching approaches need to be evaluated by considering whether they were targeted well and implemented efficaciously (with appropriate competence, organisation, and leadership). In RTF 5, we focused on key teaching approaches, with differentiated teaching as the primary approach.

There are many frameworks that can assist in evaluating differentiated teaching practice. In Australia, the focus of the Professional Teaching

Standards on differentiated instruction (AITSL, 2011) is helpful. In a contemporary context, teaching expertise in differentiated instruction is deemed fundamental. It is expected that graduating teachers in Australia bring basic levels of expertise to their teaching and continue to develop this throughout their careers. The four stages of expertise in differentiation, as they are defined in the Australian Teacher Standards, are explicit: for newly graduated teachers; proficient teachers; highly accomplished teachers; and those who lead in schools. This focus on differentiated teaching (Focus area 1.5) in the Australian Teacher Standards is accompanied by three other focus areas that explicitly emphasise what students bring to their learning including their linguistic, cultural, religious, and socioeconomic backgrounds (Focus area 1.3), whether they belong to Aboriginal or Torres Strait Island cultures (Focus area 1.4), and their disabilities (Focus area 1.6). These emphases highlight major areas of diversity that can create barriers to learning at institutional and systemic levels.

Despite the expectation, as described in the Australian Teacher Standards, that newly graduated teachers will have "knowledge and understanding of strategies for differentiating teaching to meet the specific learning needs of students across the full range of abilities" (AITSL, 2011, p. 11), they are not always ready to do this in their classrooms (Brevik, Gunnulfsen, & Renzulli, 2018; McCray & Hatton, 2011; Sands & Barker, 2004; Van Geel et al., 2019; Wertheim & Leyser, 2002). Differentiation as a pedagogical approach is now taught to prospective teachers and expected to be used in their teaching when they graduate and assessed in their final practicum experience through the Australian Teaching Performance Assessment (Buchanan, Harb, & Fitzgerald, 2020).

It is important to understand how teachers develop this domain of expertise and how best to support this professional development. To that end, research has been carried out to explore the learning continuum that underpins differentiation in teaching (see, for example, Dack, 2019; Tomlinson & Murphy, 2015; Tomlinson, 2017b; Wan, 2016). Dack's (2019) model for teaching has grown out of Tomlinson's work. It pairs conceptual understanding (a way of thinking) with classroom practices and strategies, emphasising the need for an iterative relationship between these as teachers develop their expertise. Dack's (2019) study which tracked the learning of 18 pre-service teachers has helped define the learning pathway for differentiated instruction. The coding for analysis of all the data collected during this process was based on Grossman, Smagorinsky, and Valencia's (1999) five levels of appropriation of a pedagogical tool. It focuses on both the conceptual (the way of thinking about differentiation) and the practical (the strategies that allow a teacher to apply that conceptual approach in practice).

To complement the differentiated instruction learning pathway defined by Dack (2019), Tomlinson (2017) further delineated teacher growth within elements of differentiated instruction (e.g., learning environment, curriculum, assessment, instruction, leadership, and management). Tomlinson has also defined this in terms of what teachers need to know, understand, and be able to do (KUD; Tomlinson, 2017b) which can be separated into the conceptual understanding of differentiated instruction and the processes of responsively teaching using differentiation. Therefore, it is possible to synthesise key elements of how to teach for all the students through responsive differentiation. Of course, expertise in using a range of strategies in a flexible and responsive way does not always accompany conceptual understanding. Instead, practical expertise continues to develop as teachers work out how best to use strategies, separately and together, in their own contexts, and evaluate the effectiveness of those strategies on their students' learning.

Other teaching approaches

Differentiated teaching draws on a range of other teaching approaches (RTF 5). Teachers' selection of the approaches aimed to teach specific aspects of curriculum and ATRiUM capabilities requires evidence-based instructional decision-making. Being clear about what was taught (the intended purpose of the teaching) assists in the evaluation of these approaches. For example, explicit teaching is best used when specific content or processes are to be learnt. If there are approximations or errors in students' performance or recall of information, it may be that this points to a need for more explicit teaching in future. Each of the following reflective questions can incorporate consideration of whether the approach met students' learning needs and in what ways the implementation of it was competent, organised, and well-led. Chapter 6 contains more prompts relevant to this evaluation.

- How well did I incorporate culturally responsive teaching?
- How well did I collaborate with others in teaching?
- How well did I use explicit teaching?
- How well did I use cooperative group teaching?

Evaluating layers of responsive teaching

When considering the position of teaching within *Layers of Responsive Teaching*, it is important for teachers to reflect on how well they accessed and worked with other teachers and professionals, and whether they have been able to access the appropriate level of intensity and targeted teaching for all students. Bela's need for intensive literacy teaching or intervention is a case in point. There are several ways to access the intensive, targeted teaching she needs in literacy. First, there may be other students in the class who would also benefit from some intensive targeted teaching of phonological awareness and phonics. Administering a screener assessment may identify a small group of students who could be provided with targeted teaching for a brief time, thus giving Bela access to the instruction she needs while supporting the establishment of skills for others.

Secondly, whole class or small group activities can be adapted to include an emphasis on phonological awareness and phoneme manipulation in games, so that there is an opportunity for Bela to practise her developing skills. Thirdly, it may be appropriate to seek the involvement of a specialist literacy teacher for a time to team-teach so that explicit teaching is more accessible for Bela (and any other students) within daily literacy lessons. Alternately, Bela's teacher could refer her for support from an in-school intervention program. The decision depends on what resourcing is available and the processes for eligibility and access. Fourthly, it may be possible to devise an individual program and seek parental assistance with skill development and practice at home each day. Regular consultation with family members could occur through a communication book or a monitoring log so that Bela can track her new learning both at home and at school. This list of possibilities is not exhaustive. The options depend on the educational setting, flexibility in the classroom, the availability of other teachers or intervention programs, and the resources of the family. However, this illustrates possibilities from Layer 1 and 2 of responsive teaching for providing short-term intensive and targeted teaching.

How well did I assess student learning, and use that information to support responsive teaching?

How well did I incorporate feedback to support learning?

As with the other steps of the *Responsive Teaching Framework*, reflection on Step 6 and Step 7 lead to in-depth consideration of the use of assessment information in making instructional decisions and the effectiveness of the feedback provided during teaching in improving learning.

Professional learning for responsive teaching

The questions that frame the *Responsive Teaching Framework* support the process of reflective practice and *Sustainable Learning*. A natural consequence of asking these reflective questions is that it affirms what teachers do well and identifies areas of development and growth that they can focus on in professional learning. Responsive teachers are always seeking new knowledge, building on their skills, questioning assumptions, and critically reflecting on their decision making.

Sustainable learners use ATRiUM capabilities to continue to learn throughout life. They also seek to connect with other professionals and resources when they want to further develop professional or cultural competences. RTF 2 and RTF 8 are specifically about teacher professional knowledge, skills, and professional development. When reflecting on the effectiveness of our teaching in RTF 8, teachers can re-visit considerations from RTF 2 and reconsider them. This is particularly relevant to teaching skills and knowledge; cultural competence; and assumptions held about learning, disabilities, giftedness, behaviour, and learning difficulties.

There are other frameworks that provide structure to support continued development of professional expertise and competence. These are related to the context of teaching – inclusive school contexts as well as to specific teaching expertise. For example, the Inclusion Index (Booth & Ainscow, 2002) focuses on whole school inclusion, while the Teacher Efficacy for Inclusive Practices Scale (Sharma, Loreman, & Forlin, 2011) is more about individual teacher practice, as is the Differentiated Instruction Scale (Roy, Guay, & Valois, 2013). Tomlinson's Teacher Growth in Differentiated Instruction (2017b) focuses on teachers' use of approaches to differentiated instruction. Likewise, ten essential skills for inclusion (Graham, Berman, & Bellert, 2015) delineates important routines and mindsets of inclusive teachers.

In summary, responsive teachers reflect on the effectiveness of their instruction. The eight steps of the *Responsive Teaching Framework* cue reflection throughout the teaching-learning cycle. Effective reflection leads to improvements which can be considered and implemented during the next cycle of the *Responsive Teaching Framework*.

Part III

Leadership for responsive teaching and sustainable learning

Introduction

Educational settings and the leaders in those educational settings can support the underpinning tenets of *Sustainable Learning – learning for all, learning that lasts*, and *teaching that matters*. Although many of the issues that determine the effectiveness of inclusion at school are embedded in classrooms and teaching, teachers do not teach on their own. While there is no doubt that individual teachers are the foundation of effective inclusion, their work is unarguably influenced and, ideally, strengthened and sustained by groups of colleagues and leaders within schools and systems. Leaders of inclusive education not only develop and lead responsive teachers in their schools, but they are also well-positioned to identify and engage with other layers of influence that sway inclusive culture, policies, and practice. They can also buffer educators from some of the contextual factors at play, so that teachers can focus on their prime responsibility – to teach responsively.

In Part III, we focus specifically on the role of educational leaders in developing and enabling teaching that makes a difference for all students. There are key principles that are enacted within a cycle of reflective practice in Responsive Leadership, and which aligns with and supports Responsive Teaching for Sustainable Learning.

13 Leadership principles

This section elaborates on what it is that leaders do to transform and maintain innovative educational communities within which responsive teaching can be practised. It is about active, distributed, and sustainable leadership that is grounded in ethical and inclusive values (*learning for all*). Leadership for RT4SL teaches for ATRiUM capabilities (*learning that lasts*) and uses evidence and reflective practice to support decisions and actions (Mitchell, 2017).

The evolution of educational leadership has included emphasis on transformative leadership since the 1970s, educational management (1980s), and distributed or distributive leadership and leading learning communities since the 1990s (Dinham, 2016). More recently, positive leadership has emphasised the need for trust, critical self-reflection, empowerment, and distributed leadership (Banwo, Khalifa, & Louis, 2021). Additionally, sustainability in leadership has become increasingly prominent (Hargreaves & Fink, 2006).

Since the first book about *Sustainable Learning* was published (Graham, Berman, & Bellert, 2015), there has also been an increased focus on ecological approaches to inclusive education (European Agency for Special and Inclusive Education, 2017) and leadership responsibilities (Óskarsdóttir et al., 2020). Leadership in education is affected by international, national, community, educational setting, and individual influences that are not mutually exclusive, and combinations are evident. For example, a blend of transformational, distributed, and instructional leadership set within an ecological context is evident in a recent European model of inclusive leadership which includes responsibilities for setting direction, human development, and organisational development (Óskarsdóttir et al., 2020).

In another example, a qualitative case study in an inclusive school in Peru, demonstrated that successful inclusive school leadership was the result of distributed and transformational leadership which used the setting of vision and goals to promote inclusive values within the school. This model of leadership also ensured that working with the school community to improve school climate for inclusion was a priority, alongside monitoring learning to provide evidence of teacher effectiveness, and developing professional learning communities to embed inclusive teaching strategies (Valdivieso, 2020). A key aspect of this successful example was partnering with families and using the information gathered from them about their children to inform teaching.

We draw on all these perspectives to define leadership in the context of *Responsive Teaching for Sustainable Learning* as:

DOI: 10.4324/9781003299813-16

- based on inclusive and ethical principles
- aimed at ensuring quality teaching and successful learning (RT4SL)
- founded on shared responsibility
- responsively transformative
- sustainable.

In the next sections, consideration of these principles draws on many models of educational leadership.

Inclusive and ethical leadership

Leadership for *Responsive Teaching and Sustainable Learning* is about inclusive cultures and pedagogy, with responsibility for all students, *learning for all*, being central (European Agency, 2019 cited in Óskarsdóttir et al., 2020, p. 531). With the presence, participation, and achievement of all students deliberately supported by evidence informed policies and practices, leadership needs to be based on clear and widely understood definitions of what the terms inclusion and equity mean (Ainscow, 2020). The establishment of inclusive values (Booth & Ainscow, 2002; Valdivieso, 2020) involves developing a community philosophy of inclusion such that all students are equally valued, there are high expectations for all students, staff, and students treat one another as human beings as well as occupants of a 'role', staff seek to remove barriers to learning and participation in all aspects of the school, and the school strives to minimise discriminatory practices (Booth & Ainscow, 2002).

The *Responsive Teaching* practices contained within Part II of this book are grounded in notions of inclusion and equity. The aim is for all students to access the teaching and resourcing that they need to be successful learners. Inclusive practice rejects the traditional practice of sorting or classifying students (Mitchell, 2018) and instead endeavours to set the conditions so that teachers know each student as a learner and teaching is responsive and differentiated. The basis of differentiated instruction is that students are provided with learning opportunities and teaching strategies that meet their needs. Using multi-tiered or layered approaches to academic, social, emotional, and behavioural learning (Corwin Visible Learning Plus, 2021; Mitchell, 2018) allows schools to be supportive of the development of all ATRiUM capabilities, complete with appropriate explicit teaching, acknowledgement, and feedback (RTF 5). An emphasis on prevention of problems in learning and development, and early intervention, inherent in *Layers of Responsive Teaching*, is important for school culture and climate (Mitchell, 2018). In this way, all students have the opportunity to learn and to practise skills that equip them to be active in their relationships with teachers, and thus in their learning, and to be integral members of educational settings.

Inclusive and supportive cultures underpin all the actions of teachers and learners and are important in shaping educational settings within communities, since inclusion is a community matter (Mitchell, 2018) and all students need to belong to the educational community, and to be valued (Westwood, 2018). A valuing of diversity underpins inclusive education. Over the past two decades, work on what inclusive schools look like and feel like has used the UK-developed Index for Inclusion (Booth & Ainscow, 2002).

The Index for Inclusion is a structured blueprint for inclusive school development and is available in more than 30 versions used around the world (CSIE, 2023). The Index has indicators for school communities to use in reviewing and then focusing development on the creation of inclusive cultures (Booth & Ainscow, 2002; Booth, 2011). Inclusive cultures provide the foundation for inclusion and policies and practices (Booth & Ainscow, 2002). Inclusive leadership for responsive teaching is not only about making sure students who have disabilities or learning difficulties are taught well but is also vitally concerned with cultural inclusion. Inclusive education has an ethic of care at its base (Gay, 2018) which is described as "care for others and for being among others" (Hargreaves & Fink, 2006, p. 18). Building community based on inclusive values involves a culture within which everyone is made to feel welcome and wants to help each other. In such a culture, collaborative relationships are built on trust and local communities are involved in the school (Booth & Ainscow, 2002; European Agency, 2019 cited in Óskarsdóttir et al., 2020).

Leadership based on principles of Indigenous education is a slowly developing field of study (Fan & Liu, 2020). High-expectation relationships are foundational to this approach, however, as they are to inclusive, equitable, and culturally responsive teaching and leadership (Sarra et al., 2020). A commitment to students' needs and citizenship (Ballangrud & Aas, 2022) as well as fair decision-making (Webster & Litchka, 2020) means that leadership based on principles of Indigenous education is ethical and socially just (Gümüş, Arar, & Oplatka, 2021). For education to be ethical it must as a minimum do no harm (Hargreaves & Fink, 2006). Other ethical issues arise for educational leadership in relation to ensuring equity of teaching and resources. When system requirements for accountability conflict with educational visions, there are considerable ethical dilemmas (DeMatthews & Serafini, 2021).

It is vital that leadership uses reason and evidence to determine educational policies and practices (Ainscow, 2020; Mitchell, 2018), and within *Responsive Teaching for Sustainable Learning* this means drawing on research evidence, evidence from professional practice, evidence from families and students, and evidence generated within instruction and intervention (Chapter 3). Using practices that have doubts about their efficacy or do not have evidence of efficacy, despite appropriate research investigation, is unethical. However, not all strategies or approaches come with evidence, and it may be that research studies are yet to be done to determine their efficacy. That is why less formal evidence for responsive teaching, including the evidence from professional practice, from families and students, and the evidence from within teaching, is relied upon, and may become the basis for action research and realistic evaluation within practice, or larger research investigations which can more validly establish effectiveness. Research evidence is about groups of learners, and that is not always aligned with what happens for individuals. Therefore, the most important evidence is that which tells teachers how well each student is learning; it is about what works and how well it works. Scientific research helps provide direction, but the real issue is about effectiveness of teaching for individual learners.

Equity of resourcing is a responsibility of leadership, extending from governments who fund education systems and the education systems who distribute the resources to educational settings to the school level and school leaders. A basic leadership responsibility is to make sure that adequate physical environments are provided within which teaching and learning can take place (Mitchell, 2018). In Australia there is enormous variation in physical environments in schools, and this inequity stems from a complicated basis of national, state, and private funding (Thompson, Hogan, & Rahimi, 2019).

Inequity in education in Australia is evident in the outcomes of disadvantaged students in comparison to other parts of the world. For example, the opportunity to attend advantaged schools in Australia can result in gains to learning outcomes of up to three-years compared to no difference in Finland, Norway, and Poland (OECD, 2012). This indicates that the quality of education across schools in Australia is not equal, and inequities based on socioeconomic resources have become entrenched across generations. *Leadership for Sustainable Learning* must include accessing and advocating for more equitable allocation of resources, as well as making sure that material and human resources are not depleted (Hargreaves & Fink, 2006). Such ethical leadership is seen to be associated with effective leadership more generally (Webster & Litchka, 2020).

The nature of inclusive leadership, based in an ethic of care and valuing of diversity, fosters the responsive and innovative teaching of all students, and continued collaboration and engagement with all members of the school community. This was tested during the Covid-19 pandemic and affirmed the valuable work of schools and teachers (Fournier, Scott, & Scott, 2020). Teachers had to be innovative and use alternative ways of connecting and communicating with students and families during the pandemic. At the heart of inclusive and ethical leadership is the affirmation of *learning for all, learning that lasts*, and *teaching that matters. Responsive Teaching for Sustainable Learning* is anchored in inclusive and ethical values and the belief that education is a major vehicle for reducing inequity and supporting societal change and development.

Leading responsive teaching and sustainable learning

Leadership for teaching and learning, or instructional leadership has a specific focus on core activity within educational settings, that is, the teaching and learning (Dinham, 2016). Such focused leadership has had two waves, initially from the 1970s and subsequently reinvigorated in 2000 (Dinham, 2007). This emphasis on learning is about the *teaching that matters*, that is, responsive teaching. It is explicit about the conditions for successful learning, including positive learning environments, the relationships within which teaching, and learning are negotiated, collaborative and reflective practice, innovation, evaluation, and negotiating layers of influence. The emphasis on learning is evident in the OECD delineation of learning leadership in the 21st century (OECD, 2013) wherein:

- Learning leadership is critical for reform and innovation – it focuses on creating and sustaining environments that are conducive to good learning

- Learning leadership is about engaging in the design, implementation, and sustainability of powerful innovative learning environments – it emphasises setting direction and taking responsibility for making learning happen through distributed, connected activity, and relationships
- Learning leadership puts creating the conditions for 21st century learning and teaching at the core of leadership practice – it fosters continuous learning of all
- Learning leadership demonstrates creativity and often courage – it focuses on deep changes to practice, structures, and cultures, and ensures supporting conditions are in place
- Learning leadership models and nurtures 21st century professionalism – it nurtures professional learning, inquiry, and self-evaluation, blends theory and practice, provides opportunities for experimentation, and encourages learning from those experiences and through feedback
- Learning leadership is social and connected – it is grounded in carefully crafted collaborative activity that deepens to spread and maintain learning, including professional learning communities and networks
- Learning leadership can come from non-formal partners
- Transformative learning leadership is multi-level
- Learning leadership is needed at the system level (OECD, 2013, pp. 53–54)

The Australian Institute for Teaching and School Leadership (AITSL) has made a distinction between teaching practice and standards, and the leadership expected to support teaching (Principal Standard) which is specifically for appointed principals of schools. This separation of responsibility meets the needs of the education system. A strong emphasis in the Principal Standard is that leaders are themselves sustainable learners; they are expected to constantly build their capabilities as they engage in a cycle of leadership practice. The cycle of leadership practice – reflection on practice, and responsiveness to feedback (AITSL, 2017b) – aligns with the *Responsive Teaching Framework*. As well, the focus on capabilities aligns with RT4SL and the ATRiUM capabilities of learners. Additionally, the focus on teaching and learning, professional development, school change, and engaging and working with community provides an ecological perspective on leadership (AITSL, 2011).

Further articulation of these dimensions is contained in the resources for school principals so that these dimensions can be the focus of reflective practice. Principals can ask what they bring to this leadership responsibility.

We note that in the past few years, the Covid-19 pandemic has added more complexity to all education-related roles. Subsequently, recent discussions have emphasised the need for leaders to be adaptive, draw on their capabilities in multiple domains of responsibility, and respond to the changing needs of their communities (Gurr & Drysdale, 2020). Understanding the context, developing the organisation, setting direction, developing people, influencing, improving teaching and learning, and leading self are all facets of leadership supported by capabilities (p. 27).

Within the context of *Sustainable Learning*, we can also consider models of leadership which have been created specifically to develop inclusiveness in educational settings. As already mentioned, a prominent model is the Index for Inclusion which offers a set of indicators that describe how an educational setting can improve its practices (Booth, 2011). These practices support the engagement of all students in learning. They are based on high expectations and authentic opportunities for full participation in school life. A focus on practices of teaching for learning is accompanied by consideration of inclusive culture and policies. These work together to establish and maintain conditions for effective teaching and *learning for all*.

Leadership principles derived from special and inclusive education have an emphasis on schoolwide culture, policies and practices that link to family and community resources, collaborative teaching, built-in time for planning and evaluation, and the use of assessment to support teaching decisions (Westwood, 2018). This model highlights key aspects of inclusive educational settings – the development of individual learning profiles, differentiated and individually responsive teaching strategies, and collaboration with allied health professionals to provide a multi-tiered or layered system of responsive teaching. A spotlight on leadership for differentiation has a focus on classroom and schoolwide systems and cultures that produce learning success and quality teaching (Tomlinson & Allan, 2000).

Responsively transformative leadership

Leadership for *Responsive Teaching and Sustainable Learning* needs to be responsively transformative – to become conscious of and to work towards responsive and sustainable cultures and practices. Since education has considerable power to make a difference for individuals and for society, leadership needs to build on the strengths of educational settings and further their development taking into account cultural and community contexts and drawing on available resources. The literature on inclusive education underlines the crucial role of leadership in fostering innovation and promoting inclusive change (Ainscow & Sandill, 2010; Mac Ruairc, Ottessen, & Precey, 2013; Watt, Donnelly, & Kefallinou, 2019). In addition, the Australian Institute for Teaching and School Leadership specifies that leading improvement, innovation, and change is one of the five core professional practices of school leaders (AITSL, 2017b).

With inclusive and ethical practice at the heart of leadership for responsive teaching, the aim is for an educational setting to use inclusive, ethical, and evidence-based practices to remove barriers and discrimination (Booth & Ainscow, 2002). We advocate that education settings need to apply "persistent identification of oppressive structures and practices that are normal and therefore invisible" so they can be changed (Banwo, Khalifa, & Louis, 2021, p. 45).

Transformative leadership also ensures that responsiveness is fundamental to teaching practice, and all students can access learning that meets their needs. A primary directive of this approach is that teaching and learning are constantly monitored and evaluated so that all instruction is informed by evidence. This includes planning for screening, assessment, and the monitoring of learning and the allocation of time to interpret assessment information so that teaching is informed, both by evidence of student learning and by data related to the effectiveness of teaching.

If we accept that inclusive and ethical education is based in social justice, then leadership needs to understand how equity is supported through practice. As Shields (2010) has noted, "Transformative leadership, therefore, inextricably links education and educational leadership with the wider social context within which it is embedded" (p. 588). This means that "any genuine efforts towards transformation for inclusion necessarily require actively working towards a culture of inclusion within and beyond education settings and systems, including directly working to identify and disestablish ableism in all forms and at all levels" (Cologon, 2019, p. 43).

Transformative leadership, therefore, links to both educational and broader social change and perceives schools as an instrument for reducing social inequalities. Educational settings are often the centre of communities and can influence the opening of opportunities and possibilities for individuals and their families. When schools are an integral part of communities learning extends to teachers and families which can increase the community's capacity to support all students and possibilities for their futures.

A particular focus for transformative leadership in inclusive educational settings is on youth from minority groups. For these students, it is necessary to promote culturally responsive teaching and establish culturally responsive relationships with families (Banwo, Khalifa, & Louis, 2021). Leadership also involves persistent identification and removal of oppressive structures and practices that function as barriers for learners or their families (Banwo, Khalifa, & Louis, 2021). The components of leadership and teaching within this context align with the processes of the *Responsive Teaching Framework*. As teachers become conscious of their assumptions about culture, race, learning, learning difficulties, and behaviours (RTF 2) and deliberately seek to know their students as learners and what they bring culturally and in terms of educational and life experiences (RTF 3), so must leaders. Leadership is, therefore, charged with the responsibility of transforming educational settings and their communities into culturally responsive contexts and supporting teachers to be culturally competent and responsive in their teaching. Some teachers will be more culturally responsive than others, and leadership will need to monitor and intervene to transformatively support the development of all teachers (Khalifa, Gooden, & Davis, 2016). A particular role within some contexts will be to "affirm and protect indigenous student identities" and proactively confront issues for these students as learners. It is also important to include Indigenous contexts, languages, and protocols in the content, culture, and climate of the educational setting (Khalifa, Gooden, & Davis, 2016, p. 33).

A more direct challenge for education systems is the fact that they are a perpetuation of colonial systems in many countries and this specific context creates generational barriers for learners. In this situation is it vital for leadership to examine the presence, or perceived presence, of continued colonialism in school practices and work towards positive changes (Table 13.1).

The aim of this emphasis in leadership, which is drawn from many contexts around the world, is to empower the community through affirming Indigenous knowledges, accessing and responding to their voices, providing opportunities for self-determination, acknowledging, and including Indigenous cultural practices and languages, and understanding and engaging with the

Table 13.1 Decolonising school leadership

Strand	
Strand 1 Prioritising self-knowledge and self-reflection	• Recognise integrity of Indigenous knowledge systems • Integrate Indigenous ways of knowing/learning through experience • Create culturally responsive professional development opportunities for teachers • Develop curriculum, and pedagogy influenced by Indigenous knowledge systems • Promote the co-constriction of knowledge with students, teachers, and communities
Strand 2 Enacting self-determination for community empowerment	• Recognise inherent growth tendencies and psychological needs that are the basis of Indigenous self-motivation and personal well-being • Engage in tasks that are of value to the individual and community • Resist dominant narrative to promote autonomy • Support teacher-student co-construction of knowledge • Have a critical indigenous consciousness
Strand 3 Committing to community voices and values	• Able to leverage community resources and support children's academic success • View student diversity as an asset • Engage with students and families in culturally appropriate ways • Play an important role in local communities • Advocate for students and school community • Draw on community's shared cultural experience of historical exclusion to help build community consensus • Commit to indigenous ideals in spite of external pressure • Promote social justice and equity • Learn/draw from expertise of parents, grandparents, and community members • Value relationships, family, and community over self or individual • Form partnership between school and community members/organisations • Embody commitment to community
Strand 4 Serving through altruism and spirituality	• Embrace students' spirituality • Embody a sense of altruism and service-based leadership • Serve by example
Strand 5 Prioritising collectivism in communication	• Value family, relationships, and interpersonal harmony in communications • Support collective decision making and consensus • Engage in mutual dialogue with students • Integrate learning through storytelling

Khalifa et al., 2019, pp. 19–20.

collectivism of communities (Khalifa et al., 2019). Much of this model aligns with *Responsive Teaching for Sustainable Learning*, which also has an explicit focus on the context of colonised Indigenous peoples and what they bring to educational systems and settings.

Responsive Teaching for Sustainable Learning is embedded within a complex ecology, and so too is its associated leadership framework. The implications of this are that leadership can have influence and exercise power not only at the school level, to improve teaching and learning, but also into outer layers of the ecology. Two models of leadership help us to understand the implications of nested layers of influence and the bidirectionality of influence within responsively transformative leadership. Mitchell (2018) and the European Agency (2019) both use an ecological framework. These kinds of models acknowledge that some changes can be made within educational settings, but that many other types of changes need to affect other layers of influence; however, it is possible for actions in educational settings to influence change more widely.

Distributed or shared leadership

Leadership is traditionally a sole endeavour; however, distributed or shared leadership is a closer fit for inclusive educational settings. Distributed leadership has more than one leader, and responsibilities and activities are distributed or shared (Fitzsimons, James, & Denyer, 2011). The leadership responsibilities are shared either by allocating distinct and separate tasks and activities to different people, or by having a collaborative or collective structure for leadership, within which a group of people make joint decisions (Dinham, 2016). Distributed or shared leadership has become common in educational settings allowing the operation of two principles important to inclusive leadership: (1) that "there should be an emphasis on whole-school approaches, in which teachers are supported in developing inclusive practices"; and (2) "policies should draw on the experience and expertise of everybody who has an involvement in the lives of children, including families and the children themselves" (Ainscow, 2020, p. 130). Shared leadership also contributes to building community, with priority given to collaboration of staff and positive relationships between staff and students, families, and community (Booth & Ainscow, 2002). Leaders at "classroom, school and district levels have key roles to play and teams of leaders will have more influence on teaching and learning" that observed with other models (Tomlinson & Allan, 2000, p. 136).

The notion of professional learning communities (Hord, 1997) is also pertinent in this context, whereby an educational setting collectively takes action to increase the learning of students through continuous inquiry and improvement, using supportive, shared power, authority, and decision making. Within such professional learning communities, teachers take on roles of leadership. In addition to the formal positions of leadership, teachers are leaders when they function in professional communities to affect student learning, contribute to school improvement, inspire excellence in practice, and empower stakeholders to participate in educational improvement (Childs-Bowen, Moller, & Scrivner, 2000). In this way, the success of leadership and influence depends on teachers' competence in classrooms, credibility with peers, approachability and adeptness in interpersonal skills, and membership of a context that celebrates teacher expertise and innovation (Childs-Bowen, Moller, & Scrivner, 2000).

Such a view of teacher leadership involves leading among colleagues with a focus on instructional practice, as well as working at the organisational level to align personnel, financial, and material resources to improve teaching and learning (York-Barr & Duke, 2004). Fundamentally, every teacher is a leader in their teaching, through their collaboration, and by diligently attending to their responsibilities (Dinham, 2016). As Hargreaves and Fink (2006) note, leadership spread across people is more likely to last.

Sustainable leadership

The final emphasis for leadership for RT4SL is that it is lasts, in other words, that it is sustainable. Seven principles for sustainable leadership were posited by Hargreaves and Fink (2006):

1. Sustainable leadership matters: leadership for learning; caring for others and being among others
2. Sustainable leadership lasts: leadership across and beyond individual leaders over time
3. Sustainable leadership spreads: it is distributed
4. Sustainable leadership does no harm and actively improves the surrounding environment: it is socially just
5. Sustainable leadership promotes cohesive diversity: it fosters and learns from diversity in teaching and learning and moves things forward by creating cohesion and networking among its richly varied components
6. Sustainable leadership develops and does not deplete material and human resources
7. Sustainable leadership honours and learns from the best of the past to create an even better future: leadership revisits and revives organisational memories, and the wisdom of memory bearers to learn from, preserve and then move beyond the best of the past (Hargreaves & Fink, 2006, pp. 18–20)

These principles of sustainability reinforce the other emphases we have highlighted – a focus on teaching and learning that is culturally responsive, inclusive, ethical, responsively transformative, and distributed. These emphases and principles inform practice that supports sustainability, particularly the development and implementation of policies that achieve improvements in the way schools respond to student diversity (Booth & Ainscow, 2002).

14 The responsive leadership framework

Leadership for responsive teaching and *Sustainable Learning* emphasises a core inclusive and ethical focus on teaching and learning, and a responsibility for responsively transforming educational settings using distributed leadership with a view to sustainability. Using the structure of the *Responsive Teaching Framework*, and with a nod to the AITSL reflective practice cycle, we have adapted our approach to responsive teaching practice to encompass a leadership perspective. By unpacking the same focus areas as within the RTF, leaders who use the *Responsive Leadership* Framework (RLF) are reminded of the central work of *Responsive Teaching for Sustainable Learning*. This framework encourages leaders to construct a connected understanding of what is involved in teaching and learning that acknowledges the vital complexity they are leading. Both the RTF and RLF are shown together in Figure 14.1.

In this figure we have retained the RTF questions as they articulate the core of RT4SL. In addition, we have generated leadership-focused questions to align with what it is that responsive educators do. Similar language and the same broad focus for each step of the *Responsive Leadership Framework* (RLF) allows shared understandings of what responsive teachers and responsive leaders do.

The RLF is inclusive of leadership that may or may not be attached to official positions. Our take on leadership is that it is not only that which is inherent in formal positions and explicit in leadership or executive role statements. At times, teachers take on leadership responsibilities so that groups of teachers and learners can be organised and focus on the core activities of teaching and learning. The reflective questions can be adapted to suit the contexts of formally appointed leaders or teachers who are assuming leadership responsibilities in their own classrooms. To complete this book, we briefly consider how each of the eight steps of responsive leadership can support *Responsive Teaching for Sustainable Learning*. These steps need to be considered in conjunction with the *Responsive Teaching Framework* which has been substantiated and described in detail in Chapters 5 to 12.

RLF 1. What frameworks need to be considered?

Responsive leaders mediate the influences of the larger social, structural, political, economic, and cultural environment for their education settings. They take on the expectations of these broader influences and navigate the

DOI: 10.4324/9781003299813-17

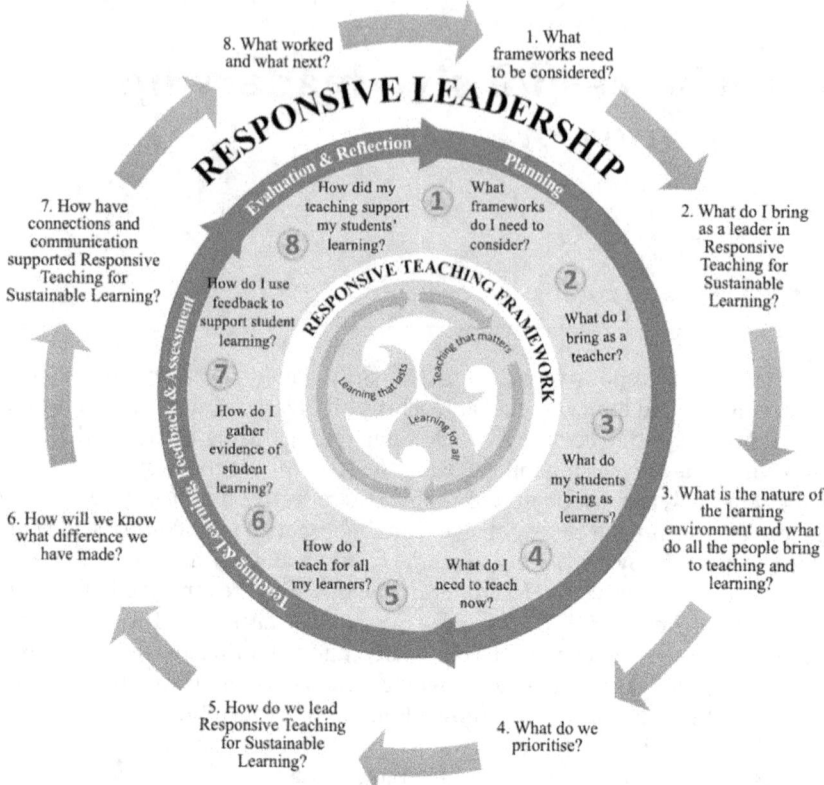

Figure 14.1 Responsive Leadership Framework.

inevitable tensions and differences in expectations. With full acknowledgement of the competing demands on educational leaders' decision making, the following sections of this chapter advocate that educational leaders give highest priority to sustainable learning and responsive teaching for all students in their communities.

In addition to the *Responsive Teaching Framework*, it is appropriate to consider the specific frameworks that influence the work of anyone with leadership responsibilities, starting with international frameworks that guide inclusive education. Universal and quality inclusive education is a long-standing global priority, and each educational setting, leader and teacher is responsible for contributing to the vision that every child in the world has access to education that meets their individual learning needs.

National legislation is also important for guiding educational leaders who need to ensure their educational settings are functioning within the laws of the land and are not discriminating against students or families. In Australia, the Disability Standards for Education and the Nationally Consistent Collection of Data are significant frameworks that influence educational leadership.

Similarly, for leaders in Australian educational settings, the Australian Professional Standard for Principals have defined the key emphases and practices which delineate the management and organisational responsibilities of school leaders.

In summary, this RLF 1 reminds us that there are expectations from the system and more widely, that influence how formal leadership is enacted (operationally, relationally, strategically, and systemically), and how it is reported on. Inclusion of the term 'management' also raises tension between educational vision and the administration of complex educational settings. We stress, however, that management is not the primary purpose of leadership, instead management needs to support the primary functions of settings, which are related to fostering *Responsive Teaching for Sustainable Learning*.

RLF 2. What do I bring as a leader in responsive teaching and sustainable learning?

Professional practice in leadership involves advanced skills and knowledge that can be unpacked in terms of the ATRiUM capabilities. The following sections offer a brief examination of the capabilities associated with responsive leadership: Active leadership; thinking; relating to others; using language, symbol systems, and ICT; and managing self.

Active leadership

Leaders for RT4SL have a vision, or way of seeing, or world view for education that is grounded in inclusive principles. It includes a belief that all students can learn, and that all students have the right to a quality education within their community which is resourced in such a way that teaching and learning are successful.

Leadership in educational settings also has an outward looking influence, whereby the strengths of the educational community influences strength building in the wider community. Leaders make ethical decisions, ensuring no one is harmed, and optimising the support for all students. Active leadership includes active learning. Sustainable learners constantly seek new knowledge and understandings and develop shared meanings with their colleagues.

Thinking

Knowledge and understanding are central to leadership. The scholarship of leadership is not a fixed body of knowledge but a constantly evolving set of understandings. A key responsibility of leadership is translating knowledge in such a way that it is accessible by all the people associated with the educational setting. This refers to not only understanding how students learn but also being able to interpret this understanding for teachers, teacher assistants, students themselves, and their families.

The reflective questions from the integrated model of thinking (Moseley et al., 2005) are helpful here in Figure 14.2:

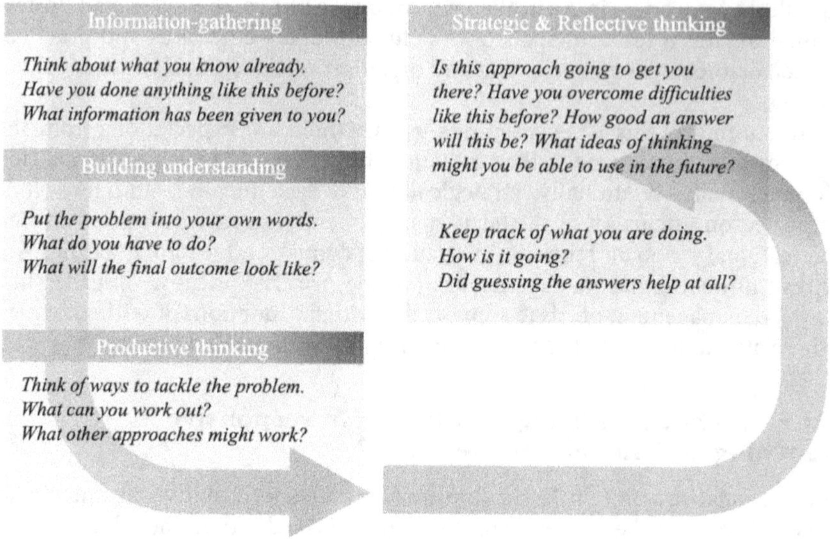

Information-gathering

Think about what you know already.
Have you done anything like this before?
What information has been given to you?

Building understanding

Put the problem into your own words.
What do you have to do?
What will the final outcome look like?

Productive thinking

Think of ways to tackle the problem.
What can you work out?
What other approaches might work?

Strategic & Reflective thinking

Is this approach going to get you there? Have you overcome difficulties like this before? How good an answer will this be? What ideas of thinking might you be able to use in the future?

Keep track of what you are doing.
How is it going?
Did guessing the answers help at all?

Figure 14.2 Reflective questions from the integrated model for understanding thinking. Moseley et al., 2005.

Relating to others

Relationships are central to effectiveness in leadership. Leaders are only as good as the team around them. The essence of social learning relationships, which we have advocated within responsive teaching, are applicable to leadership situations. The *Deliberate Actions of Responsive Teachers* (DARTs) can be reframed for leadership, with little change in their intent. The reflective questions for leaders constructed directly from the DARTs are:

1. How have I set and maintained expectations about the intention of the teaching and learning?
2. How have I established expectations of sharing that will be needed to reveal the unique differences between teachers and learners and make learning explicit or evident?
3. How have I defined goals for learning and processes for noticing growth and change through learning of students and teachers?
4. How have I explicitly tuned in to current competence, as well as providing challenge for developing competence for student and teachers?
5. How do I interpret and share the meaning?
6. How have I highlighted the relevance of learning for other times and in other situations?
7. How have I developed consciousness and self-regulation of thinking and behaviour in learning for myself, the teachers, and the students?

This kind of emphasis can also be extended to families and community members using another framework which assists with reflection on relationships within dialogic teaching (Alexander, 2018):

- Is the school a site of collective learning and enquiry?
- Do teachers and students (and families) listen to each other, share ideas, and consider alternative viewpoints?
- Do teachers and students (and families) feel able to express ideas freely, without risk of embarrassment over 'wrong' answers, and they help each other to reach common understandings?
- Do teachers and students (and families) build on their own and each other's contributions and chain them into coherent lines of thinking and understanding?
- Is classroom talk, though open and dialogic, structured with specific learning goals in view?

These focus areas for reflection are central to all teaching and learning and give direction about how leaders can strengthen these capabilities for themselves and for everyone else in their settings.

Using language, symbol systems, and ICT

High level communication skills are usually specified in position statements for leadership positions, and it is worth considering what this means for responsive leadership. Supporting relationships with people in the education system, with those in the educational setting, and in the school community requires a form of code shifting. Teachers are experts at code switching as they move between talking with their students and talking with professional colleagues. This complex use of the nuances of language is required at an even higher level in leadership. Constructing shared understandings and being able to receive conflicting information and take it into account are important skills for all leadership aspirants.

Managing self

Leaders should be experts at managing themselves, able to contribute to dealing with day-to-day issues without becoming emotionally debilitated or reactionary. Leaders need to accept that they are "responsible for how their actions shape their students' complex identities" (Banwo, Khalifa, & Louis, 2021, p. 324). Leaders need to acknowledge that their actions can have a profound effect on the futures of their students.

RLF 3. What is the nature of the educational setting?

In response to Step 3 of the *Responsive Leadership Framework*, we reiterate the importance of dynamic and wholistic learning environments, the agency of learners and their uniquely different individual learning needs (RTF 3), and the importance of the social nature of learning, which is influenced by connections with family and community, and what teachers bring to their teaching (RTF 2). All these important factors underpin the following questions:

- What do the students bring to their learning? What do their families bring to the community? What does the community bring to the education?

- What cultural contexts are relevant?
- What do the teachers bring to their teaching?
- What record of learning does the educational setting have? And what factors support effective teaching and successful learning? What barriers exist, what hinders the effectiveness of the teaching and learning.
- What data are available – what are measured and collected? What interpretation is made of that data? What is not assessed?
- What resources are available?
- What consultations, connections, distribution of leadership, and shared decision-making are operating?

RLF 4. What do we prioritise?

As educational settings are constantly changing, leadership strives to build on strengths and to increase capacity for *Responsive Teaching for Sustainable Learning*. Deciding what to focus on is pivotal to success. It is also important to consider the order of focus since imposing policy change without associated changes in vision, culture, and climate will result in conflict and disruption. Instead, for example, identification of essential questions or problems of practice can instigate a process of setting priorities (City, 2022). As with priority setting in responsive teaching, there is a need for collaboration and the development of shared understandings from which priorities arise. If transformative change is required, carefully phased planning, with built-in monitoring and collaborative decision-making will be necessary.

All the leadership models considered emphasise the need to start at a foundational level, with the consolidation of environments that provide the right conditions and culture for inclusive teaching (Booth & Ainscow, 2002; OECD, 2013) and *Sustainable Learning*. The four-phase model proposed by Day, Sammons, and Gorgen, (2020; i.e., foundational, developmental, enrichment, and renewal) reinforces the need for whole-school cultural change and positive behaviour support to improve teaching and learning. Initial efforts are made to establish foundational school-wide changes in teaching and learning, physical environments, and behaviour if these are not already sound. Then, the focus can change to achievement through consolidating good practice and using data to inform teaching. As a school transforms, a focus on the empowerment of students through personalised curriculum and of staff through distributed leadership can begin. The timing, selection, relevance, application, and continuity of strategies for change are determined collaboratively for best results (Day, Sammons, & Gorgen, 2020).

RLF 5. How do we lead responsive teaching for sustainable learning?

Responsive leaders, like responsive teachers, value a collective and enquiring approach to relating to each other (R) within educational settings (Alexander, 2018). This kind of leadership is exemplified by instructional rounds (City et al., 2009). Instructional rounds are about developing a network within which teachers dialogically enquire into their practice and develop shared understandings of what works (City, 2022). This is a process of strengthening teaching which is currently advocated by the Australian Institute for Teaching and School Leadership (AITSL, 2017c). Within this process there is a debrief response following identification of a problem of practice. The network or professional learning community observes, analyses the evidence gathered, and then asks:

- If you were a student in these classes today and you did everything the teacher asked you to do, what would you know and be able to do?

Answers to this kind of question guide responsive leaders to support all members of their school communities.

RLF 6. How will we know what difference we have made?

Responsive leaders will be informed by information gathered at earlier stages of the framework and use their command of all types of evidence to assess the impact of teaching on learning. They will also use data-based decision making to interpret the available assessment information and make plans to gather further data to answer subsequent priority questions.

RLF 7. How have connections and communication supported RT4SL?

When the vital importance of all members of the school community is acknowledged, connections and communication are the primary vehicles for all processes of leadership and change. Therefore, this reflective question asks leaders to consider how processes that foster connections and communication are established and maintained. How do these processes support leadership initiatives and change? How is the complexity of communication and consultation managed so messages are clear and there is ample opportunity for involvement?

RLF 8. What worked and what is next?

Three components of implementation science can inform responses to Step 8 of the *Responsive Leadership Framework*. These components are the competence of the people, organisation, and leadership. As we have emphasised in the previous step, people and communication are central to leadership and learning outcomes. This reflective question seeds further contemplation, such as: How did I make change within the leadership? What has been learned? Was the vision realised? To what extent, and in what ways? What needs to happen now to consolidate the strengths of the educational setting and to work towards continued change and the sustainability of inclusive practice?

In summary, leadership for RT4SL is anchored in the same ideals and vision as RT4SL. It is about *learning for all, learning that lasts*, and *teaching that matters*. Specifically, it is about *leading for all, is leadership that lasts* (is sustainable), and *leadership that matters* (makes a difference for students, families, communities, and our broader society). The actions of leaders within RT4SL are drawn from a range of leadership models that are complementary. The leadership cycle provides a scaffold for leaders to use as they reflect on their responsibilities, whether these responsibilities are a function of a formal role or negotiated as part of shared leadership. For teachers new to leadership, it is valuable to consider what others in leadership positions have done that made a difference, and what did not work. Importantly, responsively transformative leadership involves critical self-reflection within which leaders emphasise how developing students' sense of belonging requires establishing relationships based on humility and service (Banwo, Khalifa, & Louis, 2021).

Conclusion

This book contains frameworks which explain how teaching can respond to the learning needs of all students. It has drawn together a considerable evidence-base to explain how *Responsive Teaching for Sustainable Learning* can be put into practice. We started with the foundations of *Sustainable Learning*, our conceptualisation of inclusive education, which is *learning for all, teaching that matters*, and *learning that lasts*. These three themes are threaded throughout the book and act as signposts to guide our decisions about teaching and about leadership. The main ideas of *Responsive Teaching for Sustainable Learning*, including leadership considerations, are summarised in Figure 14.3.

Our emphasis is on people, those who are teachers, learners and their families, and leaders. These people and their relationships and interactions are central to everything involved in responsive teaching. It is our vision that all students will become sustainable learners, equipped with adaptable and flexible ATRiUM capabilities, so that they can learn throughout their lives. Responsive teachers and responsive leaders are expected to continually learn as they collaborate to establish and maintain innovative learning environments that are conducive to teaching and which can support the learning needs of all students.

The *Responsive Teaching Framework* and the *Responsive Leadership Framework* both include eight steps of reflective practice that are organised to support in the following ways: As teachers and leaders understand the influences on teaching and learning (RTF 1), they maintain awareness of what they bring to their own learning, and leadership teaching expertise (RTF 2 & 8). They focus on student learning and school outcomes (RTF 3 & 6), and respond by determining what and how to teach to their students and prioritise as leaders (RTF 4 & 5).

To end, we return to the voices of Australian Aboriginal parents who want teachers to believe in their children (Lewthwaite et al., 2017). Responsive teachers and leaders believe all students are learners and work towards understanding their learning needs so that teaching and school experiences can be as responsive and effective as possible.

The responsive leadership framework 209

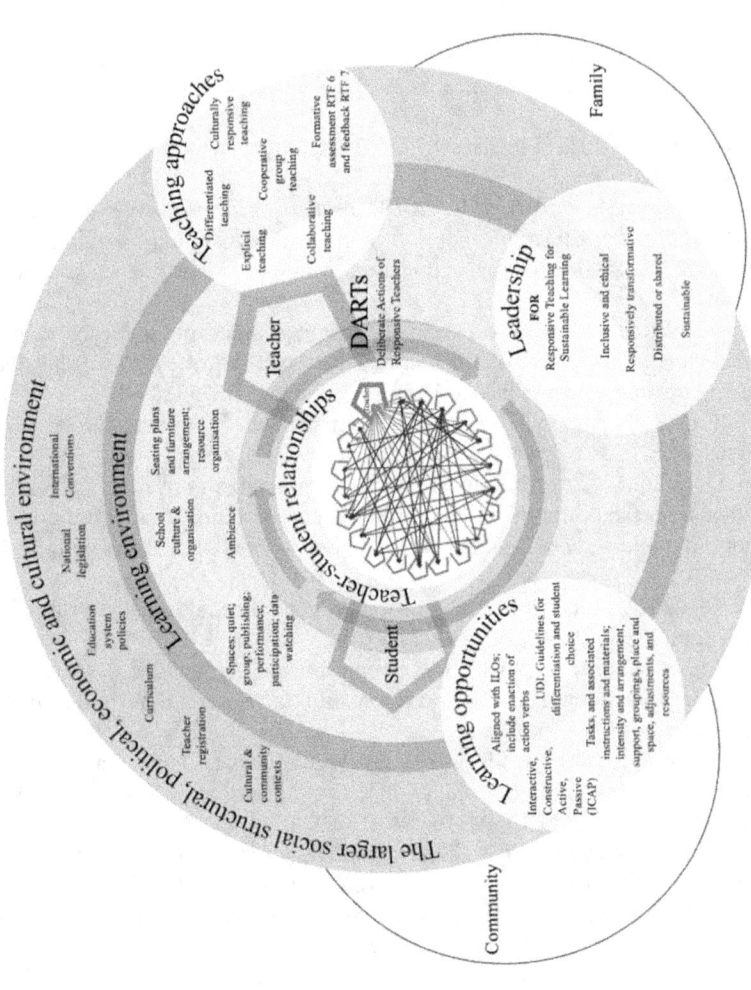

Figure 14.3 The full complexity of Responsive Teaching for Sustainable Learning.

References

ACT Government (2022). *Education Act 2004*, https://www.legislation.act.gov.au/a/2004-17

Adams, R., Jackson, J., & Turner, R. (2018). *Learning progressions as an inclusive solution to global education monitoring*, Australian Council for Educational Research Centre for Global Education Monitoring. https://research.acer.edu.au

Adelman, C. (2015). To imagine a verb: The language and syntax of learning outcomes statements. Occasional Paper #24. *National Institute for Learning Outcomes Assessment*. https://files.eric.ed.gov/fulltext/ED555528.pdf

Adelman, H., & Taylor, L. (2005). Classroom climate. In Lee, S., Lowe, P., & Robinson, E. (Eds.), *Encyclopedia of school psychology*. Sage.

Afriyani, D., Sa'dijah, C., & Muksar, M. (2018). Characteristics of students' mathematical understanding in solving multiple representation task based on solo taxonomy. *International Electronic Journal of Mathematics Education, 13*(3), 281–287.

Ainscow, M. (2020). Inclusion and equity in education: Making sense of global challenges. *Prospects, 49*(3), 123–134.

Ainscow, M., & Sandill, A. (2010). Developing inclusive education systems: The role of organisational cultures and leadership. *International Journal of Inclusive Education, 14*(1), 1–16.

Ainscow, M., Slee, R., & Best, M. (2019). Editorial: The Salamanca Statement: 25 years on. *International Journal of Inclusive Education, 23*(7-8), 671–676. https://doi.org/10.1080/13603116.2019.1622800

Akçayır, G., & Akçayır, M. (2018). The flipped classroom: A review of its advantages and challenges. *Computers & Education, 126*, 334–345.

Alegre, F., Moliner, L., Maroto, A., & Lorenzo-Valentin, G. (2020). Academic Achievement and Peer tutoring in mathematics: A comparison between primary and secondary education. Sage Open. https://doi.org/10.1177/2158244020929295

Alexander, R. (2018). Developing dialogic teaching: genesis, process, trial. *Research Papers in Education, 33*(5), 561–598, https://doi.org/10.1080/02671522.2018.1481140

Alzahrani, T., & Leko, M. (2018). The effects of peer tutoring on the reading comprehension performance of secondary students with disabilities: A systematic review. *Reading & Writing Quarterly, 34*(1), 1–17.

American Psychiatric Association [APA] (2013). *Diagnostic and statistical manual of mental disorders* (5th ed).
American Psychiatric Association [APA] (2022). *What is specific learning disorder?* https://psychiatry.org/patients-families/specific-learning-disorder/what-is-specific-learning-disorder
Anderson, L., Krathwohl, D., Airasian, P., Cruikshank, K., Mayer, R., Pintrich, P., Raths, J., & Wittrock, M. (2001). *A taxonomy for learning, teaching and assessing: A revision of Bloom's taxonomy of educational objectives (Complete edition).* Longman.
Anderson-Levitt, K., Bonnéry, S., & Fichtner, S. (2017). Introduction to the dossier: 'Competence-based' approaches as 'traveling' reforms. *Cahiers de la recherche sur l'éducation et les savoirs 16*, 27–45.
Andrade, H. (2019). A critical review of research on student self-assessment. *Frontiers in Education, 4*:87. https://doi.org/10.3389/feduc.2019.00087
Apple, M. (2004). *Ideology and curriculum (3rd ed).* Routledge Falmer.
Armstrong, D., Armstrong, A. C., & Spandagou, I. (2011). Inclusion: By choice or by chance? *International Journal of Inclusive Education, 15*(1), 29–39.
Arnicane, A., & Souza, A. S. (2022). Tracking attentional states: Assessing the relationship between sustained and selective focused attention in visual working memory. *Attention, Perception, & Psychophysics, 84*(3), 715–738.
Ashman, A., & Conway, R. (2018). *Using cognitive methods in the classroom*, Routledge Library Editions: Psychology of Education. Routledge.
Atmaca, F., Yağbasanlar, O., Yıldız, E., Göncü, A., & Baloğlu, M. (2022). The backstage of twice-exceptionality: A systematic review of the movies. *Roeper Review*, 1–15.
Aubusson, P., Burke, P., Schuck, S., Kearney, M., & Frischknecht, B. (2014). Teachers choosing rich tasks: The moderating impact of technology on student learning, enjoyment, and preparation. *Educational Researcher, 43*(5), 219–229.
Australian Childhood Foundation (2018). *Making SPACE for learning: Trauma informed practice in schools*, https://professionals.childhood.org.au/app/uploads/2018/08/ACF325-Making-Space-For-Learning-Book-v4.pdf
Australian Childhood Foundation and Queensland University of Technology (2020). *National guidelines for trauma-aware education*, https://professionals.childhood.org.au/app/uploads/2020/10/National-Trauma-Aware-Guidelines-web-version-Folder_National-Trauma-Aware-Guidelines_Web_26102020.pdf
Australian Children's Education and Care Quality Authority [ACECQA] (2017). *Developmental milestones and the early years learning framework and the national quality standards.* https://www.acecqa.gov.au/sites/default/files/2018-02/DevelopmentalMilestonesEYLFandNQS.pdf
Australian Curriculum, Assessment and Reporting Authority [ACARA] (2020a). *Version 3 of National Literacy and Numeracy Learning Progressions.* https://www.australiancurriculum.edu.au/resources/national-literacy-and-numeracy-learning-progressions/version-3-of-national-literacy-and-numeracy-learning-progressions/
Australian Curriculum, Assessment and Reporting Authority [ACARA] (2020b). *National Literacy Learning Progression.* https://www.ofai.edu.au/media/01nixkio/national-literacy-progressions-v3-for-publication.pdf

Australian Curriculum, Assessment and Reporting Authority [ACARA] (2022a), *General Capabilities (Version 8.4).* https://www.australiancurriculum.edu.au/f-10-curriculum/general-capabilities/

Australian Curriculum, Assessment and Reporting Authority [ACARA] (2022b). *Australian Curriculum Version 9,* https://v9.australiancurriculum.edu.au/

Australian Curriculum, Assessment and Reporting Authority [ACARA] (2022c). *Information and Communication Technology (ICT) Capability (Version 8.4).* https://www.australiancurriculum.edu.au/f-10-curriculum/general-capabilities/information-and-communication-technology-ict-capability/

Australian Government (2005). *Disability Standards for Education Plus Guidance Notes.* Canberra: Department of Education, Skills, and Employment.

Australian Institute for Teaching and School Leadership [AITSL] (2011). *Australian Professional Standards for Teachers,* https://www.aitsl.edu.au/standards

Australian Institute for Teaching and School Leadership [AITSL] (2017a). *Teaching Performance Assessment* https://www.aitsl.edu.au/deliver-ite-programs/teaching-performance-assessment

Australian Institute for Teaching and School Leadership [AITSL] (2017b). *Australian Professional Standard for Principals,* https://www.aitsl.edu.au/tools-resources/resource/australian-professional-standard-for-principals

Australian Institute for Teaching and School Leadership [AITSL] (2017c). *Instructional Rounds,* https://www.aitsl.edu.au/tools-resources/resource/instructional-rounds

Australian Institute for Teaching and School Leadership [AITSL] (2021). *Spotlight: Informing Teaching, Navigating and Translating Education Best Practice,* https://www.aitsl.edu.au/research/spotlights/informing-teaching-navigating-and-translating-education-best-practice

Australian Institute for Teaching and School Leadership [AITSL] (2022). *Indigenous Cultural Competency in the Australian Teaching Workforce, Final Report for Indigenous Cultural Competency Project,* https://www.aitsl.edu.au/teach/intercultural-development/indigenous-education

Australian Psychological Society (2016). *The Framework for Effective Delivery of School Psychology Services: A Practice Guide for Psychologists and School Leaders,* https://psychology.org.au/aps/media/resource-finder/framework-delivery-school-psych-services-practice-guide.pdf

Baker, J., & Gladstone, N. (2021). A complex problem: Richest school claim most HSC disability provisions. *Sydney Morning Herald,* 23 November. https://www.smh.com.au/national/nsw/a-complex-problem-richest-schools-claim-most-hsc-disability-provisions-20211122-p59ayg.html

Bakker, A., Smit, J., & Wegerif, R. (2015). Scaffolding and dialogic teaching in mathematics education: Introduction and review. *ZDM, 47*(7), 1047–1065.

Ballangrud, B., & Aas, M. (2022). Ethical thinking and decision-making in the leadership of professional learning communities. *Educational Research,* 1–15.

Banks, T. (2014). Creating positive learning environments: Antecedent strategies for managing the classroom environment & student behaviour. *Creative Education, 5,* 519–524. https://doi.org/10.4236/ce.2014.57061

Banwo, B., Khalifa, M., & Louis, K. (2021). Exploring trust: Culturally responsive and positive school leadership. *Journal of Educational Administration, 60*(3), 323–339. https://doi.org/10.1108/JEA-03-2021-0065

Bartlett, C., Marshall, M., & Marshall, A. (2012). Two-eyed seeing and other lessons learned within a co-learning journey of bringing together indigenous and mainstream knowledges and ways of knowing. *Journal of Environmental Studies and Sciences*, *2*(4), 331–340.

Bartley, V. (2021). *Australian educators' perspectives of gifted education*, [Doctor of Philosophy Dissertation], University of New England, Australia.

Bates, S. (2018). *Exploration of the role of cultural mismatch on risk and protective factors for high school dropout* [Doctoral dissertation], The Ohio State University, https://etd.ohiolink.edu/apexprod/rws_etd/send_file/send?accession=osu1524141561488306&disposition=inline

Beauchamp, M., & Anderson, V. (2010). SOCIAL: An integrative framework for the development of social skills. *Psychological Bulletin*, *136*(1), 39.

Bellert, A., & Graham, L. (2013). Neuromyths and neurofacts: Information from cognitive neuroscience for classroom and learning support teachers. *Special Education*, *22*(2), 7–20.

Bellert, A., & Graham, L. (2017). Educational approaches for students experiencing learning difficulties. *From the Laboratory to the Classroom. Translating Science of Learning for Teachers*, 229–249.

Berkeley, S., Scanlon, D., Bailey, T., Sutton, J. C., & Sacco, D. (2020). A snapshot of RTI implementation a decade later: New picture, same story. *Journal of Learning Disabilities*, *53*(5), 332–342.

Berman, J. (2001). *An application of dynamic assessment to school mathematical learning*, Unpublished PhD thesis, University of new England, Armidale, NSW, Australia.

Berman, J., & Graham, L. (2018). *Learning intervention: Educational casework and responsive teaching for sustainable learning*. Routledge.

Berman, J., & MacArthur, J. (Eds.) (2018). *Student perspectives on learning and teaching: Informing inclusive practice*. Brill Sense.

Bevan-Brown, J. (2003). *Cultural Self-review: Providing culturally effective, inclusive education for Māori learners*. NZCER.

Bevan-Brown, J. (2015). Introduction. In Bevan-Brown, J., Berryman, M., Hickey, H., Macfarlane, S., Smiler, K., Walker, T., … & McDowell, S. *Working with Māori children with special education needs* (pp. 3–29). NZCER.

Bialystok, E. (2018). Bilingual education for young children: Review of the effects and consequences. *International Journal of Bilingual Education and Bilingualism*, *21*(6), 666–679.

Biggs, J., & Collis, K. (1982). *Evaluating the quality of learning: The SOLO taxonomy (Structure of the Observed Learning Outcome)*. Academic Press.

Biggs, J., & Tang, C. (2011). *Teaching for quality learning at university*. McGraw-Hill Education.

Biggs, J., & Tang, C. (2022). *Teaching for quality learning at university* (5th ed.). McGraw-Hill Education.

Bishop, J., & Rinn, A. (2020). The potential of misdiagnosis of high IQ youth by practicing mental health professionals: A mixed methods study. *High Ability Studies*, *31*(2), 213–243.

Bishop, R., & Berryman, M. (2006). *Culture speaks: Cultural relationships and classroom learning*. Huia Publishers.

Blasé, K., Van Dyke, M., Fixsen, D., & Bailey, F. (2012). Implementation science: Key concepts, themes and evidence for practitioners of educational psychology. In Kelly, B., & Perkins, D. (Eds.), *Handbook of implementation science for psychology in education* (pp. 13–34). Cambridge University Press.

Blumen, S. (2021). Innovative practices to support high-achieving deprived young scholars in an ethnic-linguistic diverse Latin American country, Chapter 10 in Smith, S. (Ed.), *Handbook of giftedness and talent development in the Asia-Pacific*, Springer https://doi.org/10.1007/978-981-13-3041-4_9 203

Blumen, S., & Lanao, M. (2006). Una mirada desde el Rorschach hacia la niñez con talento intelectual en riesgo. *Revista de Psicología*, 24(2), 267–299.

Boonk, L., Gijselaers, H., Ritzen, H., & Brand-Gruwel, S. (2018). A review of the relationship between parental involvement indicators and academic achievement. *Educational Research Review*. http://doi.org/10.1016/j.edurev.2018.02.001

Booth, T. (2011). *Index for inclusion: Developing learning and participation in schools-Revised*, http://www.csie.org.uk/resources/inclusion-index-explained.shtml

Booth, T., & Ainscow, M. (2002). *Index for inclusion: Developing learning and participation in schools*, Centre for Studies on Inclusive Education (CSIE). http://www.csie.org.uk/resources/inclusion-index-explained.shtml

Bradley, R., Danielson, L., & Doolittle, J. (2005). Response to intervention. *Journal of Learning Disabilities*, 38(6), 485–486.

Brady, P. (2005). Inclusionary and exclusionary secondary schools: The effect of school culture on student outcomes. *Interchange*, 36(3), 295–311.

Brennan, A. (2019). Differentiation through choice as an approach to enhance inclusive practice. *REACH: Journal of Inclusive Education in Ireland*, 32(1), 11–20.

Brennan, A., King, F., & Travers, J. (2021). Supporting the enactment of inclusive pedagogy in a primary school. *International Journal of Inclusive Education*, 25(13), 1540–1557.

Breunig, M. (2005). Turning experiential education and critical pedagogy theory into praxis, *Journal of Experiential Education*, 28(2) 106–122.

Brevik, L., Gunnulfsen, A., & Renzulli, J. (2018). Student teachers' practice and experience with differentiated instruction for students with higher learning potential. *Teaching and Teacher Education*, 71, 34–45.

Brien, J. (2018). How can the right of young children with disability to be heard be enacted within the policy constructs of participant choice and control? *The International Journal of Children's Rights*, 26(3), 423–445.

Brien, J., Page, J., & Berman, J. (2017). Enabling the exercise of choice and control: How early childhood intervention professionals may support families and young children with a disability to exercise choice and control in the context of the National Disability Insurance Scheme. *Australasian Journal of Early Childhood*, 42(2), 37–44.

Brighton, C., Moon, T., & Huang, F. (2015). Advanced readers in reading first classrooms: Who was really "left behind"? Considerations for the field of gifted education. *Journal for the Education of the Gifted*, 38(3), 257–293.

Bronfenbrenner, U. (1977). Toward an experimental ecology of human development. *American Psychologist*, 32(7), 513–531.

Brown, A., & Palincsar, A. (1987). *Reciprocal teaching of comprehension strategies: A natural history of one program for enhancing learning*. Technical Report No. 334, https://files.eric.ed.gov/fulltext/ED257046.pdf

Buchanan, J., Harb, G., & Fitzgerald, T. (2020). Implementing a teaching performance assessment: An Australian case study. *Australian Journal of Teacher Education, 45*(5), 5.

Calhoun, L., & Tedeschi, R. (Eds.) (2014). *Handbook of posttraumatic growth: Research and practice*. Routledge.

Callingham, R., Watson, J., & Oates, G. (2021). Learning progressions and the Australian curriculum mathematics: The case of statistics and probability. *Australian Journal of Education, 65*(3), 329–342.

Campbell, A., Craig, T., & Collier-Reed, B. (2019). A framework for using learning theories to inform 'growth mindset' activities, *International Journal of Mathematical Education in Science and Technology*, https://doi.org/10.1080/0020739X.2018.1562118

Can, D., & Ginsburg-Block, M. (2013). Peer tutoring school-age children. *International Guide to Student Achievement*, 375–378.

Capp, M. (2017). The effectiveness of universal design for learning: a meta-analysis of literature between 2013 and 2016. *International Journal of Inclusive Education, 21*(8), 791–807. https://doi.org/10.1080/13603116.2017.1325074

CAST (2018a). *About Universal Design for Learning*. https://www.cast.org/org/impact/universal-design-for-learning-udl

CAST (2018b). *Universal Design for Learning Guidelines version 2.2*. http://udlguidelines.cast.org

Centre for Studies on Inclusive Education [CSIE] (2023). *Index for inclusion: Developing learning and participation in schools*. https://www.csie.org.uk/resources/inclusion-index-explained.shtml

Chaffey, G. (2008). Is gifted education a necessary ingredient in creating a level playing field for Indigenous children in education? *Australasian Journal of Gifted Education, 17*(1), 38–39.

Chaffey, G., Bailey, S., & Vine, K. (2003). Identifying high academic potential in Australian Aboriginal children using dynamic testing. *Australasian Journal of Gifted Education, 12*(1), 42–55.

Chaffey, G., Halliwell, G., & McCluskey, K. (2006). Identifying high academic potential in Canadian Aboriginal primary school children. *Gifted and Talented International, 21*(2), 61–70.

Chen, H. (2005). The rationale for critical pedagogy in facilitating cultural identity development, *Curriculum Teaching and Dialogue 7*(1/2), 11–24.

Chen, J., Lin, T., Anderman, L., Paul, N., & Ha, S. (2021). The role of friendships in shy students' dialogue patterns during small group discussions. *Contemporary Educational Psychology, 67*, 102021.

Cheptoo, R., & Ramadas, V. (2019). The "Africanized" competency-based curriculum: The twenty-first century strides. *Shanlax International Journal of Education. 7*, 46–51.

Chi, M., Adams, J., Bogusch, E., Bruchok, C., Kang, S., Lancaster, M., Levy, R., Li, N., McEldoon, K., Stump, G., Wylie, R., Xu, D., & Yaghmourian, D. (2018). Translating the ICAP theory of cognitive engagement into practice. *Cognitive Science, 42*(6), 1777–1832.

Chi, M., & Wylie, R. (2014). The ICAP framework: Linking cognitive engagement to active learning outcomes. *Educational Psychologist, 49*(4), 219–243.

Childs-Bowen, D., Moller, G., & Scrivner, J. (2000). Principals: Leaders of leaders. *NASSP Bulletin*, *84*(616), 27–34.

Chita-Tegmark, M., Gravel, J., De Lourdes, M., Serpa, B., Domings, Y., & Rose, D. (2011). Using the Universal Design for Learning framework to support culturally diverse learners. *The Journal of Education*, *192*(1), 17–22.

City, E. (2022). *Learning from instructional rounds.* https://www.ascd.org/el/articles/learning-from-instructional-rounds

City, E., Elmore, R., Fiarman, S., & Teitel, L. (2009). *Instructional rounds in education* (Vol. 30). Harvard Education Press.

Cohen, J., McCabe, L., Michelli, N., & Pickeral, T. (2009). School climate: Research, policy, practice, and teacher education. *Teachers College Record*, *111*(1), 180–213.

Collaborative for Academic, Social, and Emotional Learning [CASEL] (2022). *What is the CASEL framework?* https://casel.org/fundamentals-of-sel/what-is-the-casel-framework/

Cologon, K. (2019). *Towards inclusive education: A necessary process of transformation.* Macquarie University for Children and Young People with Disability Australia (CYDA), Australian Department of Social Services. https://www.cyda.org.au/images/pdf/towards_inclusive_education_a_necessary_transformation.pdf

Commission of the European Communities (2005). *Proposal for a recommendation of the European Parliament and of the Council on Key Competences for Lifelong Learning.* Publications Office of the European Union.

Commission of the European Communities (2007). *Key Competences for Lifelong Learning: European Reference Framework*, Publications Office of the European Union.

Commonwealth of Australia (2018). *Curricula project.* https://www.indigenous.gov.au/teaching-guides/curricula-project

Commonwealth of Australia (2022a). *Right to Education*, Attorney General's Department, https://www.ag.gov.au/rights-and-protections/human-rights-and-anti-discrimination/human-rights-scrutiny/public-sector-guidance-sheets/right-education

Commonwealth of Australia (2022b). *Australia's Anti-Discrimination Laws*, Attorney General's Department, https://www.ag.gov.au/rights-and-protections/human-rights-and-anti-discrimination/australias-anti-discrimination-law

Commonwealth of Australia (2022c). *Nationally Consistent Collection of Data on School Students with Disability: Guidelines Revised*, Education Ministers Meeting Schools Policy Group https://www.nccd.edu.au/

Cortese, D. (2007). A vision of individualized medicine in the context of global health. *Clinical Pharmacology & Therapeutics*, *82*(5), 491–493.

Corwin Visible Learning Plus (2021). Visible Learning Meta X, https://www.visiblelearningmetax.com

Corwin Visible Learning Plus (2023). *The Visible Learning research*, https://www.visiblelearning.com/content/visible-learning-research

Coubergs, C., Struyven, K., Vanthournout, G., & Engels, N. (2017). Measuring teachers' perceptions about differentiated instruction: The DI-Quest instrument and model. *Studies in Educational Evaluation*, *53*, 41–54.

Council for Exceptional Children (2005). *Universal design for learning: A guide for teachers and education professionals*. Arlington, Council for Exceptional Children, Pearson Custom [and] Merrill Education.
Craig, S. (2013). Questioning. In Hattie, J., & Anderman, E. (Eds.), *International guide to student achievement* (pp. 414–415). Routledge.
Crick, N., & Dodge, K. (1994). A review and reformulation of social information-processing mechanisms in children's social adjustment. *Psychological Bulletin, 115*(1), 74.
Cuevas, J. (2015). Is learning styles-based instruction effective? A comprehensive analysis of recent research on learning styles. *Theory and Research in Education, 13*(3), 308–333.
Dack, H. (2019). Understanding teacher candidate misconceptions and concerns about differentiated instruction. *The Teacher Educator, 54*(1), 22–45.
Dack, H., & Tomlinson, C. (2015). Inviting all students to learn. *Educational Leadership, 72*(6), 10–15.
Dalton, E. (2020). UDL and connected laws, theories, and frameworks. In Gronseth, S., & Dalton, E. (Eds.), *Universal access through inclusive instructional design: International perspectives on UDL* (pp. 3–16). Routledge.
Davies, O., & Mansour, N. (2022). Exploring the use of cognitive science approaches alongside SOLO taxonomy as a pedagogical framework to build deeper knowledge in science and foundation subjects at primary schools. *Education Sciences, 12*(8), 523.
Day, C., Sammons, P., & Gorgen, K. (2020). Successful school leadership. *Education Development Trust*.
De Nobile, J., Lyons, G., & Arthur-Kelly, M. (2017). *Positive learning environments*. Cengage Learning.
Deans for Impact (2015). *The Science of Learning*, http://deansforimpact.org/wp-content/uploads/2016/12/The_Science_of_Learning.pdf
Degener, T. (2017). A human rights model of disability. In Blanck, P., & Flynn, E. (Eds.), *Routledge handbook of disability law and human rights* (pp. 47–66). Routledge.
Dekker, S., Lee, N., Howard-Jones, P., & Jolles, J. (2012). Neuromyths in education: Prevalence and predictors of misconceptions among teachers. *Frontiers in Psychology*, 429.
DeMatthews, D., & Serafini, A. (2021). Do good principals do bad things? Examining bounds of ethical behavior in the context of high-stakes accountability. *Leadership and Policy in Schools, 20*(3), 335–354.
Dinham, S. (2007). The waves of leadership. *The Australian Educational Leader, 29*(3), 20–21, 27.
Dinham, S. (2016). *Leading learning and teaching*. ACER Press.
Dirth, T., & Branscombe, N. (2018). The social identity approach to disability: Bridging disability studies and psychological science. *Psychological Bulletin, 144*(12), 1300–1324.
Disability Discrimination Act (1992), https://www.legislation.gov.au/Details/C2018C00125
Doran, G., Miller, A., & Cunningham, J. (1981). There's a SMART way to write management's goals and objectives, *Management Review, 70*(11), 35–36.

Douglas, H., Headley, M., Hadden, S., & LeFevre, J. (2020). Knowledge of mathematical symbols goes beyond numbers. *Journal of Numerical Cognition*, 6(3), 322–354.

Dreyfus, S. (2004). The five-stage model of adult skill acquisition. *Bulletin of Science, Technology & Society*, 24(3), 177–181.

Duchesne, S., & McMaugh, A. (2019). *Educational psychology for learning and teaching* (6th ed.). Cengage.

Dumont, H., Istance, D., & Benevides, F. (Eds.) (2010). *The nature of learning: Using research to inspire practice*, OECD. https://read.oecd-ilibrary.org/education/the-nature-of-learning_9789264086487-en#page3

Durie, M. (1998). *Whaiora: Māori health development*. Oxford University Press.

Duschl, R., Maeng, S., & Sezen, A. (2011). Learning progressions and teaching sequences: A review and analysis. *Studies in Science Education*, 47(2), 123–182.

Dweck, C. (2006). *Mindset: The new psychology of success*. Random House.

Dweck, C. (2017). *Mindset-updated edition: Changing the way you think to fulfil your potential*. Hachette UK.

Early Childhood Intervention Australia [ECIA] (2016). *National guidelines: Best practice in early childhood intervention*, https://www.flipsnack.com/earlychildhoodintervention/ecia-national-guidelines-best-practice-in-eci/full-view.html

Education Endowment Foundation (2022). *Teaching and learning toolkit: An accessible summary of education evidence.* https://educationendowmentfoundation.org.uk/education-evidence/teaching-learning-toolkit

Education Services Australia (2020). *Australian student wellbeing framework*. Student Wellbeing Hub. https://studentwellbeinghub.edu.au/educators/framework/

Elliott, J., & Grigorenko, E. (2014). *The dyslexia debate*. Cambridge University Press.

Erdem, D. (2020). Multicultural competence scale for prospective teachers: Development, validation and measurement invariance. *Eurasian Journal of Educational Research*, 87, 1–28.

Erickson, F. (2004). Culture in society and educational practices. In Banks, J., & McGee Banks, C. (Eds.), *Multicultural education: Issues and perspectives (5th ed)* (pp. 31–60). John Wiley & Sons.

European Agency for Special and Inclusive Education (2017). *Raising achievement for all learners: Self review.* https://www.european-agency.org/sites/default/files/raising_achievement_self-review.pdf

Evans, R. (1996). *The human side of school change: Reform, resistance and the real-life problems of innovation*. Jossey-Bass.

Fan, X., & Liu, P. (2020). Exploring Indigenous education leadership research in Canada, the United States, Australia and New Zealand. *International Journal of Comparative Education and Development*, 22(4), 281–297, https://doi.org/10.1108/IJCED-02-2020-0007

Faragher, R., & Clarke, B. (2013). Mathematics profile of the learner with Down syndrome. In Faragher, R., & Clarke, B. (Eds.), *Educating learners with Down syndrome* (pp. 119–145). Routledge.

Faragher, R., & Clarke, B. (2020). Inclusive practices in the teaching of mathematics: some findings from research including children with Down syndrome. *Mathematics Education Research Journal*, 32(1), 121–146.

Faragher, R., Stratford, M., & Clarke, B. (2017). Teaching children with Down syndrome in inclusive primary mathematics classrooms. *Australian Primary Mathematics Classroom, 22*(4), 13–16.

Farrand, K., & Deeg, M. (2020). Dramatic inquiry: An inclusive approach to learning with collaboration and multiple modes. *Teaching Exceptional Children, 52*(3), 128–137.

Fergusson, D., McNaughton, S., Hayne, H., & Cunningham, C. (2011). From evidence to policy, programmes and interventions. In P.D. Gluckman (Ed.), *Improving the transition: Reducing social and psychological morbidity during adolescence* (pp. 287–300). Office of the Prime Minister's Science Advisory Committee, Auckland.

Fisher, D., & Frey, N. (2008). Homework and the gradual release of responsibility: Making "responsibility" possible. *English Journal*, 40–45.

Fitzsimons, D., James, K., & Denyer, D. (2011). Alternative approaches for studying shared and distributed leadership. *International Journal of Management Reviews, 13*(3), 313–328.

Fournier, E., Scott, S., & Scott, S. (2020). Inclusive leadership during the COVID-19 pandemic: How to respond within an inclusion framework *International Studies in Educational Administration, 48*(1), 17–23.

Fox, R., Sharma, U., & Leif, E. (2022). A study of Victorian teachers' beliefs about student behaviour and their perception of preparation and confidence to engage in evidence-based behaviour support. *Australian Journal of Teacher Education, 47*(1), 14–29.

Frey, N., Fisher, D., & Hattie, J. (2018). Developing assessment capable learners. *Educational Leadership, 75*(5), 46–51.

Fuchs, L., & Fuchs, D. (1986). Effects of systematic formative evaluation: A meta-analysis, *Exceptional Children, 53*(3), 199–208.

Gauthier, C., Dembélé, M., Bossonnette, S., & Richard, M. (2004). Quality of teaching and quality of education: A review of research findings. *UNESCO.* https://unesdoc.unesco.org/ark:/48223/pf0000146641_eng

Gay, G. (2018). *Culturally responsive teaching: Theory, research, and practice.* Teachers College Press.

Gheyssens, E., Coubergs, C., Griful-Freixenet, J., Engels, N., & Struyven, K. (2020). Differentiated instruction: The diversity of teachers' philosophy and praxis to adapt teaching to students' interests, readiness and learning profiles. *International Journal of Inclusive Education*, 1–18. https://doi.org/10.1080/13603116.2020.1812739

Giangreco, M. (2021). Maslow's Hammer: teacher assistant research and inclusive practices at a crossroads. *European Journal of Special Needs Education, 36*(2), 278–293, https://doi.org/10.1080/08856257.2021.1901377

Giangreco, M., Dennis, R., Cloninger, C., Edelman, S., & Schattman, R. (1993). "I've counted Jon": Transformational experiences of teachers educating students with disabilities. *Exceptional Children, 59*(4), 359–372.

Gibbs, G. (2006). How assessment frames student learning, Chapter 2 in Bryan, C., & Clegg, K. (Eds.), *Innovative assessment in higher education* (pp. 23–36). Routledge.

Gibbs, G., & Simpson, C. (2004). Does your assessment support your students' learning. *Journal of Teaching and Learning in Higher Education* 1, 1–30.

Gillies, R. (2019). Promoting academically productive student dialogue during collaborative learning. *International Journal of Educational Research, 97*, 200–209.

Gillies, R. (2020). Cooperative group work. In Hupp, S., & Jewell, J. (Eds.), *The encyclopedia of child and adolescent development*. John Wiley & Sons, https://doi.org/10.1002/9781119171492.wecad264

Gleeson, M. (2022). Is supporting the needs of emergent bilingual learners in mainstream classes a cultural or linguistic issue? How do policy, curricula, and secondary teacher education programmes in Australia and New Zealand compare? *International Journal of Bilingual Education and Bilingualism, 25*(8), 2962–2975.

Goodall, J., & Montgomery, C. (2014). Parental involvement to parental engagement: A continuum. *Educational Review, 66*(4), 399–410.

Goral, D., & Bailey, A. (2019). Student self-assessment of oral explanations: Use of language learning progressions. *Language Testing, 36*(3), 391–417. https://doi.org/10.1177/0265532219826330

Graham, L., & Berman, J. (2012). Self-regulation and learning disabilities. *Special Education Perspectives, 21*(2), 41–52.

Graham, L., Berman, J., & Bellert, A. (2015). *Sustainable learning: Inclusive practices for 21st century classrooms*. Cambridge University Press.

Grospietsch, F., & Lins, I. (2021). Review on the prevalence and persistence of neuromyths in education: Where we stand and what is still needed. *Frontiers in Education, 6*, 665752. Frontiers Media SA.

Gross, M. (1989). The pursuit of excellence or the search for intimacy? The forced-choice dilemma of gifted youth. *Roeper Review, 11*(4), 189–194.

Grossman, P., Smagorinsky, P., & Valencia, S. (1999). Appropriating tools for teaching English: A theoretical framework for research on learning to teach. *American Journal of Education, 108*(1), 1–29.

Gümüş, S., Arar, K., & Oplatka, I. (2021). Review of international research on school leadership for social justice, equity and diversity. *Journal of Educational Administration and History, 53*(1), 81–99.

Gurr, D., & Drysdale, L. (2020). Leadership for challenging times. *International Studies in Educational Administration, 48*(1), 24–30.

Guskey, T. (2010). Lessons of mastery learning. *Educational Leadership, 68*(2), 52.

Hadwin, A., Järvelä, S., & Miller, M. (2017). Self-regulation, co-regulation, and shared regulation in collaborative learning environments. In Schunk, D. H., & Greene, J. A. (Eds.), *Handbook of self-regulation of learning and performance* (pp. 83–106). Routledge.

Halász, G., & Michel, A. (2011). Key competences in Europe: Interpretation, policy formulation and implementation. *European Journal of Education, 46*(3), 289–306.

Hall, T., Meyer, A., & Rose, D. (2012). An introduction to universal design for learning: Questions and answers. In Hall, T., Meyer, A., & Rose, D. (Eds.), *Universal design for learning in the classroom: Practical applications* (pp. 1–8). The Guilford Press.

Halstead, J., & Taylor, M. (2000). Learning and teaching about values: A review of recent research. *Cambridge Journal of Education, 30*(2), 169–202.

Hampden-Thompson, G., & Galindo, C. (2017). School–family relationships, school satisfaction and the academic achievement of young people. *Educational Review, 69*(2), 248–265.

Hanley, M. (2006). Education: Transmission and transformation. *Journal of Thought, 41*(3), 51–55.

Hargreaves, A., & Fink, D. (2006). *Sustainable leadership*, Jossey-Bass.

Harris, A., & Goodall, J. (2008). Do parents know they matter? Engaging all parents in learning. *Educational Research, 50*(3), 277–289.

Hattie, J. (2009). *Visible learning: A synthesis of over 800 meta-analyses relating to achievement*. Routledge.

Hattie, J. (2017). *High impact teaching strategies: Excellence in teaching and learning*. Department of Education and Training, State of Victoria.

Hattie, J. (2018). *Hattie ranking: 252 influences and effect sizes related to student achievement*. https://visible-learning.org/hattie-ranking-influences-effect-sizes-learning-achievement

Hattie, J., & Anderman, E. (Eds.) (2012). *International guide to student achievement*. Routledge.

Hattie, J., & Donoghue, G. (2016). Learning strategies: A synthesis and conceptual model. *NPJ Science of Learning, 1*(1), 1–13.

Hattie, J., Fisher, D., & Frey, N. (2018). *Developing assessment capable visible learners (K–12): Maximizing skill, will, and thrill*. Corwin Press.

Hattie, J., Hodis, F., & Kang, S. (2020). Theories of motivation: Integration and ways forward. *Contemporary Educational Psychology, 61*, 101865.

Hattie, J., & Timperley, H. (2007). The power of feedback. *Review of Educational Research, 77*(1), 81–112.

Hedin, L., & DeSpain, S. (2018). SMART or not? Writing specific, measurable IEP goals. *Teaching Exceptional Children, 51*(2), 100–110.

Heller, K., Holtzman, W., & Messick, S. (Eds.) (1982). *Placing children in special education: A strategy for equity*. National Academy Press.

Hempenstall, K. (2020). Teaching reading through Direct Instruction: A role for educational psychologists? *The Educational and Developmental Psychologist, 37*(2), 133–139.

Hempenstall, K., & Buckingham, J. (2016). *Read about it: Scientific evidence for effective teaching of reading*. Centre for Independent Studies Limited.

Henderson, R. (2008). A boy behaving badly: Investigating teachers' assumptions about gender, behaviour, mobility and literacy learning. *The Australian Journal of Language and Literacy, 31*(1), 74–87.

Henderson, R. (2021). Diversity matters: Some reflections. *Literacy Learning: The Middle Years, 29*(1), 28–36.

Hernández-Saca, D., Gutmann Kahn, L., & Cannon, M. (2018). Intersectionality dis/ability research: How dis/ability research in education engages intersectionality to uncover the multidimensional construction of dis/abled experiences. *Review of Research in Education, 42*(1), 286–311.

Hickey, H. (2015). Tatau tatau: Engaging with whānau hauā from within a cultural framework, Chapter 3. In Bevan-Brown, J., Berryman, M., Hickey, H., Macfarlane, S., Smiler, K., & Walker, T. (Eds.), *Working with Māori children with special education needs: He mahi whakahirahira* (pp. 70–84). NZCER.

Hickey, H., & Wilson, D. (2017). Whānau hauā: Reframing disability from an Indigenous perspective. *MAI Journal*, *6*(1), 82–94. https://doi.org/10.20507/MAIJournal.2017.6.1.7

Hilaski, D. (2020). Addressing the mismatch through culturally responsive literacy instruction. *Journal of Early Childhood Literacy*, *20*(2), 356–384.

Hoffnung, M., Hoffnung, R., Seifert, K., Hine, A., Pause, C., Ward, L., Signal, T., Swabey, K., Yates, K., & Burton, R. (2018). *Lifespan development, 4th Australasian edition*. Wiley.

Hood, S., Barrickman, N., Djerdjian, N., Farr, M., Magner, S., Roychowdhury, H., Gerrits, R., Lawford, H., Ott, B., Ross, K., Paige, O., Stowe, S., Jensen, M., & Hull, K. (2021). "I like and prefer to work alone": Social anxiety, academic self-efficacy, and students' perceptions of active learning. *CBE—Life Sciences Education*, *20*(1), ar12. https://doi.org/10.1187/cbe.19-12-0271

Hook, P., & Cassé, B. (2013). *SOLO taxonomy in the early years: Making connections for belonging, being and becoming*. Essential Resources.

Inter-Agency Commission (1990). *World declaration on education for all and framework for action to meet basic learning needs*. World Conference on Education for All, Jomtien, Thailand.

International Educational Assessment Network [IEAN] (2020). *Learning progression: Implications for curriculum and assessment*, https://www.iean.network/gallery/iean-learner-progression-implications-dec2020v2.pdf

IRIS Center (2021). *Perspective and resources*, Peabody College Vanderbilt University. https://iris.peabody.vanderbilt.edu/module/udl/cresource/q2/p05/#content

Järvelä, S., & Hadwin, A. (2013). New frontiers: Regulating learning in CSCL. *Educational Psychologist*, *48*(1), 25–39.

Jerrim, J., Oliver, M., & Sims, S. (2020). The relationship between inquiry-based teaching and students' achievement. New evidence from a longitudinal PISA study in England. *Learning and Instruction*, 80. https://doi.org/10.1016/j.learninstruc.2020.101310

Johnson, D., & Johnson, R. (2008). Social interdependence theory and cooperative learning: The teacher's role. In Gillies, R., Ashman, A., & Terwel, J. (Eds.), *The teachers' role in implementing cooperative learning in the classroom* (pp. 9–37). Springer.

Johnson, D., & Johnson, R. (2018). Cooperative learning: The foundation for active learning. In Brito, S. (Ed.), *Active learning*. https://doi.org/10.5772/intechopen.81086

Katherine High School (2018). *Plans and policies*. https://www.katherinehighschool.com.au/our-school/plans-and-policies/

Khalifa, M., Gooden, M., & Davis, J. (2016). Culturally responsive school leadership: A synthesis of the literature. *Review of Educational Research*, *86*(4), 1272–1311.

Khalifa, M., Khalil, D., Marsh, T., & Halloran, C. (2019). Toward an indigenous, decolonizing school leadership: A literature review. *Educational Administration Quarterly*, *55*(4), 571–614.

King, A. (2008). Structuring peer interaction to promote higher-order thinking and complex learning in cooperating groups. In Gillies, R., Ashman, A., & Terwel, J. (Eds.), *The teachers' role in implementing cooperative learning in the classroom* (pp. 73–91). Springer.

Kirschner, P. (2017). Stop propagating the learning styles myth. *Computers & Education, 106*, 166–171.

Kluger, A., & De Nisi, A. (1996). The effects of feedback interventions on performance: a historical review, a meta-analysis, and a preliminary feedback intervention theory. *Psychological Bulletin, 119*(2), 254.

Krathwohl, D. (2002). A revision of Bloom's taxonomy: An overview. *Theory into Practice, 41*(4), 212–218.

Kulik, J., & Kulik, C. (1988). Timing of feedback and verbal learning. *Review of Educational Research, 58*(1), 79–97.

Lauchlan, F., & Carrigan, D. (2013). *Improving learning through dynamic assessment: A practical classroom resource*, Jessica Kingsley Publishers.

Lazonder, A., & Harmsen, R. (2016). Meta-analysis of inquiry-based learning: Effects of guidance. *Review of Educational Research, 86*(3), 681–718.

Lee, M., & Louis, K. (2019). Mapping a strong school culture and linking it to sustainable school improvement. *Teaching and Teacher Education, 81*, 84–96.

Leung, K. (2019). An updated meta-analysis on the effect of peer tutoring on tutors' achievement. *School Psychology International, 40*(2), 200–214.

Lewthwaite, B., Boon, H., Webber, T., & Laffin, G. (2017) Quality teaching practices as reported by Aboriginal parents, students and their teachers: Comparisons and contrasts, *Australian Journal of Teacher Education, 42*(12), 80–97.

Liem, G., & Martin, A. (2013). Direct instruction. In Hattie, J., & Anderman, E. (Eds.), *International guide to student achievement* (pp. 366–368). Routledge.

Lloyd, J., Moni, K., Cuskelly, M., & Jobling, A. (2021). Exploring the complexity of implementing National Disability Insurance Scheme plans for adults with intellectual disability: Parents' perspectives. *Journal of Intellectual & Developmental Disability, 46*(3), 281–290.

Lloyd, N., Lewthwaite, B., Osborne, B., & Boon, H. J. (2015). Effective teaching practices for Aboriginal and Torres Strait Islander students: A review of the literature. *Australian Journal of Teacher Education, 40*(11), 1–22.

Locatelli, C., Onnivello, S., Antonaros, F., Feliciello, A., Filoni, S., Rossi, S., ... & Lanfranchi, S. (2021). Is the age of developmental milestones a predictor for future development in down syndrome? *Brain Sciences, 11*(5), 655.

Locke, E., & Latham, G. (2019). The development of goal setting theory: A half century retrospective. *Motivation Science, 5*(2), 93.

Mac Ruairc, G. Ottessen, E., & Precey, R. (Eds.) (2013). *Leadership for inclusive education: Values, vision and voices*, 18. Springer Science and Business Media.

MacArthur, J., Berman, J., & Carroll-Lind, J. (2018). Children's rights and inclusive education. Chapter 1. In Berman, J., & MacArthur, J. (Eds.), *Student Perspectives on School* (pp. 1–20). Brill.

Macfarlane, A., Blampied, N., & Macfarlane, S. (2011). Blending the clinical and the cultural: A framework for conducting formal psychological assessment in bicultural settings. *New Zealand Journal of Psychology 40*(2), 5–15.

Macfarlane, A., & Macfarlane, S. (2019). Listen to culture: Māori scholars' plea to researchers. *Journal of the Royal Society of New Zealand, 49*(suppl), 48–57.

Macfarlane, A., Webber, M., McRae, H., & Cookson-Cox, C. (2014). *Ka Awatea: An iwi case study of Māori students' success: Report for Ngā Pae o te Māramatanga*. Christchurch: Te Rū Rangahau, University of Canterbury. http://www.maramatanga.co.nz/project/ka-awatea-iwi-case-study-m-ori-students-experiencing-success

Mahmud, M. (2019). The role of wait time in the process of oral questioning in the teaching and learning process of mathematics. *International Journal of Advanced Science and Technology, 28*(16), 691–697.

Malik, S., Tawafak, R., & Shakir, M. (2021). Aligning and assessing teaching approaches with solo taxonomy in a computer programming course. *International Journal of Information and Communication Technology Education, 17*(4), 1–15.

Marika, R. (2000). Milthun latju wanga romgu Yolngu: Valuing Yolngu knowledge in the education system. *TESOL in context, 10*(2).

Martin, S. (2011). *Using SOLO as a framework for teaching. A case study in maximising achievement in science*. Essential Resources Educational Publishers.

Martín-Arbós, S., Castarlenas, E., & Dueñas, J. (2021). Help-seeking in an academic context: A systematic review. *Sustainability, 13*(8), 4460.

Marton, F. (2006). Sameness and difference in transfer. *The Journal of the Learning Sciences, 15*(4), 499–535.

Maxwell, B. (2018). *Mechanisms, contexts and outcomes of interprofessional education in a student-run interprofessional clinic-a realist evaluation approach to developing programme theory* [Doctoral dissertation]. Bournemouth University, http://eprints.bournemouth.ac.uk/31107/1/MAXWELL%2C%20Barbara_Ph.D._2018.pdf

Maynard, B., Farina, A., Dell, N., & Kelly, M. (2019). Effects of trauma-informed approaches in schools: A systematic review. *Campbell Systematic Reviews, 15*(1–2).

McCray, E., & Hatton, P. (2011). "Less afraid to have them in my classroom": Understanding pre-service general educators' perceptions about inclusion. *Teacher Education Quarterly, 38*(4), 135–155.

Meo, G. (2008). Curriculum planning for all learners: Applying Universal Design for Learning (UDL) to a high school reading comprehension program, *Preventing School Failure: Alternative Education for Children and Youth, 52*(2), 21–30, https://doi.org/10.3200/PSFL.52.2.21-30

Messiou, K. (2012). Collaborating with children in exploring marginalisation: An approach to inclusive education. *International Journal of Inclusive Education, 16*(12), 1311–1322.

Messiou, K. (2019). The missing voices: Students as a catalyst for promoting inclusive education. *International Journal of Inclusive Education, 23*(7–8), 768–781.

Messiou, K., & Ainscow, M. (2020). Inclusive inquiry: Student–teacher dialogue as a means of promoting inclusion in schools. *British Educational Research Journal, 46*(3), 670–687.

Meyer, A., Rose, D., & Gordon, D. (2014). *Universal design for learning: Theory and Practice*. CAST Professional Publishing.

Mezirow, J. (1985). Concept and action in adult education. *Adult Education Quarterly, 35*(3), 142–151.

Mezirow, J. (1991). *Transformative dimensions of adult learning*. Jossey-Bass.

Milroy, D. (2006). *Understanding the dance of life*. https://www.ranzcp.org/practice-education/aboriginal-torres-strait-islander-mental-health/the-dance-of-life

Ministerio de Educación, Peru (2013). *Hacia una educacion bilingue de calidad. Propuesta pedagogica* (2nd ed.). MINEDU.

Ministry of Education (2013). *Summary of Ka Hikitia – accelerating success 2013-2017; The Māori education strategy.* https://www.education.govt.nz/assets/Documents/Ministry/Strategies-and-policies/Ka-Hikitia/KaHikitiaAcceleratingSuccessEnglish.pdf

Ministry of Education, Aotearoa New Zealand (2020). *Key competencies.* https://nzcurriculum.tki.org.nz/Key-competencies

Mitchell, D. (2014). *What really works in special and inclusive education: Using evidence-based teaching strategies.* Routledge.

Mitchell, D. (2016). *Diversities in education: Effective ways to reach all learners.* Routledge.

Mitchell, D. (2018). *The ecology of inclusive education: Strategies to tackle the crisis in educating diverse learners.* Routledge.

Mitchell, D., & Sutherland, D. (2020). *What really works in special and inclusive education: Using evidence-based teaching strategies.* Routledge.

Mogensen, F., & Schnack, K. (2010). The action competence approach and the 'new' discourses of education for sustainable development, competence, and quality criteria. *Environmental Education Research, 16*(1), 59–74. https://doi.org/10.1080/13504620903504032

Monteiro, A., Miranda-Pinto, M., & Osório, A. (2021). Coding as literacy in preschool: A case study. *Education Sciences, 11*(5), 198.

Moosa, V. (2021). Review of collective teacher efficacy research: Implications for teacher development, school administrators and education researchers. *International Journal of Theory and Application in Elementary and Secondary School Education, 3*(1), 62–73.

Morrison, A., Rigney, L., Hattam, R., & Diplock, A. (2019). *Toward an Australian culturally responsive pedagogy: A narrative review of the literature.* University of South Australia.

Morrow, B., & Kanakri, S. (2018). The impact of fluorescent and led lighting on students' attitudes and behavior in the classroom. *Advances in Pediatric Research, 5*(15). https://doi.org/10.24105/apr.2018.5.15

Moseley, D., Baumfield, V., Elliot, J., Gregson, M., Higgins, S., Miller, J., & Newton, D. (2005). *Frameworks for thinking: A handbook for teaching and learning,* Cambridge.

Mosley, C., Broyles, T., & Kaufman, E. (2021). A case study of teacher-student relationship development. *Journal of Classroom Interaction, 56*(1), 18–32.

National Assessment Program (2022). *National Assessment Program Special Provisions.* https://www.nap.edu.au/naplan/accessibility/adjustments-for-students-with-disability

National Disability Insurance Agency [NDIA] (2021). *What principles do we follow to create your plan?* https://ourguidelines.ndis.gov.au/how-ndis-supports-work-menu/what-principles-do-we-follow-create-your-plan

National Disability Insurance Scheme [NDIS] (2022). *The early childhood approach.* https://www.ndis.gov.au/understanding/families-and-carers/early-childhood-approach

National Reading Panel, US (2000). *Report of the National Reading Panel: Teaching children to read: An evidence-based assessment of the scientific research literature on reading and its implications for reading instruction: Reports of the subgroups.* National Institute of Child Health and Human

Development, National Institutes of Health, https://www.nichd.nih.gov/sites/default/files/publications/pubs/nrp/Documents/report.pdf

Newton, C., & Fisher, K. (Eds.). (2009). Some concluding remarks by the co-editors. In *Take 8: Learning spaces: The transformation of educational spaces for the 21st century* (pp. 133–137). Australian Institute of Architects.

Nikora, L., Karapu, R., Hickey, H., & Te Awekotuku, N. (2004). *Disabled Māori and disability support options. A report prepared for the Ministry of Health*. Māori & Psychology Research Unit, University of Waikato.

Nordengren, C. (2019). Goal-setting practices that support a learning culture. *Phi Delta Kappan, 101*(1), 18–23.

Nordin, A., & Sundberg, D. (2021). Transnational competence frameworks and national curriculum-making: The case of Sweden. *Comparative Education, 57*(1), 19–34. https://doi.org/10.1080/03050068.2020.1845065

Norman, E. (2020). Why metacognition is not always helpful. *Psychology, 2*(11) 1537. https://doi.org/10.3389/fpsyg.2020.01537

Northern Territory Government of Australia (2022). *Aboriginal languages in NT*. https://nt.gov.au/community/interpreting-and-translating-services/aboriginal-interpreter-service/aboriginal-languages-in-nt

Northern Territory Government, Department of Education (2022). *Bilingual education guidelines; Curriculum, assessment, reporting and certification: early childhood to year 12 policy statement*. https://education.nt.gov.au/__data/assets/pdf_file/0007/1108699/bilingual-education-guidelines.pdf

NSW Department of Education (2020a). *Policy: Assisting students with learning difficulties*. https://education.nsw.gov.au/policy-library/policies/pd-2006-0342

NSW Department of Education (2020b). *Schools: Language diversity in NSW*. https://education.nsw.gov.au/content/dam/main-education/about-us/educational-data/cese/2020-language-diversity-bulletin.pdf

NSW Department of Education (2021a). *Personalised learning and support*. https://education.nsw.gov.au/teaching-and-learning/disability-learning-and-support/personalised-support-for-learning/personalised-learning-and-support

NSW Department of Education (2021b). *Early learning: Early intervention*. https://education.nsw.gov.au/teaching-and-learning/curriculum/early-learning/early-intervention

NSW Education Standards Authority [NESA] (2021a). *Life skills*. https://educationstandards.nsw.edu.au/wps/portal/nesa/k-10/diversity-in-learning/special-education/life-skills

NSW Education Standards Authority [NESA] (2021b). *HSC disability provisions guide for teachers and parents*. https://educationstandards.nsw.edu.au/wps/portal/nesa/11-12/hsc/disability-provisions/hsc-disability-provisions-guide-for-teachers-and-parents

NSW Government (2016). *NSW Department of Education Disability Inclusion Action Plan 2016-2020*. NSW Department of Education.

Nunaki, J., Damopolii, I., Nusantari, E., & Kandowangko, N. (2019). The contribution of metacognitive in the inquiry-based learning to students' thinking skill based on SOLO Taxonomy. *Journal of Physics: Conference Series, 1321*(3). IOP Publishing.

Organisation for Economic Co-operation and Development [OECD] (1996). *The knowledge-based economy*. OCDE/GD (96)102. https://www.oecd.org/officialdocuments/publicdisplaydocumentpdf/?cote=OCDE/GD%2896%29102&docLanguage=En

Organisation for Economic Co-operation and Development [OECD] (2000). *Measuring student knowledge and skills: The PISA 2000 Assessment of Reading, Mathematical and Scientific Literacy*. Statistics and Indicators Division of the Directorate for Education, Employment, Labour, and Social Affairs.

Organisation for Economic Co-operation and Development [OECD] (2002). *Understanding the Brain: Towards a New Learning Science*. OECD.

Organisation for Economic Co-operation and Development [OECD] (2008). *Students with Disabilities, Learning Difficulties and Disadvantages: Policies, Statistics and Indicators*. OECD Publishing, https://doi.org/10.1787/9789264027619-en.

Organisation for Economic Co-operation and Development [OECD] (2012). *Equity and Quality in Education: Supporting Disadvantaged Students and Schools*. OECD Publishing.

Organisation for Economic Co-operation and Development [OECD] (2013). *Leadership for 21st Century Learning*. Centre for Educational Research and Innovation. https://read.oecd-ilibrary.org/education/leadership-for-21st-century-learning_9789264205406-en#page4

Organisation for Economic Co-operation and Development [OECD] (2017). *The OECD Handbook for Innovative Learning Environments*. Educational Research and Innovation, OECD Publishing. https://doi.org/10.1787/9789264277274-en

Óskarsdóttir, E., Donnelly, V., Turner-Cmuchal, M., & Florian, L. (2020). Inclusive school leaders–their role in raising the achievement of all learners. *Journal of Educational Administration, 58*(5), 521–537.

Owens, R. (2004). *Organizational behavior in education: Adaptive leadership and school reform (8th ed)*. Pearson Education.

Pameijer, N. (2016). *Assessment for intervention: A practice-based model*. Keynote address, International School Psychology Association Conference, Amsterdam, July.

Parekh, G., Brown, R., & Robson, K. (2018). The social construction of giftedness: The intersectional relationship between whiteness, economic privilege, and the identification of gifted. *Canadian Journal of Disability Studies, 7*(2), 1–32.

Patterson, B. (2021). Analysing student understanding of cryptography using the SOLO taxonomy. *Cryptologia, 45*(5), 439–449.

Pawson, R., & Tilley, N. (2001). Realistic evaluation bloodlines. *American Journal of Evaluation, 22*(3), 317–324.

Peng, D., & Yu, Z. (2022). A literature review of digital literacy over two decades. *Education Research International, 2022*, Article ID 2533413.

Pere, R. (1997). *Te Wheke: A celebration of infinite wisdom* (2nd ed.). Ao Ako Global Learning.

Perfect, M., Turley, M., Carlson, J., Yohanna, J., & Saint Gilles, M. (2016). School-related outcomes of traumatic event exposure and traumatic stress symptoms in students: A systemic review of research from 1990 to 2015. *School Mental Health, 8*, 7–43.

Perone, S., & Simmering, V. (2017). Applications of dynamic systems theory to cognition and development: New frontiers. *Advances in Child Development and Behavior, 52*, 43–80.

Peterson, C. (2013). *Looking forward through the lifespan: Developmental psychology* (6th ed.) Pearson.

Pianta, R., Hamre, B., & Allen, J. (2012) Teacher-student relationships and engagement: Conceptualizing, measuring, and improving the capacity of classroom interactions. In Christenson, S., Reschly, A., & Wylie, C. (Eds.), *Handbook of research on student engagement*. Springer. https://doi.org/10.1007/978-1-4614-2018-7_17

Pinkard, H. (2021). The perspectives and experiences of children with special educational needs in mainstream primary schools regarding their individual teaching assistant support. *European Journal of Special Needs Education, 36*(2), 248–264. https://doi.org/10.1080/08856257.2021.1901375

Pintrich, P. (2000). The role of goal orientation in self-regulated learning. In *Handbook of self-regulation* (pp. 451–502). Academic Press.

Pintrich, P. (2004). A conceptual framework for assessing motivation and self-regulated learning in college students. *Educational Psychology Review, 16*(4), 385–407.

Popat, S., & Starkey, L. (2019). Learning to code or coding to learn? A systematic review. *Computers & Education, 128*, 365–376.

Preston, A., Wood, C., & Stecker, P. (2016). Response to intervention: Where it came from and where it's going. *Preventing School Failure: Alternative Education for Children and Youth, 60*(3), 173–182.

Province of British Columbia (2022). *Core competencies*. https://curriculum.gov.bc.ca/competencies

Purpura, D., Napoli, A., & King, Y. (2019). Development of mathematical language in preschool and its role in learning numeracy skills. In Geary, D., Berch, D., & Koepke, K. (Eds.), *Cognitive foundations for improving mathematical learning* (pp. 175–193). Elsevier Academic Press. https://doi.org/10.1016/B978-0-12-815952-1.00001-3

Qayyum, A. (2018). Student help-seeking attitudes and behaviors in a digital era. *International Journal of Education Technology in Higher Education, 15*, Article 17. https://doi.org/10.1186/s41239-018-0100-7

Quackenbush, M., & Bol, L. (2020). Teacher support of co-and socially-shared regulation of learning in middle school mathematics classrooms. In *Frontiers in Education* (Vol. 5, p. 580543). Frontiers Media SA.

Queensland Government Department of Education (2021). *Inclusive Education Policy*. https://ppr.qed.qld.gov.au/pp/inclusive-education-policy

Quin, D. (2017). Longitudinal and contextual associations between teacher–student relationships and student engagement: A systematic review. *Review of Educational Research, 87*(2), 345–387. https://doi.org/10.3102/0034654316669434

Raising Children Network Australia (2021). *Vision impairment 0-6 years*. https://raisingchildren.net.au/disability/guide-to-disabilities/assessment-diagnosis/vision-impairment

Ramos Solis, R. (2020). *Competency-Based Curriculum Implementation in Peru* [Master's thesis]. Universitetet iOSLO. https://www.duo.uio.no/bitstream/handle/10852/80682/Ramos.pdf?sequence=1

Ratcliffe, S. (Ed.) (2017). *Oxford essential quotations* (5th ed.). Oxford University Press.

Reid, A. (2021). The binary of explicit instruction and inquiry-based teaching. *Professional Voice, 14* (2), Australian Education Union. https://www.aeuvic.asn.au/professional-voice-1424#:~:text=Inquiry-based

Reigeluth, C. (2011). An instructional theory for the post-industrial age. *Educational Technology*, 25–29.

Retief, M., & Letšosa, R. (2018). Models of disability: A brief overview. *HTS Teologiese Studies/Theological Studies, 74*(1).

Richmond, C. (2002). *Searching for balance: A collective case study of ten secondary teachers' behaviour management language*. [Doctoral dissertation]. University of New England, Armidale, Australia.

Richmond, C. (2007). *Teach more, manage less: A minimalist approach to behaviour management*. Scholastic.

Rohrer, D., Dedrick, R., Hartwig, M., & Cheung, C. (2020). A randomized controlled trial of interleaved mathematics practice. *Journal of Educational Psychology, 112*, 40–52.

Rosenshine, B. (1986). Synthesis of research on explicit teaching. *Educational Leadership, 43*(7), 60–69.

Rosenshine, B. (2012). Principles of instruction: Research-based strategies that all teachers should know. American Educator, *36*(1), 12–39.

Ross, K., & Tolan, P. (2018). Social and emotional learning in adolescence: Testing the CASEL model in a normative sample. *The Journal of Early Adolescence, 38*(8), 1170–1199.

Roy, A., Guay, F., & Valois, P. (2013). Teaching to address diverse learning needs: Development and validation of a Differentiated Instruction Scale. *International Journal of Inclusive Education, 17*(11), 1186–1204.

Sailor, W., Skrtic, T., Cohn, M., & Olmstead, C. (2021). Preparing teacher educators for statewide scale-up of multi-tiered system of support (MTSS). *Teacher Education and Special Education, 44*(1), 24–41.

Sánchez-Escobedo, P., Camelo-Lavadores, A., & Valdés-Cuervo, A. (2021). Gifted, talented and high-achieving students and their gifted education in Mexico, Chapter 9. In Smith, S. (Ed.), *Handbook of giftedness and talent development in the Asia-Pacific*. Springer International Handbooks of Education. https://doi.org/10.1007/978-981-13-3041-4_9 203

Sands, D., & Barker, H. (2004). Organised chaos: Modeling differentiated instruction for pre-service teachers. *Teaching & Learning, 19*(1), 26–49.

Sarra, C., Spillman, D., Jackson, C., Davis, J., & Bray, J. (2020). High-expectations relationships: A foundation for enacting high expectations in all Australian schools. *The Australian Journal of Indigenous Education, 49*(1), 32–45.

Sarra, G. (2011). Indigenous studies in all schools. *International Journal of Inclusive Education, 15*(6), 611–625.

Scarborough, H. (2001). Connecting early language and literacy to later reading (dis)abilities: Evidence, theory, and practice. In Neuman, S., & Dickinson, D. (Eds.), *Handbook of early literacy research, Vol 1* (pp. 97–110). Guilford Press.

Scarparolo, G., & MacKinnon, S. (2022). Student voice as part of differentiated instruction: Students' perspectives. *Educational Review*, 1–18. https://doi.org/10.1080/00131911.2022.2047617

Schein, E. (1992). *Organizational culture and leadership*. Jossey-Bass.
Schein, E. (1997). *Organizational culture and leadership*, 2nd Ed. Jossey-Bass.
Schein, E. (2004). *Organizational culture and leadership*, 3rd Ed. Jossey-Bass.
Schiefele, U. (1991). Interest, learning, and motivation. *Educational Psychologist*, 26(3–4), 299–323.
Schunk, D. (2005). Self-regulated learning: The educational legacy of Paul R. Pintrich. *Educational Psychologist, 40*(2), 85–94.
Schutte, N., & Malouff, J. (2020). A meta-analysis of the relationship between curiosity and creativity. *The Journal of Creative Behavior, 54*(4), 940–947.
Scruggs, T., Mastropieri, M., & McDuffie, K. (2007). Co-teaching in inclusive classrooms: A meta-synthesis of quantitative research. *Exceptional Children, 73*, 392–416.
Sedita, J. (2019). *The writing rope: A framework for explicit writing instruction in all subjects*. Brookes Publishing.
Shaddock, A., Hook, J., Hoffman-Raap, L., Spinks, A., Woolley, G., & Pearce, M. (2007). How do successful classroom teachers provide a relevant curriculum for students with disabilities in their mainstream class? Chapter 7. In *A project to improve the learning outcomes of students with disabilities in the early, middle and post compulsory years of schooling*. Australian Government Department of Education, Science and Training. https://core.ac.uk/download/pdf/30348929.pdf#page=155
Sharma, U., Loreman, T., & Forlin, C. (2011). Measuring teacher efficacy to implement inclusive practices. *Journal of Research in Special Educational Needs, 12*(1), 12–21.
Shepard, L. (2018). Learning progressions as tools for assessment and learning. *Applied Measurement in Education, 31*(2), 165–174.
Shields, C. (2010). Transformative leadership: Working for equity in diverse contexts. *Educational Administration Quarterly, 46*(4), 558–589.
Shvarts, A., & Bakker, A. (2019). The early history of the scaffolding metaphor: Bernstein, Luria, Vygotsky, and before. *Mind, Culture, and Activity, 26*(1), 4–23.
Sims, S., & Sims, R. (2004). *Managing school system change: Charting a course for renewal*. Information Age Publishing.
Skuy, M. (1997). *Mediated learning in and out of the classroom*. Hawker Brownlow.
Smart, J. (2004). Models of disability: The juxtaposition of biology and social construction. *Handbook of rehabilitation counseling*, 25–49.
Smith, L. (2018). *Adverse childhood experiences (ACEs): Interventions in education*. The Institute for Research and Innovation in Social Services (Iriss). https://www.iriss.org.uk/sites/default/files/2018-04/iriss-esss-outline-adverse-childhood-experiences-2018-4-23.pdf
Soares, S., Rocha, V., Kelly-Irving, M., Stringhini, S., & Fraga, S. (2021). Adverse childhood events and health biomarkers: a systematic review. *Frontiers in Public Health, 9*.
Social Ventures Australia, (2022). *Evidence for learning: Teaching and learning toolkit*. https://evidenceforlearning.org.au/education-evidence/teaching-learning-toolkit

State Government of Victoria (2019). *Your reporting and legal obligations.* Education and Training. https://www.education.vic.gov.au/school/teachers/health/childprotection/Pages/reportobligations.aspx

Sterling, S. (2001). *Sustainable education.* Green Books.

Sternberg, R. (2002). Raising the achievement of all students: Teaching for successful intelligence. *Educational Psychology Review, 14*(4), 383–393.

Sternberg, R., & Grigorenko, E. (2007). *Teaching for successful intelligence: To increase student learning and achievement.* Corwin Press.

Sweeney, T., & Geer, R. (2010). Student capabilities and attitudes towards ICT in the early years. *Australian Educational Computing, 25*(1), 18.

Tansley, R., Parsons, S., & Kovshoff, H. (2022). How are intense interests used within schools to support inclusion and learning for secondary-aged autistic pupils? A scoping review. *European Journal of Special Needs Education, 37*(3), 477–493.

Teaching Council of Aotearoa New Zealand (2022). *Tātaiako: cultural competencies for teachers of Māori learners.* https://teachingcouncil.nz/resource-centre/tataiako-cultural-competencies-for-teachers-of-maori-learners/

Tedeschi, R., & Calhoun, L. (2004). Posttraumatic growth: conceptual foundations and empirical evidence. *Psychological Inquiry, 15*(1), 1–18.

Thelen, E., & Smith, L. (1998). Dynamic systems theories. In W. Damon, & Lerner, R (Eds.), *Handbook of child psychology: Theoretical models of human development* (563–634). John Wiley & Sons.

Thompson, G., Hogan, A., & Rahimi, M. (2019). Private funding in Australian public schools: a problem of equity. *The Australian Educational Researcher, 46*(5), 893–910.

Thraves, G., & Bannister-Tyrrell, M. (2017). Australian Aboriginal peoples and giftedness: A diverse issue in need of a diverse response. *TalentEd, 29*, 18–31.

Thraves, G., Dhurrkay, M., Baker, P., Berman, J., & Nye, A. (2021). Facilitating dialogue to support 'ganma': A methodology for navigating contested knowledge. *Australian Aboriginal Studies, 2*, 3–13.

Tilley, N., & Pawson, R. (2000). Realistic evaluation: An overview. In *Founding conference of the Danish Evaluation Society* (Vol. 8), September.

Tomlinson, C. (2001). *How to differentiate instruction in mixed ability classrooms* (2nd ed.). ASCD.

Tomlinson, C. (2005). Traveling the road to differentiation in staff development. *Journal of Staff Development, 26*(4), 8–12.

Tomlinson, C. (2011). Mapping a route toward differentiated instruction. *Educational Leadership, 57*(1), 12–16.

Tomlinson, C. (2016). Why differentiation is difficult: Reflections from years in the trenches. *Australian Educational Leader, 38*(3), 6–8.

Tomlinson, C. (2017a). *How to differentiate instruction in academically diverse classrooms.* ASCD.

Tomlinson, C. (2017b). *Leading for differentiation: Growing the teachers who grow the kids.* Keynote Western Region Education Service Alliance, Summer Conference. https://wresa.org/wp-content/uploads/2017/06/Tomlinson-Administrator-Keynote-1.pdf

Tomlinson, C., & Allan, S. (2000). *Leadership for differentiating schools and classrooms.* ASCD.

Tomlinson, C., Brighton, C., Hertberg, H., Callahan, C., Moon, T., Brimijoin, K., Conover, L., & Reynolds, T. (2003). Differentiating instruction in response to student readiness, interest, and learning profile in academically diverse classrooms: A review of literature. *Journal for the Education of the Gifted, 27*(2–3), 119–145.

Tomlinson, C., & Moon, T. (2013). *Assessment and student success in a differentiated classroom.* ASCD.

Tomlinson, C., & Moon, T. (2014). Assessment in a differentiated classroom. *Proven programs in education: Classroom management and assessment,* 1–5.

Tomlinson, C., & Murphy, M. (2015). *Leading for differentiation: Growing teachers who grow kids.* ASCD.

Trinidad, J. (2021). Social consequences and contexts of adverse childhood experiences. *Social Science & Medicine, 277,* 113897.

UNICEF Ireland (2019). *Malala addresses youth delegates in UN.* https://www.unicef.ie/stories/one-child-one-teacher-one-book-and-one-pen-can-change-the-world/

United Nations [UN] (1989). *The United Nations Convention on the Rights of the Child.* https://www.unicef.org.au/our-work/information-for-children/un-convention-on-the-rights-of-the-child

United Nations [UN] (2006). *Convention on the Rights of Persons with Disabilities.* https://www.un.org/development/desa/disabilities/convention-on-the-rights-of-persons-with-disabilities/article-2-definitions.html

United Nations [UN] (2015). *The Millennium Development Goals Report 2015.* https://www.un.org/millenniumgoals/2015

United Nations [UN] (2016). *The Sustainable Development Goals Report, 2016.* https://unstats.un.org/sdgs/report/2016

United Nations [UN] (2022). *Treaty collection.* https://treaties.un.org/Pages/ViewDetails.aspx?src=TREATY&mtdsg_no=IV-15&chapter=4&clang=_en

United Nations Educational, Scientific and Cultural Organisation [UNESCO] and Ministry of Education and Science, Spain (1994). *The Salamanca Statement of principles, policy, and practice in special needs education.* https://unesdoc.unesco.org/ark:/48223/pf0000098427

University of Melbourne (2022). *Indigenous Knowledge Resource for School Curricula Project,* https://indigenousknowledge.unimelb.edu.au/curriculum#home

US Department of Education (2022). *What works clearinghouse practice guides.* https://ies.ed.gov/ncee/wwc/PracticeGuides

Valdivieso, P. (2020). School leaders and inclusive education in Peru: A case study of principal leadership in an effective inclusive school. *International Journal of Innovative Business Strategies, 6*(2), 453–461.

Van den Branden, K. (2012). Sustainable education: basic principles and strategic recommendations. *School Effectiveness and School Improvement, 23*(3), 285–304.

Van der Kleij, F., Adie, L., & Cumming, J. (2019). A meta-review of the student role in feedback, *International Journal of Educational Research, 98,* 303–323. https://doi.org/10.1016/j.ijer.2019.09.005

Van der Kleij, F., Feskens, R., & Eggen, T. (2015). Effects of feedback in a computer-based learning environment on students' learning outcomes: A meta-analysis, *Review of Educational Research, 85*(4), 475–511.

Van Geel, M., Keuning, T., Frèrejean, J., Dolmans, D., van Merriënboer, J., & Visscher, A. (2019). Capturing the complexity of differentiated instruction. *School effectiveness and school improvement, 30*(1), 51–67.

Vass, G. (2018). 'Aboriginal learning style' and culturally responsive schooling: Entangled, entangling, and the possibilities of getting disentangled. *Australian Journal of Teacher Education (Online), 43*(8), 89–104.

Verhoef, R., van Dijk, A., & de Castro, B. (2022). A dual-mode social-information-processing model to explain individual differences in children's aggressive behavior. *Clinical Psychological Science, 10*(1), 41–57.

Vogt, F., Koechlin, A., Truniger, A., & Zumwald, B. (2021). Teaching assistants and teachers providing instructional support for pupils with SEN: Results from a video study in Swiss classrooms. *European Journal of Special Needs Education, 36*(2), 215–230.

Vygotsky, L. (1978). *Mind in society: The development of higher psychological processes.* Harvard University Press.

Wade, S., & Kidd, C. (2019). The role of prior knowledge and curiosity in learning. *Psychonomic Bulletin & Review, 26*(4), 1377–1387.

Waldron, T. (2016). *Universal design: Strategies for building an inclusive learning experience.* http://ohioahead.org/topics-of-interest/udl/

Waldschmidt, A. (2017). Disability goes cultural. In Waldschmidt, A., Berresem, H., & Ingwersen, M. (Eds.), *Culture-theory-disability: Encounters between disability studies and cultural studies* (pp. 19–28). Verlag.

Wan, S. W. Y. (2016). Differentiated instruction: Hong Kong prospective teachers' teaching efficacy and beliefs. *Teachers and Teaching, 22*(2), 148–176.

Wang, M., Degol, J., Amemiya, J., Parr, A., & Guo, J. (2020). Classroom climate and children's academic and psychological wellbeing: A systematic review and meta-analysis. *Developmental Review, 57.* https://doi.org/10.1016/j.dr.2020.100912

Wasik, B., & Hindman, A. (2018). Why wait? The importance of wait time in developing young students' language and vocabulary skills. *The Reading Teacher, 72*(3), 369–378.

Watt, D., Donnelly, V., & Kefallinou, A. (2019). *Raising the achievement of all learners in inclusive education: Follow-up study.* European Agency for Special Needs and Inclusive Education, https://www.european-agency.org/resources/publications/raising-achievement-follow-up

Weaver, J., Bertelsen, C., & Dziak, E. (2020). Who are the voices? Reflective conversations within assessment. *Journal of Education and Human Development, 9*(1), 1–7.

Webber, M. (2019). The Development of mana: Five optimal conditions for gifted Māori student success. In Smith S. (Ed.), *Handbook of Giftedness and Talent Development in the Asia-Pacific* (pp. 671–691). Springer International Handbooks of Education.

Webster, K., & Litchka, P. (2020). Planning for effective school leadership: Teachers' perceptions of the leadership skills and ethical behaviors of school principals. *Educational Planning, 27*(1), 31–47.

Webster, R., Blatchford, P., & Russell, A. (2013). Challenging and changing how schools use teaching assistants: Findings from the Effective Deployment of Teaching Assistants project. *School Leadership & Management, 33*(1), 78–96.

Wertheim, C., & Leyser, Y. (2002). Efficacy beliefs, background variables and differentiated instruction of Israeli prospective teachers. *The Journal of Educational Research, 96*(1), 54–63.

Westwood, P. (2001). Differentiation as a strategy for inclusive classroom practice. *Australian Journal of Learning Disabilities, 6*(1), 5–11.

Westwood, P. (2018). *Inclusive and adaptive teaching: Meeting the challenge of diversity in the classroom.* Routledge.

Weyns, T., Preckel, F., & Verschueren, K. (2021). Teachers-in-training perceptions of gifted children's characteristics and teacher-child interactions: An experimental study. *Teaching and Teacher Education, 97*, 103215.

Whitaker, M. (2019). The Hoover-Dempsey and Sandler model of the parent involvement process. *The Wiley handbook of family, school, and community relationships in education*, 421–444.

Whyalla Secondary College (2019). *Whyalla Secondary School: Dear architect.* NoTosh Publishing. https://wsc.sa.edu.au/wp-content/uploads/2021/08/Dear-Architect.pdf

Whyalla Secondary College, Government of South Australia (2021). *ATRiUM Philosophy.* https://wsc.sa.edu.au/our-college/atrium/

Wiliam, D. (2013). Assessment: The bridge between teaching and learning. *Voices from the Middle, 21*(2), 15.

Wiliam, D. (2016). The secret of effective feedback. *Educational Leadership, 73*(7), 10–15. http://www.ascd.org/publications/educational-leadership/apr16/vol73/num07/The-Secret-of-Effective-Feedback.aspx

Willingham, D., Hughes, E., & Dobolyi, D. (2015). The scientific status of learning styles theories. *Teaching of Psychology, 42*(3), 266–271. https://doi.org/10.1177/0098628315589505

Winner, M., & Crooke, P. (2016). Beyond skills: The worth of social competence: The words of social competence matter when supporting students' social development. *The ASHA Leader, 21*(9), 50–56.

Wisniewski, B., Zierer, K., & Hattie, J. (2020). The power of feedback revisited: A meta-analysis of educational feedback research. *Frontiers in Psychology, 10*, 3087.

Witt, P., Wheeless, L., & Allen, M. (2004). A meta-analytical review of the relationship between teacher immediacy and student learning. *Communication Monographs, 71*(2), 184–207.

Won, S., Hensley, L., & Wolters, C. (2021). Brief research report: Sense of belonging and academic help-seeking as self-regulated learning. *The Journal of Experimental Education, 89*(1), 112–124.

Wood, R. (2021). Autism, intense interests and support in school: From wasted efforts to shared understandings. *Educational Review, 73*(1), 34–54.

World Health Organisation [WHO] (2012). *Early childhood development and disability: A discussion paper.* UNICEF.

York-Barr, J., & Duke, K. (2004). What do we know about teacher leadership? Findings from two decades of scholarship. *Review of Educational Research, 74*(3), 255–316.

Zhu, Y., & Edwards, F. (2019). Teacher questioning in a Chinese context: Implications for New Zealand classrooms. *Teachers and Curriculum, 19*(1), 27–33, https://doi.org/10.15663/tandc.v19i1.340

Zubrick, S., Williams, A., & Silburn, S. (2000). *Indicators of social and family functioning.* Department of Family and Community Services.

Index

Page numbers in **bold** indicate tables and *italics* indicate figures

achievement 4, 18, 24, **27**, **28**, **30**, 31, 43, 47, 59, 69, 84, 85, *86*, *87*, 90, 94, 96, 98, 105, 122, 134, 170, 179, 192, 206; assisted 104, *104*, 126, 135; assessment of 146–149; and childhood trauma 9; and class size 99; demonstration of 35; high achievement 79–80; and learning 18, 85–88; motivation 118; and specific learning disorder 82; and wait-time 173

active learning (A) 9–11, *10*, 16, **37**, 41, 51, 62, 67, 79, 95, 96, 99, 105–106, *106*, *108*, **111**, 112, **120**, 125, 140, *150*, 151–152, 153, 158, 159, 161, 165, 171, *172*; and active leadership 203; and ICAP 143; and self-feedback 175

adjustments 54, 55, 57, 140, 164, 169

assessment 11, 19, 20, 22, *26*, 26–33, 38, **68**, 71, 85–87, 93–98, 180; actions supported by **30**, 41; AS, OF and FOR learning **28**, 165–167; barriers in 162; constructive alignment of 140; criterion and/or norm-referenced 160–161; decision-making *26*, *86*, 102, 147; for diagnosis 44; dynamic 79, 115, 173–**174**; and factors supporting and hindering learning 150–160; and feedback 35, 168–171; high ability 79; the HOW of 32–33, 48, 87, **141**, 161–165, *162*; of ILOs 148–149; monitoring 39, 42, 43, 45, 163, 196; peer 175; in RTF **27**, *86*, **86**, 135, 146–167; screening 42, 43, 185, 196; self-assessment 171, *172*, **176**; specialist 39, 40, 47, 81, 92–93, 95, 97, 114; of unintended LOs 149–150; the WHAT of 30–32, **30**, 146; the WHY of 27–31, **28**, **30**, 101, 146

assessment-ready and assessment-capable learners 165

assistive technology 54, 156, 164

assumptions 17, 36, 44, 65; and behaviour 65, 80–82; and disability 74–78, **75**, **77**; and diversity 74–84; and giftedness 78–80; and school culture 60–62, 66–71

ATRiUM capabilities 9–13, *10*, 18, 19, **27**, **30**, 41, 67, 73, 79, *86*, *87*, 91, 93, 95, 96, 98, 103, 105–109, *106*, *108*, **111**, 119, **120**, 124, 143, 147, 165, 176, 177; and ecological map 106–109, *106*, *108*; as factors supporting and hindering learning 150–160; and labels 29; and Sustainable Learning Profile 110–113; and trauma 91; see also capabilities, active learning (A), thinking (T), relating to others (R), using language, symbol systems and ICT (iU), managing self (M)

Australian Institute of Teaching and School Leadership [AITSL] 18, 24, 35, 57, 58, 65, 72, 184, 195, 196, 201, 207

behaviour 13, 31, 40, 43, 60–61, 67, 69, 70, 110, 112, 127,129, 130, 134, *150*, 151, 154, 155, 159, 204; and ADHD 107; assumptions about 65, 80–81; cultural 79; severe disorder 77; support for 81, 128, 192, 206; verbs related to 121

behaviourist theory 67, **68**, 69

bilingual education 73, 156

Bloom's taxonomy **122**, *122*

capabilities approach 3, 5, 6, 7–13, 16, 23, **27**, 36, 47, 52, 70, 79, 80, 83, 90, 169; Australian General Capabilities **9**, 56;

Index

and evidence of student learning 146–160, *150*; and intended learning outcomes 113–114; and leadership 195, 203–205; and teacher reflection 180–182, 186; see also ATRiUM capabilities
classroom climate 90, 128–129, 179; dialogue 135
classroom 40–41, 127; and feedback 177; in reciprocal teaching 138–139; reflective 59; student-teacher 97, **198**
coding 157–158
collaboration 143; in leadership 193–196, 199, 200, 206; for responsive teaching 40, 46–47, 134, 140
collaborative teaching 44, 133–135; environment 45, 63, 132; and learning 12, 37, 40–41, 138, 139
collective efficacy 47, 134
community 7, 17, 19, 46, 58, 60, 63, 66, 73, 79, 89, 92, 109, *109*, 132, 133, 179; and leadership 191–199, **198**, 203–205; and professional learning 59
constructive alignment 118, 122, 140; and feedback 170
conventional assessment 32, 80, 116
cooperative group teaching 136–138, 139, 180, 185; and learning 11, 12, 129, 134, 159–160, 164
cultural competence 58, 65, 71–74, 88, 133, 186; frameworks for 59
cultural mediator 73–74
cultural mismatch 58, 88
culturally responsive teaching 133

deliberate actions of responsive teachers (DARTs) 124, *126*, 127, 168, 173; and prompt questions 204
developmental pathways 114–115
diagnosis 29, **30**, 31, 42–44, 78; and specific learning disorder 82
diagnostic labels 5, 7, 29, 31, **77**, 77–78, 80, 83, 93, 112, 114
dialogic teaching and learning 58, 127, 168, 169, 177, 204, 205
differentiated teaching/differentiated instruction/differentiation 19, 34, 54, 80, 131–133; evaluating 183–185; and feedback 171–172; and goal setting 118; and intensity of teaching 38–40; and interest 104–105; and leadership 196; and learning profile 105–106; and readiness 103–104; responsiveness 44–45, *44*, 100, 182; see also flexible groupings, layers of responsive teaching, UDL

Differentiated Instruction Questionnaire 35
digital literacy 158
direct instruction 125, 143
disabilities 133, 145; Convention on the Rights of Persons with 36, 51, 52; and language 156; and learning 42, 82, 83; named disabilities 76–77, **77**, 115; special provisions in assessment 164
disability 7, 18, 25, 29, **30**, 32, **39**, 58, 61; and anti-discrimination legislation 53–54; models of **75**, 76
Disability Standards for Education 54, 55, 202
disorders **77**, 82–83, and educational and developmental casework 92–93; autism spectrum 78, 92; specific learning 82–83; post-traumatic stress 90
diversity 16, 17, 19, 184, 192, 194; cultural 133; and curriculum 57; responding to 6–7, 34, 37, 59, 89, **198**, 200; and worldviews 70, 71
Dreyfus's model of adult skill acquisition 116–117, **117**
dynamic assessment 79, 115, 173, 176
dyscalculia 83
dyslexia 83, 112

early intervention 43, 92, 93, 192
ecological influences 14, *16*, 24, 62, 66, 103, 179; ecological theory **67**; and leadership 191, 195, 199
ecological map 23, 106–108, 181
educational casework 18, 20, 31, **39**, 40, 47, 76, 81, 85, 87, 92–93, 94–96, 110, 112, 114, 134, 165
effect size 168
effort 67, **68**, 128, 132, 136, 151, 166, 172, **174**
engagement 16, 20, 34–35, 58, 61, 81, 88, 90, 91, 97, 100, 101, 104, 105, 107, 110, 151, 158, 160, 165, 166, 170, 176, 181, 196; and ICAP 143; and parents 96; and professional 66, 71, 194; and social 127; in UDL 128, 132, 144
equity 4, 32, 33, 57, **75**, 164, 192, 193, 194, 197, **198**
ethic of care 133, 193, 194
ethical leadership 191, 192–194, 196, 197, 200, 201, 203
ethical practice 7, 35, 36, **39**, 44, 94, 135, 158
ethical understanding **9**
evaluation 14, 21, 147, **174**, 178, 180, 183, 194, 196; and layers of responsive

teaching 185–186; self-evaluation 154, 195; and student voice 182–183; of teaching approaches 183–185
evidence 14, 23, 43, 168; gathering 27, 27–33, 47; from professional experience 25; from scientific research 22–25, 42, 47, 66, 69, 83, 91, 103, 114, 116, 156; from students and families 25–26, 95–97; translation of research 24; from within teaching 26–33, 44
evidence-based practice 21, 22–33, 42, 43, 44, 55, 69, 71, 83, 87, 100, **111**, 130, 145, 183; and evaluation 178–180; and leadership 191, 192, 193, 196, 207; of teaching approaches 130–139, 160
evidence of student learning 20, 21, 41, 45, 46, 67, 81, 126, 145, 146–167
explicit teaching 19, 38, **39**, 39, 40, 45, 101, 110, 135–136, 143, 159, 177, 185, 192

factors supporting and hindering learning 150–160
family/families 11, 16, 22, 25–26, **27**, **30**, 45, 46, 47, 53, 55–56, 71–72, **75**, 76, 77, 78, 81, 89–90, *89*, 98, 107, *109*, 110, 133, 134, 147, 155, 181, 186; and educational casework 92–97; and leadership 191, 193, 197, **198**, 199, 204–205, *209*
feedback 15, 35, 38, **39**, 41, 45, 66, 82, 94, 115, 134, 136, 139, 142, 165, 166, 168–177, 192; and constructive alignment *170*; and interactions 173–175, **174**; in leadership 195; in learning theories **68**, 71; openness to 110, **111**; quality of 169–170; quantity and timing of 171–173; in RTF 20, 26, **27**, 122, 168–177, 180, 186; self-feedback 175–176; student role in 153, 165, **176**, 176–177
flexible groupings 40–41

giftedness 36, 39, 58, 65, 74, 83, 87, 110, 115, 161, 186
growth mindset 19, 35–36, 67, **68**, 108

Hattie, J. 24, 38, 43, 45, 47, 125, 127, 128, 135, 151, 153, 159, 165, 168, 169, 170, 171, *172*, 177
help-seeking 155, 159
high ability 79
high expectations 36, 37, 96, 161, 166, 177, 192, 196

ICAP taxonomy 143, 151
implementation science 178, 180, 207

inclusive education policy 55
Index for Inclusion 193
Indigenous knowledges 71, 197
individual education plans 112–113
information communication technology (ICT) 9, **9**, 12, 158, 205
information processing 11, **67**, 152, *152*, 154, *154*
Innovative Learning Environments (ILEs) 53, 62, 64, 195, 208
inquiry learning 142
instructional rounds 206
intended learning outcomes (ILOs) 19, **27**, **30**, 35, 103, 113–123, 132, 134, 140, **141**, 145; defining 117–123; assessing 146–149, *147*, 162, 165, 166, 169, 171, 179, 180, 181
intensity of teaching 34, 173, 185; changes in 38–40, **39**, 41, 43, 44, 83, 135, 140, 177, 180, 182, 183; and explicitness 151–153, *153*; and gifted learners **174**; and layers of responsive teaching 41–46, *43*; and increasing challenge 155–159; and repeated learning opportunities 150–151; and size of group 154; and student reflection 202; as variation in time 154–155, *155*
intercultural competence 73, 88
intercultural understanding **9**
interest/interests 18, **27**, 35, **37**, 38, 85, 86, *87*, 89, *89*, 91–92, 96, 97, 103, 104–105, **111**, 122, 128, 131, 132, 133, 136, 140, **142**, 145, 149, 151, 163, 180, 181
international conventions 17, 51–52, 53

jigsaw 137–138, *138*

language **9**, 10, 11, 32, 60, **67**, 70, 73, 110, 114, 127, 135; disorder 77, 83, 156, 162
Layers of Responsive Teaching 41–44; Layer 1 44–45; Layers 2 and 3 45–46
leadership 62, 134, 178, 180, 183, 184, 189–208
learning spaces 63–64, 129
learning styles 69, 105, 133
learning environment 8, 16, 17, 19, 24, **37**, 41, 51, 53, 59, 62–64, 66, 88, 90, 110, **111**, 124, 128–130, 180, 194–195, 205; see also innovative learning environments (ILEs)
learning for all 3, 4, 5, 6–7, 13, 16, 21, 47, 48, 57, 74, 189, 191, 192, 194, 196, 207, 208
learning intervention 40, 137

learning opportunities 3, 7, 19, 20, 23, 24, 30, 34, 38, 39, 40, 44, 46, 73, 92, 104, 105, 124, 137, 139–145, 166, 169, 180, 182
learning profile 103–106, 196; Sustainable Learning Profile 109–113, **111**, 118, 122, 124, 140, 171, 180, 181
learning progressions 31, 57, 104, 113–114, 115–116, 117, 122, 135, 148
learning processes 67, 113, 143, 151, 159
learning strategies 24, 145, 153
learning that lasts 3, 4, 5, 7–13, 16, 21, 47, 57, 150, 189, 191, 194, 207, 208
learning theory 66, **67**, **68**, 69, 71, 103; Indigenous 70–71
legislation 53–55, 56, 76, 91, 202
lighting 129–130
literacy **9**, 31, 32, 38, 45, 80, 82, 110, 111, 135, 138, 156–157, 158, 162, 181, 185; literacy rope *157*

maintenance 146, 149
managing self (M) 9, **9**, *10*, 12–13, 67, 79, 108, 112, **120**, 125, 151, 159–160, 165, 169; in leadership 203, 205
mastery **68**, 135, 151
mathematical learning **9**, 115, 116, 135, 136, 157–158, 162, 171
mediation 10, 104, 73–74, 115, 118, 125, 139, 140, 173, 176, 201
metacognition 13, 122, 135, 138, 153, 154, 159
Mitchell, D. 24, 100, 125, 126, 128, 133, 134, 135, 139, 148, 154, 156, 157, 158, 159, 168, 169, 191, 192, 193, 194, 199
motivation 10, 11, 13, 16, 36, 79, 91, 104, 105, 112, 118, 143, 145, 151, 159, 164, 169, **198**
multicultural competence 72, 73, 88–89
multi-tiered system of supports (MTSS) 42, 43, 81, 128, 192, 196

Nationally Consistent Collection of Data (NCCD) 54, 202
neuromyths 69

observation **67**, 81, 110, **111**, 116, 134, 173, 176, 181

parents 26, 53, 63, 66, 73, 81, 93, 96, 128, 156, 186, **198**, 208; and websites 115; see also family/families
pathways (developmental and learning) 114–115, 122
peer assisted learning 139, 150, 155, 166, 177

peer relationships 108, 110, 181, 182
persistence 67, **68**, 107, 112, 128, 132, 151, 152
personalised learning 8, 49, 54, 55, 206
phonemic/phonological skills 31, 135, 156, *157*, 181, 185
policy 17, 51, 55–56, 60, 61; policymakers 25
positive behaviour support 81, 159, 206
positive learning environments 180, 183, 194
positive leadership 191
professional learning 56, 57–58, 65, 66, 69, 74, 107, 116, 186–187, 195; and communities 59, 191, 195, 199, 207
psychological science 77, *77*

questioning 10, 38, 41, **68**, 105, 135, 139, 160, 170

readiness 35, 103–104, *104*, 122, 126, 140, 145, 159, 165, 170, 171, 177, 180, 181
reading 8, 12, 135, 136, 157; difficulties 148, 181; reading rope 156, *157*
realist/realistic evaluation 178, 193
reciprocal teaching 138, 139
reflective practice 20–21, 49, 180, 186, 189, 191, 194, 195, 201, 208; questions *204*
relating to others (R) 9, **9**, 11–12, 41, 79, 100, 108, 112, **120**, 125, 143, 154–155, *154*, 177, 203, 204–205
relationship skills 159
reports/reporting 20, 26, 31, 54, 66, 87, 93, 94, 107, **111**, 147, 163, 179
research evidence 22–25, 42, 47, 66, 69, 83, 91, 103, 114, 116, 156
resources/resourcing 3, 4, 7, 15, 40, 46, 53, 62, 64, **75**, 76, 80, 96, 128, 129, 131, 133, 134, 138, 139, 140, 158, 164, 165, 170, 182, 186; groups in jigsaw 137–138; and leadership 192, 193, 194, 195, 196, **198**, 200, 203, 206
Response to Intervention (RtI) 41, *42*, 54
responsive differentiation 19, 35, 44–45, *44*, 100, 104, 129
Responsive Leadership Framework (RLF) 201–208
Responsive Teaching Framework (RTF) 14–21, 26, 35, 44; and assessment/evidence gathering **27**; Part II 49–186; and leadership 192, 197, 201
rights: human 51, 52, 55, **75**, 76; of persons with disabilities 36, 52, 54, 76; of children 51, 52, 97

scaffolding 135
school culture 17, 51, 59–62, 179, 192
self-assessment 116, 171, *172*, 175, **176**
self-efficacy 13, 96, 143, 155, 159, 170, 173
self-regulation 12, 127, 128, 132, 151, 153, 159, 169, 171, 204
SMART goal structures **121**, 121, 163
social and emotional learning 43, 136, 159
social information processing *154*
social justice 76, 197, **198**
social skills 45, 107, *108*, 110, 112, 136, 154, 155, 158, 173
SOLO taxonomy 116–121, **116**, **119**, **120**, 140, **141**, 152
special education needs **75**, 134
specific learning disorders 77
student relationships 100–102, *100*, *101*, 110, **111**, 129, 139, 149, 160
student voice 97, 134, 182–183
successful intelligence 140, **142**, 152
Sustainable Learning 3–13
Sustainable Learning Profile 103, 106, 109–113, **111**, 118, 122, 124, 140, 171, 180, 181

teacher registration 17, 35, 51, 57–58, 64, 65
teacher-student relationships 12, 98–100, *98*, *99*, 124–125, *125*, 128, 130, 147, 148, 159, 160, 161, 176, 177, 179, 180, 182, 183, 192, 193, 194, **198**, *209*; and DARTs 125–127, 171, 173; and leadership 204–205, 208
teaching and learning spaces 63–64, 129
teaching approaches 63, 99, 100, 104, 124, 130–145, 178, 180, 181, 182; evaluating 183–185

teaching assistants 100, 134, 182
Teaching Performance Assessment (TPA) 18, 57, 66, 184
teaching strategies 4, 19, 20, 23, **30**, 34, 43, 45, 47, 55, 56, 94, 98, 124, 134, 135, 142, 144, 191, 192, 196
teaching that matters 3, 4–6, *5*, 13, 14, 15, 16, 21, 47, 57, 189, 194, 207, 208
thinking (T) 8, **9**, 11, 12, 41, 91, 95, 105, 106, 110, 115, **120**, 125, 152–154, *152*, *153*, 158, 160, 175, 176; and leadership 203–204, *204*; and learning theories 67, 67, 69; and levels 41, 116, **116**, 118, **119**, 121, **122**, 163; see also SOLO taxonomy, Bloom's taxonomy
Tomlinson, C. 7, 34, 35, 91, 103, 104, 105, 118, 128, 133, 135, 184, 187, 196, 199
transfer 69, 127, 146, 149, **174**
twice exceptional 39

unintended learning outcomes **27**, 146, 147, 149–150, 165, 179
Universal Design for Learning (UDL) 36–38, *44*, 144–145
using language, symbol systems and ICT (iU) 9, 12, 41, 91, 95, 96, 106, 110, **120**, 125, 140, 155–158, 160, 181, 182, 203, 205; see also ATRiUM capabilities

Visible Learning 24, 47, 88, 99, 128, 134, 139, 148, 151, 156, 168, 170, 192
Vygotsky 41, 104, 166

wait time 173
wellbeing 70, 88, 93, 129

zone of readiness (ZoR) *104*, 104, 126, 145

For Product Safety Concerns and Information please contact our EU
representative GPSR@taylorandfrancis.com
Taylor & Francis Verlag GmbH, Kaufingerstraße 24, 80331 München, Germany

www.ingramcontent.com/pod-product-compliance
Lightning Source LLC
Chambersburg PA
CBHW061711300426
44115CB00014B/2639